REAL LEARNING, REAL WORK

Series Editor: James W. Fraser,
Director of the Center for Innovation in
Urban Education Northeastern University

Routledge's Transforming Teaching Series represents a commitment to support teachers in the practice of their profession. Each volume in this series will link critical educational theory to very specific examples of successful classroom practice and detailed descriptions of the kinds of curricular materials that are most useful in implementing theory in practice. Each volume will explore the political barriers and intellectual issues involved in implementing new forms of practice. While each volume and each editor will take a different approach, all of the volumes will be united in addressing primarily the concerns of teachers—and students in teacher education programs—and in combining the voices of thoughtful theorists and currently practicing classroom teachers.

Also published in the series:

Assessment for Equity and Inclusion: Embracing All Our Children
A. Lin Goodwin, editor

Teaching African American Literature: Theory and Practice
Marianna W. Davis, Maryemma Graham, and Sharon Pineault-Burke, editors

Unauthorized Methods: Strategies for Critical Teaching
Joe L. Kincheloe and Shirley R. Steinberg

REAL LEARNING, REAL WORK

School-to-Work as High School Reform

Adria Steinberg

ROUTLEDGE
New York and London

Published in 1998 by

Routledge
29 West 35 Street
New York, NY 10001

Published in Great Britain by

Routledge
11 New Fetter Lane
London EC4P 4EE

Copyright © 1998 by Routledge

Printed in the United States of America

Library of Congress Cataloging-in-Publication Data

Steinberg, Adria.
    Real learning, real work: school-to-work as high school reform / Adria Steinberg.
        p. cm. — (Transforming teaching)
    Includes bibliographical references and index.
    ISBN 0-415-91792-1 (hardcover). — ISBN 0-415-91793-X (pbk.)
    1. Career education—United States. 2. School-to-work transition—
United States. 3. Education, Cooperative—United States.
4. Student services—United States. I. Title. II. Series.
LC1037.5.S84 1998
370.11'3—DC21   98-14659
                                          CIP

Contents

Foreword

Real Learning, Real Work engages one of the most pressing issues in contemporary education policy and practice. Is the school-to-work movement a new version of the old vocational education, a series of programs for the "non-college bound" students? Or is school-to-work a new paradigm for the education of all students in which the world of work becomes the point of entry for looking at a range of issues which will make the learning process come alive for all students? This fundamental question is the focus of *Real Learning, Real Work.* If the former is the case, if these programs are for the "forgotten half only, school-to-work will always remain an education for "other people's children"; the step-child of the more serious and prestigious forms of education. If the latter option is taken, however, school-to-work can become a means of fundamentally restructuring all of American education so that there are no longer winners and losers, college bound and "other" students, the upwardly mobile and the bored and desperate, but rather a range of students and a range of teachers involved in a common quest to use the world of work to master the skills and attributes needed to understand and improve the world around them.

Fortunately Adria Steinberg and her colleagues bring clear answers to these questions as well as a world of wonderful experience to writing this volume. As a former high school teacher, education researcher and advocate, and senior administrator in one of the nation's premiere vocational education programs, Adria Steinberg knows whereof she speaks. As the examples she presents show, she knows the pitfalls as well as the promises of using school-to-work to transform pedagogy across the whole curriculum of a modern high school. Teachers and administrators who worry about being asked to consider unrealistic or utopian options, need not bring such fears to this volume. The goals are certainly utopian—an educational system in which all students are engaged and all students succeed. But the reality of teaching and administration, and the many possible problems and challenges of implementing a new idea in a real world school, are fully addressed in this book, even while the reader is asked to keep their eyes on the ultimate prize of an educational system which really works for everyone.

The haunting statement with which Steinberg begins the book; the "as if I care," uttered by a student in the midst of a supposedly relevant class session, summarizes what many of us have seen far too often in visits to contemporary schools. For all of the noble efforts to make schooling more interesting, to use technology and important topics to get students interested, far too many of today's students and adults view the school experience as something totally alien to the "real world." It is only as this alienation is ended, as the world of school becomes as real as the world of work—because the two are integrated in fundamental ways—that the challenge which the bored student posed to Steinberg will be met. As this book shows so convincingly, the potential is there. The challenge for all of us as educators is to seize the opportunity which is presented in this volume and continue the efforts which will make the schools of the twenty-first century places of energy, excitement, and relevance for all who are involved with them.

While each volume will take a different approach and focus on a different topic, all of the volumes in Routledge's *Transforming Teaching* series are united in addressing the concerns of teachers in the service of a rich, equitable, and inclusive schooling for all students. This volume is fortunate in that Steinberg, Vickers, and Riordan are all three both experienced teachers and careful researchers. Rigorous theory must always be informed by practice, and indeed it is in the dialogue of theory and practice that both are refined. We will doom ourselves to an anti-intellectual mediocrity if we fail to ask the most rigorous and critical theoretical questions about both current practices and the kind of schooling which is ultimately needed for the development of an inclusive, multicultural democracy. But we will not build that new society if teachers do not have the practical tools in hand to do their work. The volumes which are made available through Routledge's *Transforming Teaching* series seek to meet both needs. If groups of teachers find these volumes to have done so, and if groups of students experience schooling as a more exciting and successful experience because of these volumes, then the enterprise will have been a success.

JAMES W. FRASER
Transforming Teaching Series' Editor
Director of the Center for Innovation in
Urban Education, Northeastern University

Acknowledgments

Jim Fraser knew I had this book in me long before I did, and has provided me with his generous support and encouragement throughout the process of writing it. Margaret Vickers and Rob Riordan not only contributed chapters to the book but also helped shape and sharpen other portions of the text.

This book would not have been possible without Larry Rosenstock, whose vision about a new vocationalism opened my mind to the possibilities, and whose leadership created space to put our ideas into practice. Many colleagues and students in the Rindge School of Technical Arts will certainly recognize themselves in this book. I am grateful for the conversations, meetings, and classes, and especially to Tony Carnabuci for keeping me focused on the important daily tasks of running school programs, and to David Stephen, John Shea, Tamara Berman, Maria Ferri, and Phyllis Bretholtz for letting me spend so much time with them and their students.

It was at "floating faculty" meetings and conferences coordinated by Barbara Roche for Jobs for the Future that I first learned of most of the other schools highlighted in this book and met many of the inspiring colleagues who I later visited and interviewed in their schools. In my new role as a program director at Jobs for the Future, I am benefiting greatly from my colleagues' knowledge of the field and their understanding of how to work at the intersection of policy and practice.

ACKNOWLEDGMENTS

Michelle Swanson, Patricia Clark, Chuck Ericksen, Scott Eddleman, Dennis Littky and Elliot Washor gave me incredible access—to their teachers and students, their original curriculum materials, and to work that students have produced.

Herb Kohl introduced me to a remarkable book on community education, published in 1938, which inspired Chapter 2 of this book. Some of the sections on Rindge are based on "Beyond the Shop: Reinventing Vocational Education," written with Larry Rosenstock for Democratic Schools (ASCD, 1995, Michael Apple and James Beane, editors) and "CityWorks: Redefining Vocational Education," also written with Larry Rosenstock for Creating New Educational Communities , the Ninety-Fourth Yearbook of the National Society for the Study of Education: Part I (NSSE, 1995, Jeannie Oakes and Karen Hunter Quartz, editors).

Allen Graubard took time from his own writing projects to read an early draft of this manuscript and offer his considerable editorial expertise. Hilary Goldhammer helped me through later phases of rewriting and preparing the mauscript.

Many of the ideas in this book began as fragments of dinner conversations about "what happened in school today" among my family and housemates at 33 Jackson Street, Steve, Sam, and Adam Seidel, Nancy Falk, and Dick and Gregory Cluster. Steve Seidel is not only my favorite person with whom to discuss children, schools, learning and teaching, but also the husband and friend who brings me tea and makes dinner for the family when I cannot seem to leave the computer.

This book is dedicated to the many students whose education (at least for a year) has been entrusted to me, and particularly to Sam, Adam, and Greg, each of whom, in his own way, has already begun to apply considerable expertise about schools to the struggle to make them better.

Introduction

Several years ago, I observed a new teacher who had designed a unit on human biology, and, as a part of the unit, a series of lessons on the effects of drug use on the body. On this particular day, students were to debate the pros and cons of legalizing marijuana, drawing on their knowledge of the biological processes that occurred when the drug enters the body. The teacher invited me to evaluate this lesson because we had been discussing the importance of finding ways to connect science to issues that matter to students and to move towards more interdisciplinary approaches.

He thought that this lesson would be a good example of his efforts to put these ideas into practice. And indeed it was. But it was evident from the first few moments of the class that it was not going well. Standing at the front of the room, he divided students into teams, coaxing them to move quickly into small groups and finish preparing for the debate. There was much noise and scraping of furniture, but little real energy to get down to work. The student sitting closest to me turned around, met my eyes, and said, "As if I care. . . ."

The phrase seemed to capture the mood of the class. As I watched the desultory debate, I realized that despite this teacher's good intentions and best efforts, he had succeeded only in inventing another purposeless classroom exercise. Students knew that it did not matter who won or lost this debate. Perhaps they would have reacted differently if this had taken place in

Baltimore, where the mayor has publicly called for legalization of marijuana, and major factions of the community are sharing in the debate. But, from where they sat, it made no difference whether they took an informed position on this issue; and the only consequence of doing sloppy work would be a lower grade.

"As if I care" has stayed with me ever since, probably because these four words embody a critique of education that I have heard, and seen acted out, countless times in my thirty years of working with high school students. I would venture a guess that virtually every high school teacher has stood on the receiving end of that critique, baffled, as this young teacher was, as to why so many students don't seem to care, despite a real effort by the teacher to seize on something "relevant." (This teacher, after all, was not asking them to write papers on cell mitosis.)

Still, at the heart of this assignment—and most high school work—is a big "as if." *As if* it really matters how well the work is done. *As if* there is enough trust in the educational experience, in the teacher making the assignment, in the institution of the school, and the value of a high school diploma to propel students through assignment after assignment that seems contrived and essentially purposeless.

VOCATIONAL APPROACHES/ACADEMIC GOALS

In my career in education, I have learned not to trust these "as if's," trying instead to create classrooms, curricula, and school programs where the purpose of learning is clear, and where students work closely with adults in pursuit of this purpose. In the last five years, my work has taken me in what many of my colleagues thought of as an unlikely direction. Leaving my job as the writer and editor of the *Harvard Education Letter* to become the academic coordinator of the Rindge School of Technical Arts, I entered the world of vocational education.

The timing was not accidental. Larry Rosenstock had just been named the Executive Director of Occupational Education in Cambridge, Massachusetts, which made him the head of Rindge (the second oldest vocational school in the nation). Prior to his appointment, he had spent two years on leave from Rindge (where he was a teacher) to serve as a staff attorney for the Center for Law and Education. During that period, the Center played a leading role in changing the terms of the national conversation about vocational education. In the fall of 1990, Congress passed the Carl D. Perkins Vocational Education and Applied Technology Act of 1990, the first significant reshaping of vocational education since 1917 when federal support began.

Moving away from defining vocational education as narrow skills training for specific occupations, the Perkins Act incorporated important new language about academic and vocational integration, and broad, "all aspects of the industry" instruction. The passage of this legislation provided a policy foothold (and some much-needed seed money) for making fundamental changes at the local level. Although I did not know it at the time, several years later, this work would be given an additional boost by the passage of the School To Work Opportunities Act, which not only reinforced the imperative to change vocational education, but also raised the possibility of a larger reorganization and reform of the institution of high school.

When Rosenstock called to tell me that he had a mandate from the superintendent to "turn the program upside down and inside out," and that he wanted me to develop a new kind of integrated academic-vocational experience for students, it was an offer I couldn't refuse. My work at Harvard had given me the opportunity to look into important new research on teaching and learning, and to write about numerous educational initiatives around the country. In the changing dynamics around vocational education, I saw a possibility to put what I had learned to good use. The promise inherent in redefining vocational education was all the more intriguing because I had previously spent ten years working in an alternative school for Cambridge students, many of whom had dropped out of the Rindge program. I was also living in a household with three teenagers, each of whom frequently voiced his own cogent analysis of what was "dumb" about school.

The strategy at Rindge was to address the "as if I care" syndrome by creating concrete, purposeful contexts for learning, using community and workplace problems, and tools and materials usually found in a vocational milieu. In part, this involved joining vocational approaches (e.g., coaching, performance assessment) with academic goals and standards.

We were aware that the trend in comprehensive high schools was to expunge any vestiges of the old "voc ed." Insofar as such courses narrowed students' future options, we agreed that they probably deserved to be cut. But we did not assume that students would necessarily be better off in traditional academic classes, reading textbooks and listening to teacher lectures, with little sense of how the knowledge being covered might connect to their present or future lives. Although the setting for our work was a vocational program, we assumed that the lessons we learned would have implications for students throughout the different tracks or programs of the comprehensive high school.

Because vocational education had remained unchanged for so long, the efforts at Rindge attracted attention from the beginning. Although the

Perkins Act called for a fundamentally different approach to vocational education, and the School To Work Opportunities Act created new support for combinations of learning and work, practitioners and policy-makers did not as yet have a clear vision of what these ideas might actually look like in practice. Rindge was one of a relatively few programs around the country ready to seize the opportunity to redefine the purposes and content of vocational education.

A BROAD VIEW OF VOCATION

Of course, in a sense what we were doing was not new at all. To find a source of inspiration and direction for this work, we had only to return to the writings of John Dewey, a prominent educational thinker in the first several decades of this century. Dewey, more than any scholar since, recognized that all education is, in some sense, vocational, and that Americans ignore this fact at their own peril.

"Education through occupations consequently combines within itself more of the factors conducive to learning than any other method," Dewey wrote in his 1916 book, *Democracy and Education*.[1] Like current-day cognitive scientists, Dewey saw learning as an act of construction and meaning-making. The learner doesn't simply "take in" information handed to him, but rather creates knowledge and understanding by active engagement with problems and efforts at resolution that involve transforming the environment in some way.

It is important to note that "vocation" to Dewey was not limited to paid work. In his view, every person has various vocations, occupations, or callings (terms he used synonomously) that go far beyond gainful employment and include, for example, their family and community lives, their participation in the political process, and their artistic endeavors. Thus when he called for "education through occupations" he was not talking about narrow training for a specific occupation, but rather a broad, purposive education that would help students to develop the full range of their capacities and, ultimately, to find fulfilling lives. To Dewey: "The vocation acts as both magnet to attract and glue to hold."[2] This is vocational education in the broadest sense.

Although many graduate students read Dewey in their preparation to enter the field of education, up until recently, the national ambivalence about vocational pursuits at the high school level has kept educators from building on his work. Happily, this is beginning to change. The past six years of activity in reforming vocational programs and creating new school-to-work programs has opened the door to working with Dewey's ideas in a new way. The potential is there to transform and revitalize our high schools.

Certainly, it will not be easy. Proposals to integrate vocational and academic curricula, or to create school-to-work programs that offer career pathways and internships to high school students have met with opposition from a number of quarters. No matter how many students from such programs proceed to college (and most do), some parents, teachers, and students fear that such changes might represent a new, more sophisticated tracking mechanism or a further "dumbing down" of the content of education. While understanding that infusions of business support could help reinvigorate the schools (especially in urban and rural districts with eroding tax bases), some people are also loathe to risk any form of corporate control of schools.

Cynics dismiss "integration" or "school-to-work" as still another bandwagon in a long parade. They may be right that these movements will go the way of other reform efforts of the past few decades. But, the issues that created the imperative for such reforms will not go away. Worldwide economic trends are causing changes in the very nature of work. As we head into the twenty-first century, the disjunctures between school and work are becoming more apparent, as are the consequences of these disjunctures for young people, many of whom are having increasing difficulties finding decent jobs with a living wage. Attention to the role of vocational factors in high school education is long overdue.

THE VALUE OF STORIES

To illustrate what Dewey's ideas could look like in practice today, this book draws on stories from pioneering programs that I was fortunate enough to see and learn about during my years at Rindge and, more recently, through my work at Jobs for the Future, a national nonprofit organization that assists schools, districts, and states in their efforts to link learning and work. I am aware that there are dangers in focusing too intently on specific programs. As soon as one begins to tell the details of a particular story in a particular school, the audience is likely to focus on differences between this story and their own, and might begin to feel even less clear or hopeful about achieving change in their circumstances.

I noticed this problem as we embarked on the changes at Rindge, and found ourselves simultaneously entertaining a steady flow of visitors from other schools, coming to observe and ask questions. This show of interest was extremely encouraging—especially insofar as it indicated a growing acceptance of the need to integrate academic and vocational learning and to connect school to the "real world" through project-based approaches. However, unfortunately, it was often hard to know how to be helpful.

Typically, those who came were already open to the idea of academic and vocational integration and happy to see examples of it in action. Their most pressing need was to find out how this particular group of people in this school and district were able to achieve such changes. A typical dialogue would go something like this:

Question: "You keep referring to team meetings. How do your teachers have time for those?"

Response: "Each of our design teams of teachers has common planning time during the school day at least once or twice a week."

Question: "How have you managed to schedule that?"

Response: "Within our house, we're able to schedule our own students and teachers. We've made the planning time a high priority, and have even canceled some things we thought were not working—like the old vocational exploratory—to free teachers up to meet in integrated teams."

On one level it makes perfect sense for visitors to ask such questions. But behind all of the specific questions was the larger query: What special circumstances enabled you to do something that seems so difficult, if not unattainable, to us? You can almost hear the discouraging thoughts: "we don't control our own scheduling," "we don't have any vocational teachers," "teachers in our school won't give up a prep period."

I do not mean to suggest that schools cannot learn from one another. Teachers can and do take inspiration from seeing one another's most innovative project and curricular designs, and particularly from seeing examples of the resulting student work. In fact, all of the programs described in this book have been part of networks that have provided them with some models and coaching, and have encouraged them, in turn, to articulate their own thinking to others. At various times during my years at Rindge, we borrowed approaches or even specific assignments from both the Oakland Health Academy and the Communications Academy at Francis Drake High School in Marin County, California—two of the programs described in chapter 1.

One school community may not be able to look to another for a blueprint or manual for making changes, but it can still be very helpful to have models of how others are thinking their way to a different form of practice—the theories they draw on, the places they look for evidence of success, the ways they evaluate that evidence and rethink what they are doing. It is with this hope and in this spirit, that I have written this book.

It is also important to note that portraits of schools are snapshots that, at best, capture a complex institution at a particular moment in time. Not surprisingly, recent months have brought changes in a number of these programs. For example, the successes of the Oakland Health and Bioscience Academy (described in chapters 1 and 2), have been instrumental in the district's recent decision to create similar academies, with links to broad career and industry areas, in all of the district's high schools. Although viewed by the Health Academy as an affirmation of their work, this district initiative means that some members of the staff are being pulled away to create new academies.

Program growth has also led to changes in the rural school district of Flambeau, Wisconsin (described in chapter 2). The emphasis on entrepreneurial community development has led to so many student-run enterprises that they are setting up a limited liability corporation. One half of the profits will go into a scholarship fund to be paid out at graduation, based on a student's contributions to the business, and the other half will go back into the business. On a less positive note, the Rindge School of Technical Arts is struggling to maintain its focus on academic and vocational integration amid key leadership changes and a sweeping restructuring of the larger high school of which it is a part.

Whether the programs written about here become models for large-scale changes or are themselves scaled back, they offer images of teaching and learning approaches that are very different from those typically found in high school classrooms. Hopefully, such images will be of use to practitioners, parents, community partners and policymakers as they search for ways to reform our high schools. The intent is to inspire rather than to enshrine.

Chapter 1 starts with the crisis of disengagement—hinted at by the "as if" of the student quoted earlier. It is a crisis that is much more widespread than many people admit. This chapter describes the attempts of three very different high schools to develop projects that will serve as "the magnet to attract and glue to hold" their students. These stories from the field lead into a discussion of how the research of cognitive scientists, such as Howard Gardner, provides new support for Dewey's theories and suggests new approaches for putting them into practice. The last section offers some guidelines for designing projects that are both academically rigorous and grounded in community and workplace realities.

Chapters 2 and 3 look at two important contexts for active learning—community issues (chapter 2) and workplace problems (chapter 3). In most communities today, students have far too few opportunities to work alongside adults on issues that adults take seriously. One of the consequences of this is that young people do not develop a sense of what is involved in accomplished performance or internalize a set of real world standards. The school programs described in these chapters are creating curricula and partnerships that make this kind of learning possible.

In chapter 2, the focus is on school programs that are bridging the often considerable gap between classroom learning and community life. These programs are grappling with the challenges of involving students in community-based projects and community development activities, without sacrificing their academic pursuits or their preparation for the future. Through their involvement, students are finding ways to resolve the tension they have come to feel between personal advancement and social contribution, or put more simply, between doing well and doing good. Again, Dewey's thinking provides a framework for understanding how we can move beyond such false dichotomies.

In chapter 3, the focus is on work-based learning, and particularly, on the learning experiences and opportunities being created by school-to-work programs. This chapter delves into why students in such programs routinely say that they learn more at work than at school, and explores a range of school and work combinations, from individual students doing internships in business or community settings to whole classes becoming involved in field studies in which they become "consultants" to a business or community group. The emphasis throughout is on what students can learn from their involvement in integrated work-based learning projects.

The authors of chapters 4 and 5 combine expertise in key academic domains with experience in school-to-work programs. I invited Rob Riordan and Margaret Vickers to explore more specifically how intellectually rigorous, work and field-based learning experiences can become a strategy for deepening understanding of key concepts in the sciences and for exploring central themes in the humanities. In focusing on the humanities and sciences, I do not mean to suggest that other disciplines are less important, or less easily taught through "real world" projects. Rather the examples these authors describe are suggestive of approaches that could be used in any academic domain.

Concerned that science in high school resembles an "elimination race" that most students will never complete, Margaret Vickers describes teachers and schools that are forging a very different approach. Instead of introducing science topics by asking students to memorize a series of definitions or formulas, the units of study described in chapter 4 start by giving students experience with solving problems in real situations. Guided by their teachers and by other adults with technical expertise relevant to the problem, students learn the scientific concepts and skills that will help them understand and tackle the problem. The second half of the chapter reviews several critical turning points in the history of science as a school subject, and suggests how changing the balance between abstract thought and practical problem solving can help schools achieve the goal of scientific literacy for all.

In chapter 5, Rob Riordan shares stories of how students interning in a variety of workplaces have become actively engaged in "the business of the humanities," which he defines to include: "articulate the self, encounter the world, acknowledge difference, yet find common ground." Through keeping journals, writing biographies of co-workers, as well as autobiographies, and doing projects that make a contribution back to their internship site, students deepen their understanding of how people and institutions deal with human events. This chapter suggests several design principles for constructing a more "hands-on" humanities, and also provides guidelines for supporting writing and reflection as a part of students' project work.

Finally, chapter 6 explores some of the opportunities and challenges involved in creating more programs like the ones featured in this book. In particular, this chapter considers: new approaches to professional development, a reintegration of vocational education into the life of the comprehensive high school, a reconfiguration of teachers' roles, key changes in how schools award credits for graduation, and the role businesses and other community partners might play in developing guarantees of quality. While much of the discussion centers on the reform of existing high schools, chapter 6 also considers the potential for innovation offered by a growing number of new, small schools, exemplified by the Metropolitan Regional Career and Technical Center (MET) in Providence, Rhode Island. Forming within public school systems, or being chartered via special legislation, these schools are basing their entire educational program on the types of community learning and school-to-work approaches written about in this book.

Very recently, I learned about two others that deserve special mention here. From its beginnings as a community-based organization, to its current incarnation as a school and leadership center for young people and adults, El Puente Academy for Peace and Justice in the Williamsburg section of Brooklyn is deeply rooted in the life, work, and spirit of that community. As part of the emphasis on community activism and democratic participation, students publish a bilingual newspaper for their community; in their classes, they investigate and propose action on issues that concern the long-term health of the community. In a recent study they investigated the environmental impact of the Williamsburg bridge—from the effects of traffic on the air quality of the area to the levels of lead caused by flaking paint.

Another small school, the School of Environmental Studies takes advantage of the work experiences and study opportunities presented by being adjacent to the Minneapolis zoo. A magnet program for juniors and seniors, the "Zoo School" offers a living laboratory for the study of environmental and biological sciences. In physical design, this new school resembles the way some technology companies are organized—with small clusters of individual work stations and larger group meeting spaces for discussions and seminars. George Copa, one of the designers, credits the set up of the space, in part, to a visit to the CityWorks room at Rindge (described in chapter 1).

The formation of new small schools is an encouraging and intriguing educational development. Like the other issues and trends described in chapter 6, it is worthy of its own chapter (if not its own book). Taken together, these topics underscore the feasibility, as well as the importance, of changing how, where, and what learning takes place in school. It is my hope that readers will find here the starting points for an ongoing conversation among the constituencies which ultimately must work together on the reform of our high schools.

NOTES

1. John Dewey, *Democracy and Education,* in *John Dewey: The Middle Works, 1899–1924* ed. Jo Ann Boydston (Carbondale and Edwardsville: Southern Illinois University Press, 1980), 319. The author is indebted to Israel Scheffler for his interpretation of Dewey's thought in: "John Dewey on Work and Education," in V.A. Howard and Israel Scheffler, *Work, Education and Leadership: Essays in the Philosophy of Education* (New York: Peter Lang Publishing Inc., 1995) 27–44

2. Dewey, Democracy and Education, 319.

1

—

Project-Based Learning

"Spilling into Life"

Parents send their children to school to learn. Almost no one (except, perhaps, a small number of home-schoolers) questions the wisdom of that act or the faith in schooling that it implies. Yet many young people do not emerge from high school educated in the ways we claim to value. As a learning context, the typical classroom of twenty-five or thirty students and one teacher may work for some young people. But, as teachers admit and parents fear, many teenagers neither put in nor get much out of their time there.

It is possible to get an inkling of the magnitude of the problem from the frequent complaints of teachers about the high percentage of students who do a sloppy job on or fail to complete homework assignments, who come late or cut class altogether, or who seem to have no other goal than to receive a passing, or respectable enough (for college) grade. Another signifier can be found in the criticisms from college teachers about the poor study habits and skill levels of entering students, as well as the justifications employers offer for not hiring young people. But the clearest indications come from students themselves.

They either express their disdain by tossing off comments like "as if I care," or by launching a tirade of complaints aimed directly at school: "It's boring." "This homework is stupid." "My teacher doesn't know what he's talking about." After conducting a survey of more than twenty thousand high school students, Laurence Steinberg of the University of California concluded: "Across the country, whether surrounded by suburban affluence or urban poverty, students' commitment to school is at an all-time low."[1] Four in ten of the teenagers surveyed by Steinberg indicated that they are just "going through the motions."[2] These are the young people who "drop in" to

1

their classes, tolerating forty or so minutes of instructional time as the price they must pay to join their peers in the hallways, lunchrooms, and practice fields, and eventually to reach the ritual of graduation. Although they see most schoolwork as irrelevant to their lives, they are afraid to give up on school altogether, still believing that school may have something to do with reaching future goals.

Research into what actually transpires in a typical classroom or school day helps to explain why students are so quick to call school boring. One method researchers have invented to collect such data is to select a random sample of students and give them digital watches, programmed to beep at eight random times each day for a week. Students are to respond to the signal immediately by filling out a detailed self-report form. Using this "Experience Sampling Method," Barbara Schneider, Mihaly Csikszentmihalyi, and Suanti Knauth collected data on 376 students, as part of a comprehensive longitudinal study, known as the Sloan Study of Youth and Social Development.[3]

Concluding that schooling is primarily a passive activity, the research team reports that students spend less than 5 percent of the time in their academic classes in discussions, although students reported spending more than twice as many minutes chatting with classmates. Very few moments are spent in individual interactions with the teacher. The largest blocks of time are spent listening to lectures or waiting to do something (roughly one-fourth of their time) and engaging in independent work, such as individual "seatwork" and tests or quizzes (roughly one-third of the time).

Students are asked to state not only what they are doing, but also whether the activity is challenging and whether they feel motivated by it (the latter is gauged by students' indicating whether the activity is interesting to them, they wish to be doing the present activity, and enjoy what they are doing). Unfortunately, the activities that challenged students the most, were also largely ones in which their motivation was low and their anxiety high. On the whole, the researchers find that students feel more challenged in academic courses than in art, music, or shop, but they also feel less motivated. Interestingly, students who reported feeling both challenged and engaged were more likely in the follow-up interviews to see some connection between school-related activities and their future.

"Life Was Happening"

One of the best ways to understanding what is happening for students, and particularly why so many disengage from school, is to listen to the way they make sense of their experiences. In her research on drop-outs, Michelle Fine conducted in-depth interviews with numerous young people, like Tony, a twenty-one-year-old bellhop in Manhattan who left high school years earlier.

> I was always taught that you went to elementary school to prepare for junior high to prepare for high school which prepared you for college which prepared you for life. But life was happening when I was fourteen, and I was stuck in school. I wasn't being prepared, I was being held back, constrained . . . I had energy, passions, physical life to lead and that was set back.[4]

Tony's words struck me when I first read them several years ago. Recently, I reread them after receiving a letter from Greg, a young friend in his first semester at a well-regarded, selective liberal arts college. He had been a top student at the high school where I work, and one of the only students I ever spoke to there who could talk with genuine enthusiasm about the study of mathematics. He passed advanced placement tests in both calculus and physics while in high school, received great scores on the college boards, and was generally considered to be a model student. Yet, within two months of starting college he wrote us a letter that was powerfully reminiscent of Tony's thoughts:

> I realized that academic education beyond learning to read and basic arithmetic should not begin until age 30. Our society forces us to waste our youthful bodies sitting . . . to take our wonderfully multi-interested minds and force them into one channel . . . maybe college should be based around group-oriented physical activities, such as . . . playing sports, or even picking potatoes in the hot sun. There is much time left as our bodies deteriorate and our minds tire of constant switching for us to begin to enter academic fields.

Teachers at the high school would be shocked to read this letter, probably chalking it up to a youthful identity crisis. Perhaps some of the sentiment can be explained as first-semester college adjustment issues. But, the hunger for experience and activity that Greg expresses should not be ignored. (He has since decided to take a leave from college and spend the next semester teaching in an urban fourth-grade classroom.)

It is possible that Greg's enjoyment of the subject matter and success in meeting the school on its own terms made him willing—through high school—to put up with the disjunction between life in school and life in the society. After all, school was less painful for him than it was for Tony. What is striking is that despite the differences between these young men, both in background and probable futures, neither could envision school as a way of being a part of, rather than missing out on the world.

One of the primary demands that adolescents make of one another is to "be for real" or "get real." Teenagers do not abide hypocrisy; they even have difficulty with hyperbole. Disdainful of anything or anyone phony, they have made the term "wannabe" into an insult. Psychologists say that the drive for authenticity and identity are a central preoccupation of the teenage years. Sadly, these drives put teenagers at odds with the very institution that is there to educate them: the schools in which they spend much of their time.

In school, students are expected to learn fragmented bits or chunks of subject matter which seem to be important only as a gateway to more of the same. They move from class to class, in batches of thirty, with few opportunities, except perhaps disruptive behavior, to distinguish themselves from their peers. They have little respect for teachers, who have been given the impossible job of commanding attention to material that seems lifeless and useless. Disengaged from the enterprise of schooling, students can be harsh critics of their teachers, even when teachers try to tap into their concerns (as the biology teacher leading a debate on drug use was doing); not suprisingly, they are as likely to resist as to applaud such a move.

Over two thousand years ago Plato wrote that the most important task of educators is to teach young people to "find pleasure in the right things."[5] Try as they might, most of those working with teenagers in high schools today are finding this difficult to accomplish. How, teachers ask, can we compete with television? or rap music? or the seemingly never-ending desire to "chill." Some teachers make a point of emulating entertainers in order to catch the attention of their students. The problem with this approach is that it accepts as a given that students, seeing no real purpose to what they are doing in school, will only be motivated to learn if they are being diverted or entertained. It might be more instructive to derive lessons from a different set of "competitors"—the teams, workplaces, and youth groups where teens seem more inclined to roll up their sleeves and get down to work.

Relatively few young people are lucky enough to find such arenas (most of which are outside of school), where they come to realize that true enjoyment does come from Plato's "right things," activities that require skill, concentration, and involvement. This is most likely to happen to students who have a clear talent or passion—perhaps for the arts, music, or sports, or to students whose early successes in an academic discipline like mathematics or science lead them to become deeply involved in solving intriguing problems or carrying out experiments.

4

Most young people are not yet sure where their interests or talents lie; they need to connect with people, ideas, and events to help guide them in their search. Instead, they attend schools that are dissociated from the productive life of the community. The first section of this chapter looks at three school programs that are trying to make schoolwork more like the real work and real projects that young people willingly embrace: The Communications Academy of Sir Francis Drake High School in Marin County, CA (ComAcad); the Health and Biosciences Academy of Oakland Technical High School, in Oakland, CA (Health Academy); and the Rindge School of Technical Arts of Cambridge Rindge and Latin High School in Cambridge, MA (Rindge).

The ComAcad and the Oakland Health Academy are both examples of what Dewey might have envisioned in 1916 when he called for education through occupations. In each, a major industry provides thematic coherence to a program of integrated academic and vocational education. Interestingly, although similar in form, these two programs developed in very different settings and circumstances.

Sir Francis Drake is a comprehensive high school in the affluent suburban Tamalpais Union school district outside of San Francisco—a community that views high school mainly as a way station to college. In the 1980s, with real estate prices soaring and student enrollment shrinking, the district was faced with the threat of closing one of its three high schools. The likely candidate was Drake where issues of student disengagement and under-performance had become a concern, especially in comparison to the other two high schools in the district. Believing that a more integrated, interdisciplinary, and project-based approach could revitalize the school (and perhaps even draw students who might otherwise go to private schools) the Superintendent, with the support of the Marin-based Autodesk Foundation, encouraged teachers to step forward with new ways to organize teaching and learning. Over a six-year period, faculty members started five school-within-a-school programs: an interdisciplinary cluster for freshmen, and four clusters for tenth through twelfth graders, each organized around a broad industry theme. (In addition to communications, there are academies for engineering, environmental sciences, and leadership/public service.)

In contrast to Sir Francis Drake, Oakland Tech is a technical/vocational high school in an urban district with a very high concentration of African American and immigrant students. Over a decade ago, when staff began to develop the Health Academy, their major goal was to decrease a startlingly high drop-out rate by giving low-income students hope about future careers. A focus on health careers made sense in an area with a burgeoning health and biomedical industry. The success of the Health Academy has since led to the formation of additional academies with other industry themes, not just at Oakland Tech but at all six of the high schools in Oakland.

Cambridge Rindge and Latin School combines demographic characteristics from each of the other two schools. A merger of a vocational school (named after industrialist and philanthropist, Frederick Rindge) and a "Latin" school for the college bound, it is a comprehensive high school in a small city where substantial populations of African American and immigrant students coexist with the children of families who work in universities in the Boston area. In 1990, when the Rindge School of Technical Arts took its current name and form, it continued to be (despite the merger) a somewhat separate entity within the high school, defined more by its demography and the probable destinies of its students than by an intentional focus or theme. The challenge was to overcome a long legacy of tracking poor and minority students into a vocational program structured around selecting a trade and preparing for it, and instead create a variety of community and workplace contexts within which students could learn academic skills and experiment with different work identities.

Despite differences in origin and structure, the three programs are all— each in its own way—trying to address the crisis of student disengagement from school studies. All three have made more permeable the walls between academic and vocational, school and community, and school and work. As a pedagogical approach, all three have chosen to involve students in substantial projects grounded in real world issues and concerns, and guided by adults from outside as well as inside the school. Their stories point to the practices and theories we will need if high schools are to capture the attention and allegiance of youth, and ultimately, help them to take pleasure in the "right things."

I. STORIES FROM THE FIELD

The Communications Academy: Focus on the Arts

"I think all those years of creativity-free, spoon-fed learning drained my ability to learn . . . ComAcad doesn't just stop at a test or report card, it goes on and spills into life. That's the most rewarding thing."

A high school junior wrote this in her first quarter evaluation of the Communications Academy (ComAcad) at Sir Francis Drake High School. It is rare to find this kind of glowing testimonial about high school. Yet students in the ComAcad routinely praise the program in their evaluations. Their enthusiasm becomes more understandable when one views some of the performances, videos, and multi-media productions that these students work on during their two-year experience in ComAcad. This is clearly a program in which creativity is valued and fostered.

The challenge for the staff has been to strike an appropriate balance between artistic endeavors and academic pursuits. As juniors and seniors, students come to ComAcad for half of their school day. The curriculum includes subject matter required of students in most high school college preparatory programs (e.g., American Literature, World Literature, Economics, U.S. Government, and U.S. History). But rather than encountering this material simply as school assignments—something one must get through to earn a diploma and move on beyond high school—ComAcad students are expected to transform their academic studies into a series of multi-media and performance projects, many of which require sophisticated applications of technology.

To ensure that students develop the skills to create such projects, the schedule also includes "craft time" when they can select a course in an area such as theater arts or video. Students are also required to participate in a second craft period, choosing from an array of after-school, evening, and weekend offerings. By extending the school day in this way, the program can bring in professionals from the San Francisco Bay area to serve as adjunct staff. "We want them to learn to use the medium to a professional standard," explains Michelle Swanson, a founder of the program.

The ComAcad has managed to bring "inside" the curriculum the kinds of activities many students find particularly engrossing outside of school— such as dance, drama, and film-making. Within the context of exploring and experiencing the fields of communication, performance, and media arts, ComAcad students combine academic work with concentrated studies in theater arts, sound design and engineering, video production, and computer-based interactive applications and presentations.

Such activities are not only a regular part of their school day, but are also supported by special opportunities for students to work closely with visiting artists and technical experts. In the past several years, local playwrights have created original works with and for the students to perform; and students have worked with professional directors, choreographers, and performance artists, as well as lighting, sound, and camera technicians. Working alongside professionals has not only helped students enhance their skills, but also has led them to recognize and reach high standards of production.

Swanson describes the process: "We say to our visiting directors or choreographers, we want you to direct this as a professional production. We'll be in the room with you while you work, so that if we discover Johnny doesn't have good rehearsal discipline, or doesn't know how to break down the script outside of class, we can coach him and offer more explicit instruction on how to meet the standard being set." The students may not reach the standard the first time, but at least they understand what good work looks like and know when they are moving closer to it.

Perhaps the most unusual aspect of the program is that the multi-media projects do not just come out of special arts or media production courses, but are an integral part of the academic program as well. Throughout their study of American history and literature, ComAcad students engage in artistic production activities. These productions are not just expressions of what students have learned, but are a means to understanding important themes in American life and culture.

For example, during a study of social revolutions in American history, one group of students produced, shot, acted in, and edited a satire of the early television situation comedy, "Leave It to Beaver." In their script, the students drew on their understanding of three social trends of this era: McCarthyism, the Beatnik movement, and the rise of suburbia. In conducting their research for this project, students obtained actual commercial footage from the era, which they combined with original footage using students and teachers as actors. The result was a hilarious, high quality television program take-off, "Leave It to The Beav."

In another project in American history, teams of students created screenplay adaptations of scenes from Toni Morrison's *The Bluest Eye*, drawing both from their reading of that novel and from an extensive study of the civil rights movement. Later in the semester, students used interviews they had conducted with Vietnam veterans to produce audio-visual portraits of the war, as seen through the eyes of those who fought it. These types of productions are not just created for a classroom audience or grade. They are shown at the quarterly ComAcad public exhibition. Students at the ComAcad can expect to have their work viewed by hundreds of people, both from within the school and larger community.

"What I like a lot about the craft areas is that they all demand a synthesizing of content, thinking, and technical skills," explains Swanson. "Even if you know how to shoot or edit video, if you want to produce a piece, you have to know what you want to say with it. Artists make choices. The staff expect students to be able to discuss how these kinds of choices convey meaning. We didn't want the kids showing a piece and only being able to say, 'You know, Vietnam War, the 1960s. They should be able to answer questions like: Why did you choose to shoot the piece on immigrant rights in black and white? Did you try to find Vietnam vets with a different point of view?"

A requirement after each major project is that students not only share their work with others, but also defend their work in front of an audience. One strategy for cultivating an audience beyond the high school has been to do some projects that are of immediate interest and usefulness to local citizens. For example, as part of a study of the American political process, students create advertising campaigns (including video and audio ads, as well as an interactive computer piece) for real candidates and propositions on the ballot.

The public presentation of this work takes place the night before the election. Over the years people have come to depend on it as a way of informing themselves before they vote. The evening includes straw ballots and interactive, computer-based presentations on the electoral college process, as well as specific information on the candidates and issues. After showing their work, each team of students is expected to come up to the front and field questions from the audience, who are encouraged to ask about both content and process.

People also attend the quarterly public exhibition of student work because they have become directly involved in that work, either as coaches for students, or as subjects of students' research. For example, some of the veterans who had been interviewed for the piece on the Vietnam War came to the exhibition of the piece. Their response left little doubt in the minds of the students as to the value of what they had produced. Several of the veterans were so moved by the way their stories had been told that they gave students medals they had received in the war.

As these examples illustrate, in the ComAcad, the communications industry offers an appropriate way to focus instruction, not to narrow it. Students pursue academic studies through engaging with the tools, disciplinary lenses, ideas, and skills of artists and technicians. Thus, despite the rigor and seriousness of their technical studies, students are not necessarily preparing to be communications technicians. Certainly, they can decide to go on to entry level jobs or further technical training in these areas. But, they can also opt (as many of them do) to continue their study of the liberal arts and sciences in a four-year college. Their program has prepared them to do so if they wish.

The Oakland Health and Bioscience Academy: Using Knowledge to Help People

Like the ComAcad, the Health and Biosciences Academy of Oakland Technical High School uses an industry theme to organize its curriculum. With an entirely different demography from the ComAcad, but using a similar approach, the Oakland Health Academy has achieved comparable outcomes for its graduates. Although the program began, and still functions as dropout prevention, it routinely sends the vast majority of its graduates to postsecondary institutions.

A four-year evaluation, done as part of a statewide assessment of ten career academies, found that Health Academy students had better attendance, more credits, higher grade point averages, fewer courses failed, and a lower probability of dropping out than did a matched comparison group. After noting similarly positive results in a more recent evaluation, the Far West Laboratory for Educational Research concluded that the program has "accomplished the nearly impossible with a significant number of urban at-risk youth."[6]

As in the ComAcad, students in the Health Academy spend half of every school day within their separate program. In this case, in addition to English and social studies, students take science each year (biology, physiology, and chemistry), as well as a biomedical lab, and courses in computer applications, health occupations, and advanced electives (including community college courses offered on site). Students also participate in a series of work-based learning experiences in hospitals and other health-care settings.

One of the most unusual aspects of the Oakland program is the way in which students proceed through increasingly complex school and work-based projects, with decreasing coaching and scaffolding on the part of the teachers and industry partners. In their three years in the program, Oakland students are expected to make progress along three major trajectories: 1) from doing small, short-term projects under the tutelage of a teacher of a specific course, to completing longer term integrative projects that cross curricular boundaries and draw on the expertise of industry partners; 2) from handling projects with a lot of specific work requirements, to tackling more open-ended projects with more room for student choice and creativity; and 3) from demonstrating knowledge or skills they have been taught, to undertaking projects of personal interest that make a contribution to a larger audience.

From the time students enter the Health Academy, most of their classes include at least short-term projects that relate to the subject area of the course. Because many of these projects call for newsletters, brochures, and other products, the Academy sets aside a period for instruction in computer word-processing and desktop publishing. While working on major projects, they can also use this time for meetings with their health industry mentors. In addition, the computer lab is open and available to them after school every day.

The most explicit instruction in doing a project occurs in eleventh grade, within, and then broadening beyond, the context of the physiology class. The year begins with a short-term project in which students interview relatives to develop detailed family medical histories. In November, students begin work on a major health education project that helps students develop their knowledge while at the same time practicing skills in conducting research, and producing competent written and oral communications. In small teams, students choose a health problem or issue that interests them. It can be one of particular concern to teens, or one that will potentially be of interest and relevance to a different target audience.

The first benchmark for the team is to develop a project proposal. Approval of the proposal marks the beginning of the research phase, during which students draw on basic medical knowledge about the health issue they have selected to write a description of the scope of the problem. Several requirements structure this phase of the work: students must keep a careful list of sources, and each student has to turn in a research notebook, detailing how s/he spent at least four hours of research time.

As students carry out these research activities, the physiology teacher, David de Leeuw, recruits an industry coach for each team, using the team's proposal summary to attract someone with expertise in the specified problem area. For example, this past year, de Leeuw found a local dietician to match with the team investigating the health effects of vegetarianism. The dietician met with the team to review their research findings, to suggest additional areas of research, and to help them anticipate some of the hard questions that their intended audience might ask.

After completing the research requirements, teams are expected to begin work on a newsletter, which must include at least one factual piece on the health issue, one article detailing a controversy concerning this issue, and a human interest story. They pass the next benchmark when they turn in a first draft of the articles and a summary of each team member's role in the writing/production process. After the teacher has commented on the draft, students move into the production phase, using a computer to do the page layout. Finally, they are ready to plan and rehearse the presentation that they will eventually make for a real audience. During this phase, they get help from a new set of experts—people who specialize in health education.

Patricia Clark, the coordinator of the Health Academy emphasizes the vital importance of the role the industry experts play. Such partners are critical, explains Clark, because they can provide knowledge about the industry that teachers may not have, and they make students feel that what they are learning is "the real thing." Throughout this project, the experts expose students to real-world standards. If the newsletters are good, the student not only receives a good grade, but a health clinic might make the material available to patients. If students are to present what they have learned to other groups of young people, their presentations must be good enough to meet the standards set by community groups like the Red Cross that routinely do this kind of health education.

For example, after being trained as AIDS peer educators by a representative from the Red Cross, a team of students put together presentations on AIDS-related issues for other groups of teens. Their presentations included basic scientific knowledge about HIV as well as a question and answer period which they prepared for by anticipating difficult questions peers might ask. Other groups received training as anti-tobacco and lead poisoning educators. Their audiences included parents and younger students as well as peers. As Clark notes: "Our students are well-placed to do effective health outreach. They live in medically underserved communities and are often the 'health experts' for their extended families."

In the end, students are graded not just on how well they cover the facts of their issue, but also on how likely it is that their health education strategy would bring about behavioral change around this issue. This project drives home a point that de Leeuw believes to be critical to his course: that it is important both to develop technical knowledge about aspects of physiology, and to know how to use that knowledge to help people change their behavior. "Both of these are important parts of being in health care," explains de Leeuw. "Technical vocabulary is vital, but being a health care worker does not mean reciting terms. What good is this stuff if you can't talk about it and use it to help people?"

If the health education project is an apprenticeship in project-doing, the senior project is a chance for students to do a masterwork of their own. Every student in the program is required to undertake a major independent project in their senior year, which "counts" for senior English credit. Students are encouraged to work in teams. Through undertaking this project (which can be but does not have to be directed at health education) students are required not only to demonstrate what they learned about a topic they have researched, but also to produce something of actual use to clients or professionals in the field or the Health Academy community itself.

In the research phase, students are expected to make use of community resources as well as printed material, e.g., by interviewing professionals and patients, and/or visiting offices, clinics, or advocacy programs. Periodically, they are given reflective writing prompts that ask them to think about both the process and product of their work. Finally, they present their projects to a panel that includes industry partners, and, as part of this discussion, they are expected to assess how well they set up and executed their projects.

Although facing a less structured set of work requirements, many teams use a very similar process to the one they used for their eleventh grade project—a good indicator to the staff that the students have begun to internalize the methods necessary to carry out a multi-step project. Staff are still working on "getting it right" in the structure and support of this major piece of work. The requirement that the product be "of use" seems very effective in directing students toward good topics, but it also has led to some frustration, for both students and staff. If the goal is a usable product for a real audience, much depends on the type of product the students decide to produce.

For example, one team produced a "Patients' Guide to the Emergency Room," which turned out to be a good vehicle for synthesizing what they had learned in the research phase of their project. The students visited and took photographs of emergency rooms in two different hospitals, interviewed a triage nurse, staff nurse, and a doctor, and read procedure manuals used by staff in the hospital. The guide they produced discusses typical emergency room procedures and anticipates consumer questions, such as: When does it make sense to go to an emergency room? What should I bring with me? How long should I expect to wait?

However, for other teams, the requirement to be "of use" led to final products that were more narrowly utilitarian, and hence did not fully demonstrate or make use of the depth or breadth of what they had learned. For example, after completing their research on breast cancer among women of Hispanic origin—which included an investigation of both cultural and epidemiological issues—a student produced a four-page brochure for Latinas. Although this might be a perfectly adequate and usable product in its own right, a brochure—by its very nature as a readable educational pamphlet—only skims the surface of a topic. Teachers have discovered that one way to address this issue is also to require a reflective essay, in which students analyze the experience of carrying out the project and discuss what they learned (e.g., how the student's choices of what to include in the brochure were affected by her research into common attitudes among Latinas toward breast cancer detection or treatment).

In talking about their program, the faculty of the Oakland Health Academy express an acute awareness of the dilemmas involved in project-based work, particularly the delicate line they walk between providing enough structure to ensure consistency of effort and yet also allowing for individualization. Structured work requirements serve to ensure that most teams, regardless of skill levels, end up doing a very good job. In this way, the eleventh grade health education project "is a very leveling one," according to de Leeuw. "The issue is how much choice, in what areas, with what requirements," explains Clark. The search is for a balance between too structured (hence too much like schoolwork) and too open-ended (hence confusing and leading to inconsistent results).

At the same time, de Leeuw and Clark recognize that it is important to encourage students to select an issue about which they really care, and select a target audience who will benefit from their work. These more value-laden aspects of the project, along with the opportunity to make artistic choices about the products they make (e.g., newsletters) and the presentations they do, leaves room for individuals to make their own very personal connections to the work. In a sense the design of the program in Oakland provides students with an apprenticeship in project-doing. Built into the program is the recognition that becoming adept at doing sustained project work is in itself an important goal for all students, and, as such, is worthy of school time. By engaging in increasingly complex and multi-step projects, students practice such critical skills as working in a team, dealing with real constraints, and maintaining flexibility in the face of ill-defined and changing problems—all vital skills in today's world.

Elite vs. Mass Education: Background to The Rindge School of Technical Arts

The projects that students do in the ComAcad and Oakland Health Academy grow out of and reinforce the industry focus each program has adopted. The Rindge School of Technical Arts has created a somewhat different structure and curricular organization to support project work. Like the other two programs, Rindge is a school-within-a-school. But rather than forging links to a particular industry, the task at Rindge has been to overcome a century-old separation of academic from vocational studies.

In 1917, one year after Dewey made the case for education through occupations, the Smith Hughes act was passed and a much narrower vision of vocational education found its way into federal law. Under pressure from organizations like the National Association of Manufacturers to train students in the technical skills needed by industry, lawmakers laid the groundwork for a federally funded system of vocational education, the legacy of which has lasted to this day. For years, vocational education has functioned as a largely separate track within the comprehensive school where some students (largely those from working-class and immigrant families) would train for specific trades and occupations.

The educational rationale for this policy can be found in a 1918 report, commissioned by the National Education Association, entitled *The Cardinal Principles of Education*. Proposing the introduction of a diversified program of studies adapted to the supposed needs of different students, this report provided the foundation for the comprehensive high school with separate academic and vocational programs. The new high school would include a distinct vocational strand designed to "equip the individual to secure a livelihood for himself " and a domestic program to ensure that girls will develop a "capacity for an interest in the proper management and conduct of a home."[7] These would exist alongside a liberal studies strand, a continuation of the curriculum that had dominated the high school when it was an elite institution, primarily preparing students from privileged backgrounds to become society's intellectual leaders.

With its focus on the capacity for reasoning and rhetoric, and for mathematical and scientific thought, the liberal studies curriculum was seen as appropriate for a talented minority, an increasing number of whom would proceed on to college. Because many of the occupations for which students in the vocational strand would prepare required only moderate levels of literacy, schools were under no particular pressure to develop a strong academic component for their vocational programs.

Over the next forty years, the high school went from an elite to a mass institution. In many ways, the model of the high school emerging in this period—with its separation of head and hand—mirrored the division of labor in the economy. Basic organizing principles of mass production, such as quality control, repetitive activity and interchangeability, can still be seen in our schools, in standardized ways of keeping records, furnishing classrooms, dividing up school days, dividing up curriculum (units and lessons), administering discipline, instructing, and grading.

By the 1920s, the new science of psychology had produced a theory of learning, called behaviorism, that was very compatible with the new factory system. In behaviorist theory, it is possible to identify exactly what is to be learned and then break it up into small, sequential bits. The speed and accuracy of a student's response represented the "output." This too could be quantified and measured. As in the factory, the model was hierarchical. Teachers would be treated as semi-skilled assembly-line workers, processing students for slots in society. Knowledge would be attached to the students somewhat as the parts of an automobile are attached to basic frames.[8]

The goal was to process a great many students efficiently, selecting and supporting only a few for thinking work. As millions of new immigrants entered the United States in search of a better life, intelligence testing and school tracking were invented to prove the necessity and fairness of sepa-rating out children into those who would work with their heads and those who would work with their hands. Intelligence, it was thought, was an in-herited quality that could be measured with a single instrument. The best the schools could do is test and sort the students, teaching some to work with their minds, and relegating most to work with their hands.

To this day, many school vocational programs feature lowered expec-tations and watered-down content. Requirements are met through courses like "Consumer Math" or "Business English." Instead of education through occupations, students receive (at best) education for a specific occupation; only, unlike apprenticeship, this type of occupational education is divorced from the setting where the student can see the actual need for and use of the skills. Victims of the same history, their more privileged peers in the col-lege preparatory track work their way through a program of increasingly abstract and academic pursuits, with significantly fewer opportunities to see connections between what they are learning and its uses in the world.

From Manual Training to Exploring Community Needs and Resources

A visitor to Rindge in 1990 would have found a program that had existed largely unchanged since its original design for the industrial revolution over a hundred years before. Described in 1888, as a "Manual Training School for Boys of Strong Physique and Average Talents," Rindge in 1990 still embodied the outdated and undemocratic premise that fifteen-year-olds of lower income families should choose a trade and spend their high school years preparing for it. The starkest example of that philosophy was the freshmen exploratory, in which all entering students sampled each of the shops available in the school, culminating in their selection of a vocational "major" that would structure the majority of their time in the remaining three years of high school.

The exploratory was not only the entry point for students, but also for faculty, as they tried to "sell" their programs (and hence keep enough en-rollment to secure their jobs) to the students. Although they taught the ex-ploratory course in the autonomous isolation of their own shops, these teachers had a strong interest in getting to know all of the freshmen. The system functioned rather like a series of blind dates: students went from shop to shop trying to decide with which teacher (and technical area) they would enter into a relationship.

Not surprisingly, this bred competition among the shops. Teachers in each area suspected the others of "courting" students too vigorously and making unrealistic promises. Although teachers did not propose a change, there was a recognition that a competitive norm was not particularly healthy. There was also a growing feeling of futility and desperation as the total enrollment continued to drop, and students who entered seemed happy to spend time hanging out in the shops (and hence escaping from boring academics), but not all that interested in the trades being offered.

There was virtually no integration of the exploratory with academic subjects. In fact, Rindge students "went out" to the other parts of the high school for academics. Although this was supposed to eliminate social isolation and bring vocational students into contact with a wide range of peers, the reality was that they were mixed primarily with other low-income students in low-level academic classes. Rindge students faced all the problems associated with the bottom track in high school: watered down curriculum with minimal academic content, teachers who would rather be working with a more motivated set of students, and negative labeling by other students and teachers.

Because the ninth-grade exploratory was the entry point for students and a critical year for faculty as well, it was the initial focus of the redesign efforts. In the spring of 1991, we created the first design team of faculty, who had volunteered to help create a new ninth-grade program. No one in this group had ever undertaken this type of collaborative curriculum development before. For many years, these teachers had spent virtually all of their time at school teaching narrow technical skills that were occupationally specific. Most believed that this is what it meant to be a vocational teacher. State mandated curricula reinforced this notion: manuals for each shop area listed duties and tasks that students were expected to complete. Little was left to the teacher's judgment.

We were asking these teachers not only to work together, but also to take on an ambitious task. Whatever we developed had to build on the strengths of vocational education, such as working on real projects and using appropriate tools and technology, while avoiding the assumption that students were training for a particular trade. Our ultimate goal at that point was to achieve a state of integration so that a visitor would not be able to tell whether he was in an academic or a vocational classroom.

Over the period of several months, the team created the framework for a new ninth-grade program called "CityWorks." The idea was to replace the exploration of trades with an exploration of local community needs and resources. In the process of representing what they saw, and addressing some of these needs, students would learn to use some of the tools, materials, and approaches of the various shops. They would also learn to do interviews and conduct research in local archives, and write up their findings for a variety of community audiences. In this way, CityWorks would reinforce academic skills as well.

The first task was to develop a learning space that would look neither like a classroom nor a shop, where faculty could lead students in projects grounded in community life. David Stephen, an architect and drafting teacher suggested we borrow the notion of "studios" from design schools, subdividing most of the room into small spaces, each with its own work table and locked cabinet for hand tools and art supplies. This arrangement would give participants the flexibility to team up and regroup as a project necessitated. An open area at one end of the room would be used for large group activities, such as presentations and exhibitions.

At first, no one was quite sure how to behave in this type of setting. Some students took advantage of the arrangement to pop in and out of the various studios, thus disrupting the work of other groups. Faculty longed for the privacy of their own shops. For the first year, the CityWorks team—expanded to include all twelve of the teachers leading studio groups—met on a daily basis, trying to find solutions to the many new problems we had created. Memories of that first year still produce groans and nervous laughter among the teachers who pioneered the program. But despite the pains of adjustment (or perhaps in part because of them), the unusual set-up of the CityWorks room has worked quite well. The room itself communicates to all who enter that this is indeed new territory.

The studios allow students to work individually and in teams, creating "artifacts" of Cambridge (e.g., maps, tapes, oral histories, photographs), and designing new buildings and services. Projects involve hands-on work, like making a wall-sized map of the city and wiring it to light up selected landmarks. At the same time, students engage in problem solving and social analysis, like deciding where on the map to locate a new teen center that would attract youth from all ethnic and racial communities of the city. Every few weeks, students bring their work-in-progress or finished products to the exhibition area, where they present it to the other studio groups and, periodically, to panels of experts as well.

Each year, the culminating project focuses on different neighborhoods in the throes of revitalization and redevelopment. These projects involve a mixture of simulation (e.g., designs for and models of new buildings) and real products with an immediate use (e.g., T-shirts or brochures). Community activists, local business people, and staff from community agencies are invited to help create a context for students' efforts. Staff members from city agencies and programs identify unmet community needs that students could address, and also serve as an authentic audience for students' finished products and presentations. (See Chapter 2 for more detail on the community development projects.)

This type of "hybrid" of vocational and academic education worked so well that we decided to anchor the tenth grade program in a similar way. After several failed attempts to create new hybrids, we finally came up with two new courses: Pathways and Introduction to Technology. With its emphasis on projects and on-site investigations, Pathways builds on the skills students have learned in CityWorks. The differences are that the focus shifts from community needs to work issues, and students are expected to work independently, as well as in teams. To understand how adults think about and approach their work, students do informational interviews and job shadows; they also start their own micro-enterprises, which involves learning how to do market research and write a simple business plan. The goal is for students to discover more about their own interests and how these might connect to further schooling and careers. (See chapter 3 for a description of Pathways.)

Introduction to Technology builds on CityWorks in a different way. An integrated math, science, and technology course, co-taught by the vocational and science department staff, it provides an opportunity for students to continue learning technical skills without having to "major" in a particular shop. Built in half of what used to be a large carpentry shop, the technology lab is a space in which students can do hands-on projects, using equipment ranging from computers to power tools; there is also an area that works well for discussion and even the traditional "chalk and talk."

The course draws on a combination of home-grown and published curriculum units. In one unit developed at Rindge, students learn principles of physical science through conducting a structural analysis and energy audit of the school building. Based on what they find, they design and construct something that will improve the safety and/or efficiency of the facilities. Such activities help make the connection between technical tasks and procedures and key concepts in math and science.

As juniors and seniors students apply to participate in one of a number of different internship programs offered by the school in collaboration with local businesses and educational institutions. Internship opportunities include facilities management, culinary and conference planning and university operations and services at Harvard University, early childhood and early elementary education in the Cambridge public schools (in collaboration with Lesley College), financial services in local banks, and health sciences in local hospitals and clinics.

Students spend half of their day in a combination of work and learning—interning at a work-site and attending an on-site seminar coordinated by a member of the high school faculty. In addition to the routine work tasks assigned on the job, students are expected to carry out a major project that makes a contribution to the work-site, jointly negotiated among the student, teacher, and supervisor. (See chapter 3 for a general description of the seminar and student projects, and chapter 5 for a detailed look at humanities projects.)

II. DESIGN PRINCIPLES FOR PROJECTS

Research on How People Learn

In their emphasis on projects that link schoolwork to real work, the Com-Acad, Oakland Health Academy, and Rindge all embody Dewey's notion that students should learn through engaging in activities that have a purpose and correspond to adult pursuits in the real world. In a sense, they also represent attempts to recapture an approach that hearkens back to a much earlier time, long before there were separate institutions called schools. For centuries, children had learned to carry out the occupations of their parents by observing and imitating them, working alongside adults to cultivate the land and create the products of daily living.

As societies and technologies became more complex, more formal systems of apprenticeship emerged. Through apprenticing themselves to master craftsmen, who coached them through a series of tasks and challenges, young people could learn the intricate skills and sometimes secret arts of the trades and crafts of preindustrial life. With the rapid growth of new industries in the nineteenth century, this kind of learning began to disappear—replaced by schools for some and hard labor in the mines and mills for others.

Dewey's idea of education through occupations combines the benefits of apprenticeship with those of formal schooling. He did not believe that schools should ask children to pick a vocation and then train specifically and exclusively for it. Rather he envisioned a continuous process throughout a child's schooling of focusing on activities and occupations that would evolve with the age of the child. By engaging students in the tasks and projects of a range of occupations, and exposing them to adults who competently carry out various arts and scholarly pursuits, it would be possible to make classrooms into contextualized settings where children could explore materials and tools, solve interesting problems, and devise and carry out their own projects.

Interestingly, this idea is being actively advanced again, this time by cognitive scientists whose studies of how students learn, and especially how they come to deeply understand something, has led them back to features of apprenticeship and to the work of progressive educators like Dewey. In his book, *The Unschooled Mind*, Howard Gardner concludes that "apprenticeship may well be the means of instruction that builds most effectively on the ways in which most young people learn."[9]

Features of apprenticeship and of discovery museums, argues Gardner, can help lead to a level of understanding that students rarely reach in a decontexualized classroom setting. While most high school courses try to cover a broad sweep of content and to impart a wide array of generalizable skills, the result is often disappointing. When asked to apply knowledge they have learned in a classroom context, even top students from the best universities demonstrate only a superficial understanding of key concepts and ideas. They revert to what Gardner calls their "five-year-old unschooled mind."[10]

The need and desire to try to make sense of things is a distinctly human trait. Our minds are designed for complex, situated learning. By the age of five, most of us have developed full-blown, albeit primitive, theories to help us explain and understand the world. Schools fail to acknowledge or challenge these early mind-sets, preferring to view the mind as an empty vessel into which new knowledge can be poured. (One education analyst has called school "15,000 hours of systematic training in learning *not* to learn!"[11]) Fed a steady diet of skills and drills, students do not see any relation between earlier intuitive theories (e.g., heavier things drop faster) and important concepts (e.g., gravity) that are taught in school. To survive within the constraints of school, they learn the "code," memorizing formulas, or learning propositions that they will need to regurgitate on tests. But as soon as they meet these same concepts in a non-school setting, they revert to their original intuitive theories.

Gardner describes some of the features of apprenticeship that, if adapted by present-day schools, could help address this disjunction: "They permit aspiring youngsters to work directly alongside accomplished professionals, hence establishing personal bonds as well as a sense of progress towards an end. Frequently they also feature interim steps of accomplishment, with workers situated at different levels of the hierarchy, so that a learner can see where he has been and anticipate where he is headed." And perhaps most importantly, unlike schools where students are expected to work on tasks "that appear more or less remote from the operation of the remainder of the society," in apprenticeships, "learning is heavily contextualized—that is, the reasons for the various procedures being taught are generally evident, because the master is in the process of producing goods or services for which there exist an explicit demand and an evident use."[12]

It is, of course, not simple to adapt key features of apprenticeship to to-day's classrooms. First, the apprenticeship system developed as a way to in-struct young people in trades involving physical and tangible activities. Apprentices in tailoring or plumbing could see the process of work as the master carried them out and could learn by imitating them. Today, however, in both academic and vocational domains much of the work takes place on a symbolic and conceptual level. The problem-solving strategies and cre-ative application of ideas at the heart of the work of an engineer or a com-puter programmer are not at all easily observable, nor can they be learned in the abstract.

And this leads to a second major difficulty— in apprenticeships the learn-ing take places inside the work context, with many opportunities to practice and apply the skills. It is not clear how to create this sense of urgency and au-thenticity inside a classroom, how to structure situations, such as those de-scribed by Gardner, where "youngsters enter directly into the excitement that surrounds an important, complex, and sometimes mysterious undertaking where the stakes for success (and the costs of failure) may be high."[13]

Where Do We Keep the Paper-Mache? Redefining "Projects"

Gardner's words have special resonance for those trying to reform high schools along Deweyan lines. The challenge is to find ways to connect the excitement and opportunities for practice that can be offered by vocational education at its best with the habits of mind and important ideas or con-cepts fostered by academic education at its best. For Dewey and his disci-ples, the answer lay in organizing the curriculum around projects.

Since the early years of this century, the project method (the more con-temporary term is project-based learning) has survived, mainly in progres-sive elementary schools where teachers and parents place a high value on active learning. However, as with many labels describing educational ideas, the term "projects" is used somewhat indiscriminately, to describe anything that involves "learning by doing."

Several years ago, the cartoon strip "Calvin and Hobbes" ran a series in which Calvin has to produce a diorama for school. He waits until his bed-time, the night before it is due, and then asks his mom, innocently, "Where do we keep the paper-mache?" In the last frames Calvin wonders aloud why his mother has turned into the "conniption queen" and why producing a good diorama is all that important anyway.

As in many strips in this series, creator Bill Watterson relies on readers recognizing and identifying with Calvin's frustrations and humiliations in school, as well as his wisdom about the institutional realities and his occasional triumphs over these obstacles. Miss Wormwood undoubtedly had good intentions in assigning this "hands-on" project. But, like school projects that most of us can remember, it is every bit as contrived as the worksheets that are due the next day. Is it any wonder that Calvin wants to give it the same last-minute treatment?

Unfortunately, like Miss Wormwood, many educators use the term "project" to refer to just about any activity that departs from the usual paper and pencil, lecture/recite formats of school. By this definition, school projects are simply big or messy assignments—ones that will take more than a half-hour to complete and hence "count" more than everyday assignments, or ones that require parental attention and support, such as making a diorama. As students get older, the project is most likely to be in the form of a paper, or the occasional "hands-on" assignment, such as a collage for an English class or a presentation board and model for a science fair project. The main exception to this is in vocational classes, where students might work on building a bookcase or taking the engine out of a car.

Dewey was not unaware of the charge, still made today, that involving students in "learning through doing" might limit their intellectual growth. His response was simple. The school should not oppose practice: it should "intellectualize practice" by putting it to systematic use in the promotion of learning. "The burden of realizing the intellectual possibilities inhering in work is thus thrown back on the school." Or, as he put it in another passage, it is possible to "pour acid on metal for the purpose of getting knowledge, instead of for the purpose of getting a trade result."[14] Rather than a substitute for thinking, hands-on work to Dewey was a context for intellectual development.

The Six A's of Project Design

One way to open up a discussion of project-based learning with teachers is to ask them to spend a few minutes thinking or writing about a memorable learning experience in their own lives. When I have used this technique in workshops on academic and vocational integration, I have found that people usually come up with forms of experiential learning—travels to different cultures, adventures in the wilderness, plunging into a new job with a steep learning curve—or they describe particularly stimulating extracurricular or community projects, such as producing a play or editing the school newspaper. Often their stories include a mentor who modeled a certain kind of action or behavior and expressed faith in them and their abilities. As teachers review what was said and realize how few of these experiences happened in class, it is almost possible to hear the group "Aha."

The point of such exercises is not to discourage people about their profession, but rather to help them use their own most potent learning experiences as a guide to creating powerful, effective projects for their students. When teachers identify the characteristics of projects in their own lives, they note that these have usually been things they are personally invested in doing. They also observe that such projects require substantial planning and sustained effort, often undertaken over an extended period of time, and drawing on the combined efforts of several people.

Adults have difficulty coming up with memorable learning experiences that took place inside the classroom because many of the features that characterize real projects are absent in school assignments and projects. One of the striking things about the three programs described in this chapter is that each has found a way to involve students in complex projects grounded in real world issues and problems. These programs make effective use of projects as a classroom pedagogy, by paying attention to "six A's": authenticity, academic rigor, applied learning, active exploration, adult relationships, and assessment practices.

The Six A's of Designing Projects

Authenticity

- Does the project emanate from a problem or question that has meaning to the student?
- Is it a problem or question that might actually be tackled by an adult at work or in the community?
- Do students create or produce something that has personal and/or social value, beyond the school setting?

Academic rigor

- Does the project lead students to acquire and apply knowledge central to one or more discipline or content area?
- Does it challenge students to use methods of inquiry central to one or more discipline? (e.g. to think like a scientist)
- Do students develop higher order thinking skills and habits of mind? (e.g. searching for evidence, taking different perspectives)

Applied learning
- Does the learning take place in the context of a semistructured problem, grounded in life and work in the world beyond school?
- Does the project lead students to acquire and use competencies expected in high performance work organizations (e.g. teamwork, appropriate use of technology, problem-solving, communications)?
- Does the work require students to develop organizational and self-management skills?

Active exploration
- Do students spend significant amounts of time doing field-based work?
- Does the project require students to engage in real investigation, using a variety of methods, media, and sources?
- Are students expected to communicate what they are learning through presentations and performances?

Adult relationships
- Do students meet and observe adults with relevant expertise and experience?
- Do students have an opportunity to work closely with at least one adult?
- Do adults collaborate on the design and assessment of student work?

Assessment practices
- Do students reflect regularly on their learning, using clear project criteria that they have helped to set?
- Do adults from outside the classroom help students develop a sense of the real world standards for this type of work?
- Will there be opportunities for regular assessment of student work through a range of methods, including exhibitions and portfolios?

I developed the "Six A's" as a self-assessment tool for teachers, to help them consider whether the project they are planning addresses key dimensions of project-based learning. It is probably unrealistic to expect to be able to answer "yes" to all of the questions posed. There is, it could be argued, a degree of contrivance that must be expected in schoolwork. But it is unlikely that high schools will be able to capture the hearts and minds of adolescents unless teachers attempt to find ways to meet such standards.

Authenticity: How Real Is Real Enough?

Young children seem to have an ability to invest almost any school assignment with some value. My husband, Steve Seidel, who is a researcher at Harvard's Project Zero, frequently talks with children in the elementary grades about their school work. "If you walk up to a six year old who is coloring in a stencil-produced outline of a turkey as part of a pre-Thanksgiving project, and if you ask her what she is working on, she will almost certainly say something about why she has chosen a particular color or tell you whom the finished product is for," he reports. In other words, the child has brought her own personal meaning to the work. By the time kids have reached middle school (or earlier, if they are precocious like Calvin), many have lost all inclinations to do things that appear to have no value beyond school. Their desire for authenticity is on a collision course with the school.

How Real Is Real Enough?

- Students see a reason for what they are doing beyond getting a grade.
- Students have access to appropriate technology, tools, and materials.
- The work is taken seriously by adults engaged in similar issues or work.
- The work is structured to emulate the best characteristics of high performance work environments.

As the stories in this chapter illustrate, students will often have a more positive response to school projects that involve a combination of simulation and reality. The work feels "real enough" to the students if the project resembles the work adults do and they are given the opportunity to invent, create, or contribute something that is taken seriously by adults. ComAcad students see their schoolwork as "spilling over into life" precisely because they are constantly involved in the process of creating new products and performances that are shared with real audiences.

For example, when students make campaign advertisements for local candidates, they are not producing "real" campaign material. They have not been contracted to produce these; nor are they expecting to have their work shown on television. The work feels authentic to the students because they are working within a genre they know is important in the world (television advertising). They are coached and encouraged by experts who work in that genre, have access to (and are coached in the use of) the tools and materials of the television trade, and, most importantly, are participants in an activity that adults in the world take seriously.

This is also the case in CityWorks when students design new buildings and services for Cambridge and present these to the community development department. The Oakland Health Academy frequently involves students in teaching something to others. From the time they enter the program, students are expected not simply to study the medical sciences, but to become health educators capable of conveying important information to a range of others from elementary school children to targeted underserved populations. Educational needs and opportunities in their community become a major source of projects.

Sources of "Real Enough" Projects

- Community needs and development issues: students design/create something the community needs.
- Problems/questions that arise at work: students "consult" to a local institution or business.
- Educational needs and opportunities: students teach something to others.

Academic Rigor: Mapping Backward into the Disciplines

Academic rigor is, of course, the "A" that most concerns high school academic teachers, and the dimension that probably has most to do with their reluctance to tackle sustained project work. While some elementary and middle school teachers try to incorporate substantial, long-term projects into their curriculum, such projects are still relatively rare in high schools, where class periods are shorter, and the pressures to "cover" a certain amount of subject matter are greater.

The problem is that many students simply do not see the importance of much of this subject matter, and, as Gardner and other cognitive scientists point out, learn it superficially at best. Projects that start from a real question, arising from the life and work of the community, have the potential both to spark students' interest and to lead them to an exploration of key disciplinary concepts and skills. Margaret Vickers, who writes in chapter 4 about using projects to teach science, calls this approach "mapping back-ward." It is an approach she and her colleagues used in creating the *Work-ing to Learn* curriculum.

Mapping backward involves a simple but profound shift in the way we structure learning for students. Rather than beginning with academic sub-ject matter and later asking how any of this might be applied to the "real world," this approach begins with a real problem that someone might need to solve on the job. Students learn the concepts and skills as these become important and relevant to tackling such a problem and to produc-ing a product or solution that addresses the problem. For example, a cur-riculum unit on water quality and aquatic ecology begins with the question of how communities monitor and maintain water quality and cen-ters around a series of visits to workplaces involved with water quality. With the help of teacher and workplace coaches, students learn scientific techniques for monitoring both chemical and biological factors in a river or stream and basic ecological concepts of niche, food webs, and chains of causation.

Complex projects also provide starting points to explore themes in the humanities, a subject that is discussed in chapter 5. As Rob Riordan writes, being out in the community or in a workplace raises many issues for stu-dents that can help them enter classical treatments of these same themes. In addition, in the process of doing a project, students get a lot of practice in literacy skills. For example, by the time they complete their health educa-tion projects, de Leeuw's students have done a great deal of reading from a range of texts, and have written in a number of genres, including propos-als, journals, reports, and newsletter articles.

Applied Learning: Tackling Semistructured Problems

It is possible to address concerns about academic rigor by developing proj-ects that help students engage with subject matter and practice literacy skills. Still, in the process of doing a project, students may spend substantial time learning technical skills and engaging in the "hands-on" work of de-veloping finished products and presentations. Is it legitimate to take class time for students to learn to produce a newsletter or a video? Is learning to do water quality tests essential to an understanding of ecosystems? What does rehearsing for a presentation have to do with learning biology?

One way that teachers "solve" this problem of time is by assigning proj-ects as homework—often as the culminating assignment of a unit. The logic goes this way: "First I'll teach the content and skills of my course; then, if there's time, I'll assign a project that requires students to apply what they have learned." The assumption is that students will be able to do this work at home, because they have learned the requisite skills in school. This type of linear progression from learning (in school) to application (outside of school) does have an appealing simplicity.

Underlying such assignments is an assumption that students will know how to carry out projects on their own. Whether the assignment is piecing together a diorama for a book report, or setting up a science fair project with an experimental design, this assumption is an underestimation of the effort and skill involved. One problem is that it leads to inequities between those who have parents who can help and those who do not. The quality varies tremendously, depending on the child's outside-of-school support systems. Of course, teachers realize this. It is not uncommon for teachers to wonder who to grade—the parent or student—because clearly the parent did the work. At the other extreme, teachers bemoan the shoddiness of the work kids do on their own.

The main value of projects is as an *instructional* strategy, not as an extension or demonstration of what students have learned. While projects take more time than the usual school assignment, they provide a context for deepening the learning, and of teaching important applied learning skills that students will need whether they are heading to college or directly to work. By making time during the school day for students to carry out at least some project activities, teachers can help students learn skills that will help them become more independent and persistent learners, and more collaborative and productive workers.

Most school assignments ask students to draw on a defined, finite amount of material to respond to a problem or question that has a right answer. But, in everyday life outside of and beyond school, problems are rarely so clearcut, and a person rarely has all the relevant information upfront. In fact, the act of tackling a problem often changes its very definition. And, in many real projects, it is never really clear whether the problem is "solved" or if the right decisions have been made. There is great value in creating learning contexts that allow students to meet unstructured or semistructured problems *before* they are instructed as to the "right answer" or the right way to go about addressing the problem.

It is possible that one of the reasons so many students experience difficulty (and leave) during the first year of college is that their earlier schooling has not done a good job of exposing them to just such complexities. Rather, they have moved through school, completing assignments in which the boundaries and expectations are clear. Faced with more ambiguous situations or more open-ended college assignments, they simply do not know where to begin, or how to engage in a sustained effort.

The ability to tackle semistructured problems is also a valuable competency for students to have when they enter the workforce. It is a competency that shows up regularly on the lists employers make of qualities that they are looking for when they hire or promote workers. High on the list are a number of other skills that students gain by participating in well-designed projects—most notably the ability to work well in a team, to communicate well in oral and written form, and to use technology appropriately.

Of course, students do not automatically learn applied learning skills from doing projects. These skills, like any others, require a combination of modeling, direct instruction, and opportunities for guided practice. One image that seems to help teachers envision their role is to see project work as building a tower. If the students are the builders, the role of the teachers and other adults involved is to provide the scaffolding that allows students to take their work (literally) to a higher level.

Scaffolding of this sort is very much in evidence in all phases of the the Oakland health education project. From the beginning, students understand what they will be expected to produce throughout the project. They know how and when their work will be evaluated, and have helped to establish the criteria. As with most projects one encounters at work, there are a number of "deliverables" throughout (e.g., a proposal, research notebook, newsletter, and health education presentation), not just one final product at the end. These milestones are opportunities for ongoing assessment and self-assessment. Teacher and students find out if the project is on track while there is still time for students to make adjustments that will help them complete the project successfully within the given schedule.

To help inculcate a sense of high standards, the teacher shares exemplars of completed work from previous years. As they proceed with their own efforts, he continues to guide them to useful materials and to adults who serve as coaches and mentors in the field-based components of the project. When it comes time to prepare for their health education presentations, students get direct instruction from adults whose job it is to do health education work. Finally, students have access to the technology necessary to produce high quality products, and receive instruction in the desktop publishing skills required to produce finished newsletters.

Is the outcome worth all of the time this, or any other complex project takes? The answer is yes if students learn what is involved in carrying out such a project, begin to internalize a sense of quality work, and require less and less scaffolding as they encounter future projects. In the last several years it has become increasingly popular to assign a "senior project" the second half of the senior year of high school. Certainly this can be a wonderful culmination of twelve years of education. But, without explicit attention to applied learning skills, and opportunities for students to engage in a sequence of projects earlier in their education, this could become—like the science fair—another time when students (and their parents) are rewarded or punished for skills that the school did not help them develop.

Active Exploration: From Field Trips to Field Work

"Student as worker, teacher as coach" is one of the nine principles for whole school reform articulated by Theodore Sizer of the Coalition of Essential Schools. Sizer developed this principle after months of visiting high school classrooms in which the teacher was doing the bulk of the work, while students sat there, bored and passive. The question, of course, is how to encourage students to become more actively involved in their own learning.

One reason for this passivity is that students are rarely expected to grapple with what Eleanor Duckworth of Harvard University calls the "funny, frustrating, intriguing, unpredictable complexities of the world. . ." The tendency in school, notes Duckworth is to present students with "the simplest, neatest explanation of the 'law of moments,' 'the composition of the atmosphere,' 'density,' 'buoyancy,' or whatever. . ." Yet it is through experiencing and grappling with complexities, that students learn to form their own ideas and to use these ideas to make connections to new situations.[15]

Within the context of a well-structured project, students can learn to accept the importance of exploration and investigation, of expecting and coping with the unexpected. One of the best ways I have found to change the usual classroom dynamic and move students into a more active stance is to design projects that necessitate leaving the classroom, at least for some aspect of the work to be completed.

Anyone who has spent much time visiting historic sites or museums has probably encountered a group of high school students on a field trip. School field trips are a time-honored way of getting students out of the classroom for a period, or a whole day, and are usually much-appreciated by students as a break from the usual, boring routine of the school day. Unfortunately, such trips are often of limited educational value: the students spend much of their time socializing, leading the teacher to focus more on behavior management than on the learning potential of the trip.

In the first month of Cityworks we made the mistake of piling the students into a bus to visit historic sites in Cambridge. We wanted to signal to them early on that the community would be the major "text" for the course. Although we had planned carefully (there was background information on each of the tour stops and worksheets for students to fill out), students treated it mainly as a time to socialize, not to try to learn more about their city. Several weeks later, as part of the Walkabout unit, students went out again. Each studio group had the task of gathering information and artifacts relating to an aspect of community life that interested them and on which they were going to report back to their peers (see chapter 2 for a full description of the unit). Although some students still had difficulty getting down to task, for the most part students were much more focused and productive.

It was in discussing the contrast between the first trip and the later forays out into the neighborhoods that we discovered the different between field trips and field work. Even though both activities expand the learning environment beyond the classroom, field work requires a much more active stance. Students literally become investigators and explorers, using a variety of tools and technologies to gather and codify information. This is true whether they are looking for signs of lead paint problems in city neighborhoods or monitoring the various forms of animal activity in a wildlife preserve.

In some cases, aspects of the field work may serve as a "mini-internship." For example, in the water quality project of "Working to Learn," students spend four hours in a sewage treatment plant where they learn about the water quality tests performed there and investigate the effects of the plant on aquatic life in the area. Although students have already learned in class how to test for a number of water quality factors, at the plant they have the opportunity to see how professionals run these and other tests. The direct connection of the worksite visit to students' understanding of the technical procedures involved in their project is what makes this "common workplace experience" more than an ordinary field trip.

Projects that culminate in an exhibition or panel require students to be active in the presentation, as well as the investigation and writing phases of their work. When ComAcad students show their election campaign ads or their documentaries on war, they also interact directly with the audience, explaining the choices they made in the work. Whether showing a film they have made, or simply preparing to report their results to adults in related professional and academic disciplines, students need a deep enough understanding of their project to be able to respond to questions and, if necessary, defend their ideas.

Adult Relationships

One of the major advantages of organizing instruction around a project is that it creates both the need and opportunity to involve adults from outside of the school. With the exception of teachers in long-standing school-to-work programs, such as the ComAcad and Health Academy, most teachers are simply not used to bringing in the expertise of other adults. But this can be a very important way to change the dynamic in a classroom and to personalize the link between schoolwork and real work.

In a recent workshop in Milwaukee, I met a mathematics teacher who has for several years taught key concepts in algebra by asking his students to think about the design for and economics of a new stadium that is being proposed for the city. It had not occurred to him to call upon the school's business partner to guide students in calculating the fair market value of the stadium land or to bring in people from the city planning department or tax assessor's office. He left the workshop excited about the possibility of enriching this project through the involvement of a broader community of adults.

The interaction with adults becomes most meaningful when the students themselves are working on a project that resembles work the adults do, and perhaps even makes a contribution to a problem the adults are confronting at work. For example, in the health education project at the Health Academy, each team of students receives information and coaching from experts with experience in the issue area and type of outreach the team has chosen. In the final part of the project, the teams do health presentations to otherwise underserved populations—thereby addressing a key issue facing health professionals. When students tackle a problem that is of real concern to a community of adults, they are, in effect, acting as consultants to that community. This lends a considerable sense of support and accountability to the work. (Chapter 3 includes a section on field studies.)

For younger students, even limited exposures to adult professionals can be important. One of the teachers in a ninth-grade mathematics/science team from Rindge went to a summer workshop run by *Working to Learn*. In the process of generating ideas for real problems, he began to write some questions that engineers might ask: "How can I ensure that this building will be structurally sound?" "Why do bridges collapse?" Then he realized it would not work to introduce engineering questions to a group of students who have never met an engineer (nor seen one on television, which tends to ignore the less glamourous professions) and thus have only the vaguest idea of what is involved in engineering.

He decided to begin the year by having students draw a mathematician or a scientist. Just as one might expect, most of the drawings were of the "mad scientist" variety—Einstein on "a bad hair day," as one student put it. In other words, they drew a white man with a crazed look, wearing a white lab coat with a "nerd pouch" for his pens, and grasping a test tube in his hands. Even when they brainstormed all of the people who might use math and science in their work, most students could not come up with a different image.

Within days, students hosted their first class visitors—a multicultural, mixed gender group of engineers from nearby firms, who had volunteered to come to class on a weekly basis to assist students in their studies and to host students at their workplaces. This contact helped to create a context for classroom projects. For example, as part of an integrated unit on structures, students apply basic geometric and physical principles to building the "tallest tower" possible, with a constrained set of materials; later, they move on to building a miniature, weight-bearing bridge, using materials such as toothpicks and popsicle sticks. Such projects take on more depth and resonance because of the presence of real engineers.

At the same time, the contact with engineers challenges the students' stereotypes about who is "good at science" and opens them up to new possibilities for their own futures. While constructing bridges in school, students are also expected to produce a short paper on a specific type of engineering that interests them, drawing their research from interviewing one of the engineers and from career guides available in the school library. Writing in his journal about this assignment, one student described his evolution from wanting to be a rapper to now thinking about engineering—partly, he admits, because of how much he liked the female engineer that he interviewed.

It is possible to start with any subject matter and ask students to brainstorm about how a particular skill or intellectual activity is or could be used by adults in the real world. This is a favorite question among teachers in the *Foxfire* network. When Eliot Wigginton, the founder of *Foxfire,* was a language arts teacher, he would inform students that one of the key goals of his class was for them to learn to write and then ask them to think about writing: "Where do you run into it? Where do you notice it? What kind of writing is that? What is your favorite example of this type of writing?"

Anyone who has tried this technique knows that students begin with obvious or (as in the "draw a scientist" exercise) stereotypic responses: writing is used by writers, and writers are people who wear glasses and sit at word processors all day writing books. But with some encouragement, students realize that everything from the trayliners at MacDonalds to their favorite rap songs have actually been written by someone. Many more people are "writers" than the few professorial types that they might imagine in the role.

Follow-up questions ask the students to think about specific examples of skills or knowledge in use: "Who in our local area might be using such a skill? Where could we find local experts? Which local institutions could we call?" Making contact with people who use a particular knowledge area is obviously easier for some topics or skills than others. Yet even a topic, such as the Civil War, that seems particularly divorced from current day concerns, could be of interest to documentary film-makers in the area, or to set or costume designers, or possibly a museum curator. Similarly, photosynthesis could lead students to botanists, or plant store owners, or greenhouse workers.

Once such a list has been generated, a number of possibilities present themselves: students could design a survey, invite a local expert to come into the classroom, or interview local experts and bring back the results. The point is to find a way to probe how experts use the particular knowledge area or skill in their work. What kinds of tasks or projects require this knowledge? What happens when you don't have a solid enough grasp on the knowledge or skill? What can go wrong? Do they have a story to tell about a failure or disaster that occurred? What are some of the problems they currently face in their work? Sometimes, this type of discussion could suggest a problem or issue that the class could later tackle as a field study.

Finding Uses of Knowledge

- List all of the ways this knowledge area (concept/skill/information) is or could be used in the real world.
- Who in our local area might be using such knowledge; where could we find local experts? Which institutions in our community could we call?
- What are some ways that you could develop or demonstrate your own knowledge and skills while at the same time addressing a real community need or concern?

Assessment: How Standards Evolve

Conditions for Evolving Quality Work

- Faculty meet regularly to share the work students are doing and talk about it.
- People from the community help create a context for students' efforts, by serving as presenters, coaches, and audience for student work; and
- The work—warts and all— is open to public scrutiny.

When Wigginton's students investigated the uses of writing, they decided to write articles about local folk remedies and ended up in a full-fledged oral history project that culminated in the *Foxfire* magazine—one of the most well-known examples of an authentic activity undertaken by high school students. More teachers would surely be willing to consider project-based instruction if they were certain that the end result would equal or come close to the quality of *Foxfire*. One of the obstacles teachers face as they make the transition into project learning is that they do not know how the work will turn out. This is especially problematic when there is not adequate time in the school day for students to work on their projects. In this situation, the "sixth A," assessment practices, can stop people cold.

To reach a quality standard, the work must indeed "spill out" beyond the confines of the usual definitions of school time. Project work does not necessarily fit neatly into fifty-minute blocks; nor does the life of a project necessarily conform to a school calendar of when particular lessons or units must start and end. Feeling pressured to cover a certain amount of subject matter, teachers are often reluctant to use class time on some of the time-consuming but more technical aspects of project work—e.g., mastering graphic or presentation software, editing the video, rehearsing the performance or presentation.

All three of the schools described here have found ways to create the time and support students need to bring their work to a quality standard. They have created action-learning settings that enable students, teachers, and outside experts to engage in a combination of academic and hands-on activities. In the Health Academy students have a period set aside for using the computer lab, or meeting with mentors. ComAcad students also have time during the school day to focus on the technical and production aspects of their work. When performance or final production time draws close, they routinely spend late afternoons and evenings working with visiting artists and technicians. In the Rindge program, we created new courses, like City-Works and Pathway, that are structured around community and work-based learning. In these courses, project work *is* the curriculum.

However, even when such action-learning settings are available, entering into project work with their students can feel risky to teachers. Consider their situation. They have sanctioned an expenditure of that most precious commodity of school—classroom time—without knowing exactly what, or how much, students will produce. They have moved away from the dominant paradigm of content coverage, opting instead for learning goals that are much harder to measure: deeper understanding, the development of habits of mind, and "learning-to-learn" skills.

Most importantly, they are doing all of this at the same time as they open themselves up to more public scrutiny than they may ever before have experienced. By definition, projects of the sort being described here have an audience beyond the classroom itself. The work is viewed—at various stages—by a range of adults from outside of the school. Teachers are not used to opening themselves or their students up to this kind of high stakes assessment.

It would be nice to reassure teachers that the work students do will be great, and will allay any parental or administrator worries about the quality of instruction. But, the truth is that it takes most teachers several years to begin to see student work of a high enough quality to be reassuring to anyone. One of the hardest and most critical moments in the transition towards this type of instruction occurs towards the end of the first project cycle, when it is time to make public the work students have been doing. Teachers often feel that much of the work is simply not good enough to warrant the public scrutiny they anticipate.

The paradox is that the project work students do may never reach the "good enough" standard if the work is contained within the classroom and kept private. In my work with teachers I have seen the same phenomenon over and over. It does not work to set a quality standard and only allow projects to become public if they meet that standard, because it is in the very "public-ness"—the sharing of ideas and attempts with others who take the work seriously—that a true quality standard evolves.

As the person responsible for creating new project-based courses and modules at Rindge, I learned most of these lessons the hard way. The first year that the students in the CityWorks program did community development projects, teachers were embarrassed by some of the work students had done—the drawings and designs were too childish; the models were not finished; the spelling was bad; the handwriting was impossible to read.

We had endless debates in our team meetings as to how much teachers should step in and correct or complete the work. We also had heated disagreements as to whether students should be forced to make oral presentations of their work.

In the end, people handled these issues differently, but at least we reached a point where everyone respected one another's choices. The presentations and exposition occurred. On the whole, the experts we had invited found ways to convey respect for what students had accomplished, and, at the same time, point out other possibilities or areas for improvement. Parents came in greater numbers than anyone expected, and were generally delighted to see their children's work displayed. In fact the only negative feedback came from several teachers and administrators from other (competing) programs in the high school.

As a result of our team debriefing of these projects, we made some adjustments in the way we handled the community development unit the next year. In kicking off the project with students, we brought community experts in earlier and shared exemplars from the previous year's work. We also built in a few more work requirements at the beginning (e.g., interviews had to be typed and spell-checked before being mounted onto display boards). Finally, we added a mid-project "mini-presentation," so that the students themselves would get a chance to assess their progress and the quality of their work while there was still time for improvement. This also gave them an opportunity to practice their presentation skills. Not surprisingly, the quality of the work improved.

The projects students produced this year (the fifth time through for the faculty) were deemed good enough to be shown in a special exposition in Cambridge City Hall. In the presentations to the expert panel, every student spoke; and, for the first time, students were able to handle almost any question that the experts threw at them. Finally, after five years, the standards have evolved to the point where everyone involved feels proud and comfortable with the quality of the work produced.

There is, of course, still the larger challenge of documenting what students are learning for the purposes of accountability. Despite several years of talk and workshops about portfolio assessment, the major accountability tool in most districts is still standardized tests. Such measures fail to "capture" the learning embodied in complex, long-term projects. These tests do not fully assess the growth and development of individual students, and the resulting test scores do not fairly reflect the quality of the program.

Over time, programs like the Oakland Health Academy have developed an array of prominent community partners, who are not only willing to vouch for the quality of the work, but are willing to demonstrate their satisfaction by offering summer and part-time employment to students, or scholarships and internships to graduates. Such vocal and active partners can help a great deal in allaying public concerns. The Health Academy staff are also careful to keep a set of exemplary student projects, to show to students, and to new teachers or policymakers voicing accountability concerns.

Some schools have adopted a complementary strategy that requires regular, outside review of student work. For example, community partners serve on the graduation review committees of the Central Park East Secondary School in New York. In addition, "critical friends" who have viewed student work come together regularly to assess what the work as a whole indicates about the quality of education in the school. Rindge has begun experimenting with a portfolio process used in Sheffield, England, called the "Student Record of Accomplishment and Experience." This is a four-year portfolio process, with standards developed in conjunction with an advisory group of local businesses and community partners. The partners do not review each individual student record, but they certify the process and standards being used, by "signing on" to the record.

Clearly this is still a period of experimentation. But teachers and schools cannot afford to ignore the issues of accountability and assessment. Without adequate documentation, a program is very vulnerable when staff positions are being cut or when resources are slim. Ultimately, if high schools are to embrace the sorts of projects described here, whole programs will need to be able to demonstrate that the work students are producing is good, and getting better.

NOTES

1. Laurence Steinberg, with B. Bradford Brown and Sanford M. Dornbusch, *Beyond the Classroom: Why School Reform Has Failed and What Parents Need to Do* (New York: Simon and Schuster, 1996), 13.

2. Steinberg, *Beyond the Classroom*, 3.

3. Barbara Schneider, Mihaly Csikszentmihalyi, and Shaunti Knauth, "Academic Challenge, Motivation, and Self-Esteem: The Daily Experiences of Students in High School," in Maureen T. Hallinan, ed. *Restructuring Schools: Promising Practices and Polices* (New York: Plenum Press, 1995), 175-95.

4. Michelle Fine, *Framing Dropouts: Notes on the Politics of an Urban High School* (New York: State University of New York Press, 1994) 10.

5. Mihaly Csikszentmihalyi, "Education for the Twenty-First Century," in *Daedalus: Journal of the American Academy of Arts and Sciences* 124:4 (Fall, 1995), 113.

6. David Stern, Marily Raby, and Charles Dayton, *Career Academies: Partnerships for Reconstructing American High Schools* (San Francisco: Jossey-Bass, 1992), 130.

7. George Willis et al, *The American Curriculum: A Documentary History* (Westport, CT: Praeger, 1994), 153–62.

8. Sylvia Farnham Diggory, *Schooling,* The Developing Child Series (Cambridge: Harvard University Books, 1990), 22.

9. Howard Gardner, *The Unschooled Mind: How Children Think and How Schools Should Teach* (New York: Basic Books, 1991), 124.

10. Gardner, *Unschooled Mind,* 5.

11. Farnham-Diggory, *Schooling,* 49.

12. Gardner, *Unschooled Mind,* 122.

13. Gardner, *Unschooled Mind,* 124.

14. Dewey, *Democracy and Education,* 281–83.

15. Eleanor Duckworth, "Twenty-four, Forty-two, and I Love You: Keeping It Complex," *The Harvard Educational Review* 61, no. 1 (1991), 6.

2

—

Grounding Projects in Community Life

The Search for "Utmost Satisfaction"

> Unfortunately, many of us don't realize how important it is to look around us once in a while and figure out what we can do to help the community, because basically it all comes back to us and our quest for success. And I must admit I am one of those people. You don't really realize that working to improve things . . . is what's gonna help keep you going down the road. So that's basically what I'm looking for. A method to keeping my mind open to the community and to achieve my goals in life.

Javi Mejia-Blau wrote this recently in response to an assignment in "Community Problem Solving 101," at the Cambridge Rindge and Latin High School (CRLS) in Cambridge, Massachusetts. His request does not seem at all unreasonable: he wants his school to help him to do well *and* to do good. But it is not a request that is usually met. As another student wrote recently in an editorial in the Rindge school newspaper, "We are taught the only sign of achievement of people our age is high grades." Many high schools operate on the assumption that it is only by appealing to each student's desire to succeed as an individual (or, more negatively, an individual student's fear of failure) that we can motivate students to learn.

Anyone who has worked or lived with adolescents knows that underlying much of what they do or say is their struggle to answer such fundamental questions as: "Who am I?" "What am I good at?" "Where am I going?" "Do I belong or 'fit' anywhere?" "Does anything I do matter?" Adolescents search for ways to feel valued and central. If their school and home lives do not offer them that opportunity, they are likely to find alternate routes, some of which may not be healthy for them or their community. Students who not do well in school, or do not already have a particular area of recognized talent or skill, are particularly vulnerable, often feeling (perhaps correctly) that adults do not like or respect them.

This chapter features school programs that ask teenagers to become active participants in their communities and that give them ways to contribute directly to the improvement of community life. By involving students in assessing and fashioning responses to real needs and issues in their communities, these programs try to prepare them both for their economic and social lives. The community education program in the Flambeau school district of rural Wisconsin emphasizes entrepreneurship within a context of rural community development. The Oakland Health Academy and the Rindge School of Technical Arts, introduced in chapter 1, use community projects as a primary way to achieve academic and vocational integration. Both of these programs have gained national recognition as innovative school-to-work initiatives. Their focus on community development and participation underscores the distance they have traveled from a more traditional model of vocational education.

I. STORIES FROM THE FIELD

Flambeau, Wisconsin: Carving a Place "Out of the Wilderness"

"We're tearing our hair out about this group of kids. What can you do with 'em?" This is how Chuck Ericksen describes his entry into the Flambeau school district in Rusk County of northern Wisconsin. Brought there by the Cooperative Educational Services Agency #12, his first task was to develop an alternative education program for the students perceived to be most at risk. Nearly a dozen years later, he has the title of community education coordinator, a post from which he oversees an impressive array of initiatives, special projects, and working groups, involving youth and adults, school and community people.

Flambeau is a far-flung school district (twenty-five miles by thirty-five miles) that encompasses five small towns, as well as large areas of farmland. The junior and senior high schools for the district are on one campus in the centrally located town of Tony. Although the distances within the district can make it difficult to maintain community-based activities, the size of the district also means that there are a large number of potential partners to any efforts undertaken by the schools. The groups participating in community education efforts include local businesses, county agencies (such as the Rusk County Committee on Aging), governmental departments (e.g.,

Forestry), conservation groups, and committees of citizens which take care of local sites, like the fairgrounds or the Trails End Camp.

Ericksen's work over the last dozen years traces a trajectory from focusing on disaffected students to creating programs for all children; from involving young people in discreet community service activities to combining youth and adults in highly visible community development and improvement initiatives. "I started with a lot of conversations," he explains, "and I realized that a lot of kids, parents, and teachers were frustrated with the educational system." It was not difficult for Ericksen to understand why. He arrived in the Flambeau district after having run a wilderness education program in Canada for a decade. In the wilderness, he had seen adults and teenagers go through dramatic changes. The key ingredient was the opportunity to "enter into some worlds that really challenge them." It was the desire to understand this phenomenon that inspired him to enter a graduate program in experiential education, which then led to his job in Flambeau.

Soon after beginning his program, Ericksen realized the limitations of a solitary effort: "I could only take so many kids, there was only so much of me to go around . . . I quickly realized that in order to create more opportunities and a better, richer, more challenging environment for kids we really had to have adults engaged from throughout the community." The first entry he found was through community service. Everyone could agree on the value of youth providing services to older and disabled adults. Through a partnership with the Rusk County Social Services Community Options Program, the Flambeau Beautification Project was born. Ericksen matched teenagers with adults referred by the agency, with the understanding that the young people would make regular "friendly visits," helping out with yard care and house maintenance activities as needed. As the partnership grew to include local nursing homes and the Rusk County Animal Shelter, the program eventually expanded to include animal care and recreation services for older adults. Teenagers groom and exercise dogs and cats from the shelter, and then bring them to nursing homes for "pet therapy."

Building on early successes from such efforts, the community education program was able to begin creating links between service activities in the community and more formal learning opportunities for youth. Through a "Summer of Service" initiative, the young people involved in summer service activities, such as the visiting and pet therapy programs, spend part of every day with a teacher, investigating local history, and preparing to interview the elders about their memories of the past. This learning program effectively strengthens the ties between the youth and their elders, while also teaching some valuable lessons in sociology and history.

In addition to the beautification and pet therapy crews, the summer initiative offers young people the choice of joining the Josie Creek Project, in which they work with fisheries and conservation personnel to groom trails, maintain campgrounds, and improve streams for trout habitation. The educational component of this program focuses on science (e.g., biotic features, soil conditions, and composition) and math (e.g., map topography, volume, and flow of creeks). By the summer of 1996, students could elect to work on erosion control projects, biological inventory work for foresters, or improvement of the local country fairgrounds or of an outdoor environmental education camp.

Now, nearly a dozen years into the community education program, the principles of experiential education and integrated learning embodied in the Summer of Service are informing teaching and learning in many parts of the school year curriculum as well. Three years ago, Flambeau became a site of a systemic school change initiative, the Responsive Schools Project of the Institute of Responsive Education in Boston. With its emphasis on school change through new models of family, school, and community collaboration, this initiative has ensured the broadest possible reach for Ericksen's efforts. The growing partnerships with community agencies and businesses have made it possible for teachers to extend and transform traditional school projects into occasions for youth to make meaningful contributions to their community.

For example, with the help of community partners like the Wildlife Restoration Association and the county social services, a typical seventh-grade industrial arts "build a birdhouse" project has become an opportunity to learn scientific concepts as well as to reach out to senior citizens. Rather than simply building a birdhouse or birdfeeder and bringing it home, the students place them at the residences of senior citizens throughout the community. In class, students learn about the birds that use the houses and feeders. Periodically, they go out to monitor the birdhomes on site—an occasion both for gathering data and for paying a friendly visit. Recently, the junior high students added still another element to the project. They have begun to develop sales and marketing plans for selling the houses and feeders to raise money for a summer program focusing on outdoor education and community service in the parks.

Like numerous other rural communities throughout the United States, this area of northwestern Wisconsin is geographically isolated and economically strained, facing the erosion of both their manufacturing base and the family farm. In fact, Rusk County has the lowest average household income and highest unemployment level in the state. One indicator of the economic stress is that fully two-thirds of the students get free or reduced lunch. As Ericksen talked with people in the community, he realized how widely shared (among people of all political persuasions) was the concern for their future way of life and the fear that all of their children would have to leave the area to make a living. "The future of our community requires us to be really enterprising; to do things differently. We can't wait for Madison or Washington to come up with a plan for us; we have to come back to our grandparents' tenacity and creativity. They carved places out of the wilderness. That's what we're trying to do," Ericksen concludes.

Developing Roots and Wings

On the surface, the entrepreneurial spirit of American business would seem to have little in common with the ethic of caring embodied in community service. Yet, the community education program that Ericksen oversees encompasses both. Students and teachers are encouraged to be enterprising as they develop new ways to contribute to the life and work of their community. In fact, entrepreneurial pursuits begin as early as second grade, where the students have set up their own credit union. By high school, such ventures constitute a regular feature of the curriculum. Among the thriving school-based enterprises are a graphic design business and a video business, both of which use computer technology to tailor products to a variety of clients, ranging from daycare centers to local businesses.

Darrell Gago, the welding teacher at the high school, requires all of his students to design a new product made of metal, build and evaluate a prototype, making changes as necessary, and then make a second version that they market. One of Gago's dreams is that one of his students will "come back some day to Rusk County, open a factory and hire lots of people." Based on his experiences thus far, the dream does not seem that far off. Last year, a boy who invented a bear-proof deer feeder found himself hiring some of his friends to help him meet the orders from people who saw his model at a local deer show. "He was going nuts," trying to meet the orders, according to Gago, who believes that the young man could have started a successful business. Instead, he decided to pursue a degree in metallurgy at a technical school.

Over the time they are in high school, students can also design up to four semester-long independent projects not associated with a particular class they are taking. Dave Johnson, the school-to-work coordinator estimates that between a quarter and a third of the students get involved in such projects. "In rural areas we don't have all of the opportunities that

45

everyone else does; we have to customize more," explains Ericksen. The process is straightforward. The student sits down with Ericksen or Johnson, or another teacher coordinating independent projects; together, they identify what it is the student intends to learn and how the student will demonstrate he has met his goals; they also develop a plan for carrying out this work, including what research needs to be done and who could potentially help. If the project is to be carried out in a real work setting, the employer is invited to join in this process as well.

Sometimes a student's independent project ends up sparking the interest of an entire class. For example, one student's project focused on finding alternative uses for the waste from the paper-making process at City Forest, a local paper company. Eventually, his whole science class got involved in the project, discovering from their analyses that the waste contained some decent quality clay that could be separated out. This led them to visit a turkey farm forty miles "down the road," where the owner was considering using the clay as a binding for the feed. The students also tested whether the clay could be used for making pots for plants in the small greenhouse they were setting up.

Recently, working with their biology teacher, Jim Segebrecht, twenty five students have become involved in the planning and development work involved in launching a student-run greenhouse as an entrepreneurial venture. The project took a major step forward when the school obtained a contribution of plants and trees from a major open pit copper and gold mine in the county, as well as a commitment of substantial funds for building a new, larger freestanding greenhouse. Since most people in this rural area have their own systems for growing plants to put into their gardens, students are looking for a way for their enterprise to fill a speciality niche. As part of their classwork, science students have begun to explore local history and horticulture to discover whether there might be a market for "heirloom seeds"—plants that have special meaning for particular ethnic groups in the area, and that represent the "old country" but are not currently cultivated in the area.

Another blossoming enterprise, the Technology Learning Consultants group (TLC, as they are known throughout the community) grew out of an interest expressed by a few students in learning more about computers. As these students honed their own skills, they branched out into helping others in the school and community who needed help with new software and hardware. Within the past several months, TLC, now a group of about ten students, have conducted a half-day inservice for teachers on how to use both the internet and a recently installed intranet system, helped several teachers put together "power point" presentations for conferences, designed web sites for the school, as well as for more than a half-dozen community groups, and begun accepting paid web site design work from area businesses.

When students find new uses for industrial wastes and develop new businesses like the greenhouse for heirloom seeds and the TLC, they strengthen their connections to the people, the land, and the activities (existing and possible) of their local area. In the process of making such connections, young people have the opportunity to develop their own knowledge and skills, and to discover something about their own interests and passions. They learn that while there may not be enough *jobs* in their local area, there is interesting and valuable *work* to be done, and that they may even be able to turn that work into a vocation. And even if they cannot or choose not to, they have learned transferrable skills in the process.

In other words, the goal is to help the students develop both strong roots (a feeling of connectedness to the local community through an understanding of its needs and resources) and strong wings (the knowledge and skills to succeed anywhere, rural or urban). The metaphor of roots and wings, along with several other key elements of the philosophy adopted by Ericksen and his colleagues, came to Flambeau via REAL Enterprises (REAL stands for Rural Entrepreneurship Through Action Learning), an organization founded over a dozen years ago by Jonathan Sher to promote the involvement of schools in rural community development. Many of the teachers (including Gago) have learned how to combine entrepreneurship and community development through REAL Enterprises summer institutes.

Clearly community education in the Flambeau district has come a long way from its modest beginnings as a program for at-risk young people. One measure of this distance is that the teachers coordinating gifted and talented services at the high school now play an important role in developing new projects and in finding community partners to work with the schools in these efforts. Because they are not assigned to classrooms every period of the day, they have the flexibility to do this vital kind of outreach work. It is not often that strategies developed for the most disengaged, lowest-achieving students have later become part of the mainstream program for all students, including those labeled as gifted.

CityWorks: Developing a Pedagogy of Place

The roots and wings philosophy that underlies what Sher calls a "pedagogy of place" is applicable beyond rural communities, although the issues of community development are quite different in urban areas. In developing the CityWorks program at the Rindge School of Technical Arts, we set out explicitly to discover ways to bring a community development approach into an urban vocational milieu. The process begins with an exploration of the idea and value of neighborhood and community. In the early weeks of CityWorks, students have the opportunity literally to place themselves on the map (a large map is painted on the floor) of the city and share what they know about life in Cambridge with one another. Although Cambridge is a small city, many students know little about neighborhoods outside of their own.

After a series of short activities that introduce them to the goals of City-Works and build their skills in map-making, way-finding, and teamwork, students begin the first major project of the year, Walkabout Cambridge. Neighborhood planners from the Community Development Department of Cambridge kick off the project with a slide show and discussion. They take students on a "virtual" tour of the city, outlining major aspects of city life and issues affecting the quality of life for citizens of different ages and backgrounds.

Over the next few days, students and teachers repair to their studio workspaces (see chapter 1 for a description of the CityWorks room) to decide which issue they would like to explore for their Walkabout project. They must then come up with a proposal to present orally to the other studio groups, describing the field work and other types of research they intend to pursue while investigating this issue. The only stipulations are that the field work include visits to sites within walking distance of the school (and hence doable in a class period), and interviews of speakers invited into the school. Each group is accorded one half-day field trip to allow for travel to more distant sites, or for more intensive exploration.

Students are told that they will present their proposals to a panel of teachers, who will grant their request only if they have a good, solid plan for carrying out the field work. Once approved, they have four weeks to conduct their field work and develop a presentation board, displaying visual images (maps, photos, drawings) and written information (interviews, descriptions of field work, facts/data) about the issue.

The story of one studio group's project from this year serves to illustrate what is possible when students are encouraged to bring into the classroom concerns and relationships that shape their lives outside of the school day. The group, as is typical in the first stages of this work, had a somewhat desultory discussion of which issue area to pick, with a few students immediately advocating for entertainment, and particularly the issue of recreational and entertainment facilities for youth. The group probably would have settled on that area, if not for one student's sudden, very emphatic proposal to explore health issues, and particularly the provision of services for HIV patients in the city.

A popular student, Karen was able to convince her group that this was a good idea, especially since the city hospital is only three blocks from the school and she knew people who worked in the AIDS clinic there. Karen's leadership in this process was surprising. Up to this point, she seemed to have only one strong motivation for doing schoolwork—the desire to participate in the football cheerleading squad, which requires students to maintain passing grades in all major subjects. Once her place on the squad was assured, her name began to come up frequently in ninth-grade faculty team meetings as a potentially failing student.

Over the next four weeks of field work and project development, the teacher found himself with this new, unlikely ally. Karen not only made suggestions as to who to interview, what to read and where to visit, but also she pushed her peers to take the work seriously during each step of the process. None of us had predicted Karen's turnaround, because until this project, none of us knew that her brother had died of complications from AIDS. We had no reason to think that Karen would feel an intense personal connection to healthcare issues and institutions in Cambridge. (She shared this information privately with the teacher after the first discussion in the group, and then later told the whole group.) Karen's personal connection to this issue propelled her into an active and engaged stance in school and in the community. The opportunity afforded her by this project allowed her to renew and transform her relationship to healthcare providers whom she had met at an extremely stressful time in the life of her family.

No one was more surprised than Karen when the ninth-grade teacher team recognized her accomplishment in the project by giving her the City-Works Team Leader Award at the end-of-semester awards assembly. By the third term in the year, Karen had made the school honor role, an event she lists in her end-of-year evaluation as the best thing about her year. It is still too early to tell whether this will translate into long-term results, but at this point, Karen's leadership in the Walkabout Project has had the result of revealing her potential as a student to herself and her teachers.

Of course, not every student makes this kind of deep connection through the Walkabout project. The point is that this type of project provides a context where this can happen. It suggests the *possibility* of connection, of reaching across what many students experience as an unbridgeable chasm between the tedious routines of school and the much more compelling, although sometimes distressing, non-school parts of their lives. The message is that life outside of school is a legitimate area of inquiry inside the classroom and that coursework can extend out to meet the needs of the community and perhaps even afford students a chance to make a difference.

CityWork: Encouraging Teen Visions

The Walkabout project leads right into the culminating project of the year in CityWorks, "Teen Visions for Community Development." Each year, the staff and students pick a different focus for the community development project. One year, for example, students worked with the city's tourism agency, in creating plans for a heritage museum for Cambridge. The director of the agency approached the staff with the idea of involving students in this effort. With thousands of people visiting the city each year, we agreed that it was important for students to understand the tourism industry and to help plan its development in a way that would take the needs of residents into account. We were also intrigued with the idea of creating a reason for our students to become familiar with local museums. Although several excellent museums are located within walking distance of the school, our students were virtually unaware of their existence.

To kick off the project, we asked the agency director to speak with the CityWorks students and ask for their help in planning for a heritage museum. Based on the needs explained by the director, and their own interests and strengths, each of the CityWorks teachers outlined a project for a team of students to do. Students could select the one that best suited their skills and interests. Not surprisingly, given the context of a vocational program, a number of students were most interested in preparing designs for the new heritage museum and creating scale models based on those designs. To prepare for this work, they visited a number of nearby museums. It was their job also to pick a site for the proposed building. This involved visits to some vacant lots where a new structure could be built and to several old buildings that could be renovated.

Several other teams focused on developing written products for visitors to the city. Rejecting existing brochures featuring "Old Cambridge" and Harvard University, one group designed a tour featuring places of interest to visiting teens, while another created a "Sweet Tour" for visitors seeking the best desserts in town. Still another group decided to highlight the efforts of a local hero. While videotaping an interview with John E. Gittens, a founder of the Cambridge National Association for the Advancement of Colored People, the students learned that he had led a neighborhood organizing effort to get the city to open a new playground after a child was struck by a car while playing in the street. Their brochure featured a map locating the playground as well as the story of its creation. All three brochures, along with a T-shirt designed by another group of students, were subsequently adopted by the tourist agency as products to distribute and market. Three years later, I still see people walking through the city wearing the T-shirt students made with the silkscreen of the bridge over the Charles River.

In each of the following years, planners from the city's Community Development Department has helped CityWorks staff and students identify a neighborhood of the city where there is already an active revitalization campaign or which has been slated for redevelopment. As with the heritage museum, these community development projects have the quality of being "real enough," because adults in the community are actively committed to them. All have also ended with students doing a formal presentation of their work to a panel of experts, including the director of community development for the city, local school board members, staff from city agencies, architects, designers, and community activists. The panel responds to the work, asking students questions about what they have done and offering suggestions as to how to move forward with the effort. In the evening, the school hosts an exhibition of the students' work for family and friends. Both of these audiences are vitally important, helping to "up the ante" on quality.

Other teachers in the school have expressed surprise at how seriously the freshmen in CityWorks take the projects and presentations, given that most of their ideas and products will probably not literally change the face of Cambridge. We believe that the presence of the panel and the fact that the tasks resemble the work adults actually do helps to set these projects apart from the usual classroom fare. Students can see for themselves that what they have produced matters and makes sense to adults who are engaged in similar work in the community.

In our efforts to use community exploration and community economic development as contexts for learning, Rindge, like Flambeau, has enjoyed the vital support of a larger network: the VOCED Project of the Center for Law and Education. Through the VOCED network, the model of CityWorks has been adopted and adapted by a number of schools around the United States (as well as the school system of Utrecht in the Netherlands), all of which are searching for ways to integrate academic and vocational learning, while encouraging students to be a positive force for change within their own communities.

Senior Projects: Giving Back to the School

Although CityWorks is a "stand-alone" course, the energy it creates has reverberated into other areas of our school program. This has occurred partly because so many teachers are involved in it (see chapter 6 for descriptions of the staff development component of CityWorks) and also because the work of the students becomes so public. One effect has been that a number of teachers are bringing a community focus to courses they teach outside of CityWork. For example, Rosalie Williams, whose desktop publishing students run a greeting card and calendar business, realized that beginning students could learn many of the features of sophisticated computer applications by creating coloring books and puzzle books for younger children. She brings her students to meet children from local preschool programs who then enjoy the products that the high school students create. Williams' more advanced students, who sell their cards and African-American Inventors calendar, donate one-third of the proceeds each year to a cause that they select.

After teaching CityWorks, Joel LeGault, the chef who runs the culinary program, added a community outreach and service component to the already successful lunch restaurant run by his students. For several years, students have prepared special luncheons for elders participating in a local day center. At one such event, elders were asked to bring favorite recipes as the "price of admission." These became the basis for a "Grandma's Place" recipe book, distributed at one of the CityWorks exhibitions. At another event, the class not only prepared a nutritious three-course meal, but also brought in a piano and music teacher to lead the elderly group in a "sing along" of old standards and favorites.

Inspired by such events, two culinary students decided to host a different kind of special event as their senior project. They created a luncheon for a population of students who are often forgotten within a large comprehensive high school—those with Down's syndrome or with other developmental disabilities. Their project included everything from raising the funds for the luncheon, to planning the menu, and assigning tasks to their classmates. In their presentation, they described at least two valuable lessons they had learned from this event: "how hard it is to supervise other people," and how satisfying it is to "do something for kids who really, really appreciate it."

Working with Tom Lividoti, the electrical teacher, two other students taught a group of seventh and eighth graders how to hook up their own stage lights and operate them for a class play. Although clearly pleased to use their own developing skills to mentor younger students, the high school students were considerably less enthusiastic about presenting what they had done to a small audience of teachers, parents, and students. When they finally did, one student expressed what the project had meant to him with a simple eloquence: "It made me feel tall."

Senior projects such as these attracted the interest of teachers and students outside of the vocational program. A group of teachers began to meet to discuss the feasibility of offering this opportunity to all seniors. We decided to see what would happen if we issued a call for proposals to the whole school. (See chapter 3 for a discussion of how schools support senior projects and the benefits to students of doing them.) In response to this first call, over thirty seniors at the high school declared an interest in spending a portion of their spring semester doing a senior project. Meeting together in a large conference room, they spoke, in turn, about issues or topics of interest to them.

The group of us who had organized the meeting were pleasantly surprised by the diversity of the students—running the gamut from those at the top to the bottom of their class academically, and including students from many of the racial and ethnic groups in the school. But what surprised us even more was how many students arrived at the meeting with ideas about improving or changing the high school itself—desiring to leave their mark on it in some way.

One student wanted to investigate the reasons behind the underachievement of many of her African-American peers; another proposed a similar project focusing on Latino students; four students who were recent immigrants to the United States proposed working together on preparing information for their peers about financial aid for college, especially for those without green cards; another group of three wanted to plan activities that would involve students in Pacific-Asian heritage month. Several others had specific ideas about how to improve teaching and learning: the editor of the school newspaper wanted to create a curriculum for a new English course focusing on investigative journalism; another student planned to work with a high school physics teacher and a middle school math teacher to devise ways to make technology more intriguing and understandable to students.

Several months before this event, Kaya Stone, the school newspaper editor and would-be curriculum developer, submitted an application to join the Cambridge Service Corps (see below). His words provide insight into why he and so many other students are interested in doing projects directed at improving the school and its surrounding community:

When I look at Cambridge, I see a school system that can always use improvements, a city segregated by class lines and a need for more community activities. . . . While I may have enjoyed going to the Shoot Straight basketball clinic on Saturday mornings, this program was not always in existence. Someone saw the need and acted upon it. Now I would like to do the same. If I could come back to Cambridge in ten years and see something in the city or at the school that I played a part in, it would give me the utmost feeling of satisfaction.

Clearly this is an articulate student who sees the importance of social activism and feels strong enough to get something done. Reading this, many teachers might point out that such students are a small subculture in our high schools. But, the diversity of the students who proposed and completed senior projects such as those listed above, illustrates that the need to feel a sense of efficacy, connection, and contribution, is much more widespread.

Real Time vs. School Time

Periodically one can find inspiring articles in the newspaper about a class of school children who are making headway in their efforts to save an endangered species of fresh water shrimp or a high school science class that has influenced county water policy through their studies of water quality in their town. These stories leave little doubt that the students involved have experienced the "utmost feelings of satisfaction" that Kaya describes. Less evident in the story, are the barriers that had to be overcome in order to connect classroom learning to real events, issues, and people in the community.

"Real time" community projects do not fit easily or neatly into a daily school schedule or a nine-month school calendar. Nor is it simple, as community organizers understand, to break down a compelling (and large) community issue into achievable action steps, each of which makes participants feel a sense of progress and efficacy. Such difficulties became evident to us at Rindge when we launched a new course called Community Problem-Solving 101, with the express purpose of enabling juniors and seniors to make a difference in their community. In the two years that the course was offered, students accomplished some important goals inside the school, and learned a lot in the process, but did not have the kind of impact they (and we) hoped for in the city itself.

The idea of this course was for students to select a target problem in the community, and then to organize a broad community of young people (from middle-school through college) to work with them on addressing this problem. In preparation for this, they read and discussed numerous newspaper articles about local issues, and books like Alex Kotlowitz's *There Are No Children Here,* and Jonathan Kozol's, *Rachel's Children,* went out into the neighborhoods of Cambridge to do an assessment of current local needs, and each did after-school service placements to become familiar with community resources and agencies.

In the first year, after considering a number of issues from homelessness to the lack of playgrounds in several areas of the city, students took as their focus the launching of a school-based Cambridge Service Corps. This included securing a good space within the high school to use as the resource library and "staging" area for community work. Although internal to the school, it did prove to be a rich project for the students involved, leading them to investigate everything from the way rooms are allocated in the high school to the way school budgets are constructed. In the process of identifying an appropriate space, students attended numerous School Committee and City Council meetings, negotiated with the school administration, and through conducting and analyzing surveys, kept abreast of the concerns of their peers regarding the quality of life in the city.

The project engaged their hands as well as their minds. Once the room was secured, students entered the "design and build" phase of the project. Led by their peers with carpentry and artistic skills, they crafted tables, cabinets, and bookshelves, and painted a wall mural. One section of the room immediately became a resource library to house notebooks they had produced during the neighborhood exploratory project earlier in the year. In these notebooks, students mapped the resources and services of the different neighborhoods of Cambridge, and wrote up their research into the issues and concerns of people living and working in that area, drawing from interviews, newspaper accounts, and first-hand observations.

To celebrate the opening of the center, students also planned and carried out the "First Annual Youth Summit," a full day of workshops and speakers (students were invited to come during their study halls; and some teachers signed up to bring their classes), including a lunch-time community service fair, with tables representing many of the different volunteer activities available to students, and an evening reception in the new center, attended by parents, students, the Mayor of Cambridge, and other officials.

Despite this promising beginning, the center did not reach its intended goal as a launching pad for community-wide projects. Although students learned a lot through the community needs assessment process, the teacher and class were unable to overcome the barrier of a school schedule that not only rotated the periods each day, but did so on an eight-day cycle (thus making it impossible to schedule a regular commitment to an outside group or agency). Creating a physical center and holding a youth summit were both undertakings that could be fit into a single school year. The problem was in going beyond these activities and getting involved in the real work and issues of the community.

The Oakland Health Academy: Creating An Ethos of Service

Helping students develop the skills and sensibilities to become leaders who give back to their community is central to the mission of the Oakland Health and Bioscience Academy. Recognizing the challenge of doing "real time" community projects as school assignments, staff have developed a number of interesting strategies for involving their classes in community problem-solving.

One key strategy is to work directly with community-based organizations as they address particular public health issues in the local area. For example, in one recent project, students helped a local lead paint abatement group to carry out a block by block assessment of lead paint hazards in the area. After reading a case study of a lead-poisoned child, students learned to interpret results of a blood test for lead, and to create a medical management plan, as though they were the public health nurses in charge of the case. With this background, they were ready to hear from a nurse and an industrial technologist—members of the lead paint abatement group—who came to the school to teach them how to assess the level of lead in housing. Specifically, students learned how to conduct a risk assessment from the street: where to look for lead paint flakes and how to assess whether children live and play in the immediate area.

Going out in teams, students were assigned a two block area, in which to take notes on approximately fifty structures. As they were taught, they looked for clues to help them assess the age of the building, and to help them deduce whether there were small children present. They also took note of the types of trim, and whether the surrounding land was landscaped, or bare dirt. The data gathered by the students proved to be very useful to the lead paint abatement project. "The project used the kids' maps to lead them to the most high-risk buildings. They dropped off flyers and documented the worst cases," notes David de Leeuw, the teacher orchestrating the project in the school.

A second, related strategy is to form partnerships with nearby universities. For example, each spring, seniors in the Health Academy participate in a project called, "The Urban Plan," mentored by a dozen or more graduate students in the College of Environmental Design of the University of California at Berkeley. Originally based on a simulation game for high school students, designed by the Urban Land Institute, the "Urban Plan" project is now firmly grounded in real community development and planning issues in Oakland. Each year, Berkeley graduate students select an actual site slated for redevelopment in Oakland, teaching students the vocabulary and concepts they need to become knowledgeable and active community participants in the planning process. For the Health Academy students, this is an opportunity to learn to use urban planning as a tool for creating a healthier physical and social environment.

Although the lesson plans vary somewhat from year to year, depending on the interests of the graduate students involved and the specific features of the site selected, the basic outline remains the same. The unit begins with students doing a community autobiography—they draw their own neighborhoods, using the planning concepts of boundaries, focal points, and landmarks. They also learn to map social networks and common travel routes. An Oakland history treasure hunt involves interviews with elders, followed by a search for memorabilia from the period described by the interviewee, and library research on events of that time period.

Perhaps the most important activity is a walking tour of the selected site. Divided into teams, groups of students gather information to bring back to the classroom. For example, in this year's exploration of the block surrounding the MacArthur Bay Area Transit, (BART) station, different groups focused on history, natural factors, land use, built form, and transportation. Each group then analyzes its findings and produces a graphic map appropriate to its focus, using photographs they took and icons and base maps supplied by the graduate students. In the culminating activity, students from each of the different groups recombine into design teams to come up with their own proposals for the site. Their proposal must include an analysis of opportunities and constraints, as well as financial worksheets that show that their projected revenues would match the overall costs.

The final presentations take the form of a "friendly competition," similar to one that the graduate students participate in each year. Groups present their proposals to a panel of jurors—which might include an architect, a professor from the University of California, Berkeley, a real estate expert, and an Oakland City Council member—as well as to a larger audience of peers and parents. This year, students also presented to the BART Community Planning group, and several students were invited to serve on the committee.

Although the ideas presented are those of the high school students, the graduate students help them shape these into a very professional presentation. Early in the process, they bring in examples of presentation boards they have done, as well as the tools and materials that professionals use in preparing their proposals. According to Patricia Clark, the coordinator of the Health Academy, the excitement generated by the final presentation is making it one of "the rites of passage for our seniors."

For the graduate students, the Urban Plan is an opportunity to share their knowledge of relevant planning issues and skills with high school students. In a paper that several graduate students wrote, they explain why this is so important: "urban planners . . . traditionally had such a difficult time getting people to come to community meetings. Most people do not know what urban planning is . . . disenfranchised communities are the least organized and capable of resisting the building projects in their neighborhood . . . High school students seem ripe for learning how planners think and how the decisions that affect their surroundings are made."

As the Urban Plan illustrates, high school students, mentored and coached by urban planning students, can participate in community problem-solving on a very sophisticated level. When Rindge teachers and students have presented CityWorks in conferences or to visitors who come to the school, the most enthusiastic responses have come from educators working in middle school settings. While appreciating the active nature of the investigations students do, high school educators tend to see community field studies and community service as something appropriate for younger students, before the real work of high school begins. The strategy of matching high school seniors with graduate students provides a way to maintain a focus on community issues throughout high school.

The Urban Plan also embodies elements of a third strategy employed by the Oakland Health Academy—combining simulated and real activities. This strategy has been used effectively by staff at the Oakland Health Academy to sustain student interest and involvement in a large scale project that has been ongoing in the community for over ten years: the creation of a school-based health clinic and health education and resource center. Three years ago, at a summer team workshop, staff of the Health Academy realized that they could turn their frustration over stalled efforts to open a clinic into an opportunity to create a multidisciplinary project for students. What better way to learn about all aspects of the health industry than by planning a clinic? "Imagine that you have been hired to serve as planners for a school-based (or community-based) Health Clinic . . ." begins the instructions for "HealthWorks: Sim Clinic," a six-week curricular unit. Each year, all sophomores entering the Health Academy do research and planning tasks associated with designing and operating a school-based health facility.

With the clinic now open, the experience is, in a sense, a simulation. But the desire for student input has been and remains real. And, the tasks (e.g., writing a mission statement for the center, designing and conducting a student health needs assessment survey, marketing to parents) mirror those actually carried out by professionals who design health services for young people. Another way the staff keeps Sim Clinic as close as possible to reality is by using health professionals as coaches to help students base their design ideas on real possibilities.

Furthermore, there are opportunities each year to become involved in new projects emerging from the clinic and health education center. This year, groups of students helped to organize a citywide innoculation program, worked with hospital partners to design a health risk assessment project for all ninth graders, worked with the students at the School of Public Health of the University of California at Berkeley on teen health and safety issues in the workplace, designed a school health and safety project, and trained for summer community health projects in Latin America.

The emphasis recently has shifted to HealthWorks, a component of the Academy dedicated to delivering effective health education to teenagers. This year students are working on a business plan for Healthworks, which is being run as a school-based enterprise. A new class has been added both to provide advanced training to health peer educators and to serve as a homebase for coordinated student management of Healthworks. Spin-off projects include a healthy foods cafe, a teen health newsletter, as well as a number of health education efforts. Eventually the plan is for HealthWorks to be entirely run by senior and health peer counselors. Meanwhile, a number of the projects that sophomores and juniors do in class culminate in products—like brochures or pamphlets—that are displayed and distributed via HealthWorks.

The Oakland Health Academy is a good example of a program that infuses comunity projects throughout its three-year curriculum. Academy director, Patricia Clark explains the process: "In tenth grade our students do service learning projects with elementary students in the school across the street; they also mentor junior high school students who have expressed an interest in health careers. In eleventh grade, they focus on peer health education. In the Urban Plan project and senior project, they have the experience of being coached and mentored by graduate students. When Health Academy students get to college, they become frequent volunteers in the Academy, in other schools, and in community-based organizations." The result, notes Clark proudly, is that students graduate with a long-term commitment to giving back to their community.

II. CONNECTING COMMUNITY SERVICE AND WORK-BASED LEARNING

Beyond Dualistic Thinking

The Flambeau, Cambridge, and Oakland programs have each found a different balance between classroom and community learning, and between simulated and real project work. All maintain a focus on community needs while providing students with ongoing practice in doing large-scale projects. The projects that students do go far beyond the types of activities that are usually encompassed in what schools call "community service" or "service learning."

Typically, community service is defined in terms of opportunities for individual students to volunteer to help out, most often within the high school, and sometimes in local agencies that offer services like tutoring, home visiting, daycare, or elder care. About half of the schools that support some type of service offer it only as a voluntary club activity.[1] Only a very small percentage of schools have taken steps to create time and space within the school day for what educators call "service learning"—a term which generally encompasses some form of reflection as well as the actual experience of doing something for the community. And even in those schools, it is usually a somewhat marginal elective, not structured to appeal to a broad spectrum of student from the highest to the lowest achievers, and from the most to the least economically advantaged.

When service is defined in terms of individual volunteerism, and when the student is the slender thread connecting school to community, it is not surprising to find that the quality of the experience is uneven, dependent on the particulars of the placement, or as one provider put it, on "whether the student is placed with an individual who knows what to do with him." To engage in the kind of community problem solving and community action that might result in the "utmost feeling of satisfaction" envisioned by Kaya, students need the opportunity to work together in a team and to collaborate with groups or agencies already active in defining community needs and assets. These conditions become possible when community service is brought inside the curriculum.

Perhaps most importantly, the programs described here do not see any contradiction between preparing students to make a living and preparing them to make a life as contributing members of a community. Historically, Americans have long argued between these two broad purposes for the schools. On one hand are idealists and liberals who support a Jeffersonian vision of the schools. In his advocacy of public education, Jefferson connected it to no less a purpose than the preservation of democracy itself:

"Every government degenerates when trusted to the rulers over the people alone. The people themselves therefore are its only safe depositories. And to rend even them safe, their minds must be improved somewhat."[2]

A version of Jefferson's vision can be found in virtually every school's mission statement. In some schools, the vision of building an engaged, active citizenry permeates the curriculum as well. Deborah Meier, nationally known for the success of Central Park East Secondary School, urges teachers to imagine each and every student as a juror in a trial in which the teacher has a personal interest. Teachers who think this way, Meier believes, will help students to develop habits of mind (such as empathy and the ability to search out and weigh evidence) that are basic to participation in democratic life.

On the other hand, the Jeffersonian ideal has not been the only guiding philosophy of American education. From early on, some supporters of public schools have emphasized the importance of preparing young people for the workforce and of keeping America economically viable and competitive through its educational policies. One of the confusing things about the current moment in education reform is that federal and state support for building a school-to-work system would seem to indicate the triumph (at least in policymakers' minds) of the economic over the civic function of schools. But, ironically, at the local level, school-to-work initiatives seem to be creating a climate in which students are becoming more active participants in community life.

The rhetoric, policies, and practices of the school-to-work movement are serving to remind people of the importance of joining classroom work to the real world outside the high school, a world that includes neighborhood groups and governmental agencies as well as small and large businesses. For example, in Milwaukee, a district that has embraced school-to-work as the centerpiece of its systemic reforms, all students are expected to complete a project in "community membership" as a graduation requirement. The district encourages classroom and school-based projects that involve students in doing fieldwork in the community, under the tutelage of community and business partners.

The experience of the particular programs described in this chapter suggests that by maintaining a focus on community needs and community improvement, schools may indeed improve their capacity to respond to requests, like that of the student quoted at the beginning of the chapter, for a less dualistic education. When students in the Flambeau district start a new heirloom seed business, they are both creating jobs and income for themselves and helping to create a viable economic and social foundation for their community. When Oakland students learn to assess housing for lead paint risk factors, they are acquiring valuable research skills that will serve them well in college and the workplace (e.g., analytical reasoning and statistical methods) and are helping their community deal with a serious public health issue.

In a world of separate turfs, funding streams, and professional organizations or networks, these programs defy categorization. They are academic *and* vocational; they deliver entrepreneurship education *and* community education; they provide work-based learning *and* service learning. Many years ago, John Dewey warned us about the trap of dualisms like "thinking vs. doing," or "individual vs. community." One reason Dewey focused on vocation was because he saw it as a fulcrum for balancing hands and minds, and for balancing the contributions of an individual to himself and to his community. There need not be any contradiction or competition between education for citizenship and education for productive employment. It is through vocation, Dewey wrote, that people come to realize their own distinctive capacities which then allow them to provide social service to the community.[3] Thus, with vocation at the center, schools could become democratic laboratories of learning, closely linked to community need.

It is important to remember that Dewey used the term *vocation* much more broadly than we do today. Dewey's point, recently articulated by educational philosopher, Israel Scheffler is that a vocation is an activity "which is purposive, demands attention, concentration, skill, and intelligence." As Scheffler points out, by this definition "every education is of necessity vocational in organizing a person's capability and disposition for intelligent activities."[4]

Lessons from Community Organizations: Succeeding with Disadvantaged Youth

In the not so distant past, families and communities expected young people to play roles as active and productive workers. Sometimes a household's very survival depended on the participation of all family members in controlling the environment. Now, the tendency is to include youth as part of the environment that needs to be controlled. This is a dangerous notion.

In his recent book, *The End of Education,* Neil Postman makes the important point that "motivation" is something educators have to worry about when their students are lacking a sense of purpose, when they do not see a reason for engaging in academic learning. If teachers could find a way to nurture and capitalize on students' desire to improve the world, then they might find much less need for the carrots and sticks of school life. Specifically, he suggests that schools invent ways to engage students in "social reconstruction," beginning with the care of their own schools, neighborhoods, and towns, and ultimately leading to a sense of responsibility for the planet. It would be a more cost-effective and ultimately a better moral choice than hiring more security guards in the school, or putting more youth in prison.[5]

Many people will argue that "social reconstruction" lies far outside the mission of the school. It is the job of the school to transmit important and valued skills and knowledge—any broader notion of youth or community development is the province of the family and the community. Certainly there are public and private efforts in many communities to involve youth in socially constructive activities outside of school hours. In fact, research on why some youth are more resilient than others in overcoming adversity in their lives, often reveals a connection to such a community-oriented group. But many more young people are in school than can ever be served by these programs.

After five years of studying community youth organizations that seem to be working effectively with economically disadvantaged young people, Shirley Brice Heath and Milbury McLaughlin reached the depressing conclusion that schools were often quite irrelevant to the lives and futures of these youth, and that schools were sometimes even worse than irrelevant. "Most of the young people who come to these organizations, in fact, regard school as a place that has rejected and labeled them by what they are not rather than by what they are."[6] As one neighborhood youth worker said to the researchers, "We spend at least an hour every afternoon making up for all of the negative stuff kids hear about themselves in school."[7]

In their research, Heath and McLaughlin found a key reason why some youth organizations are successful where schools and other youth efforts have failed: "The youth organizations that attracted and sustained young people's involvement gave visible and ongoing voice to a conception of youth as a resource to be developed and as persons of value to themselves and to society."[8] In recent years, schools in some urban areas have formed collaborations with local social service agencies, with the goal of better co-ordinating services to youth and their families. In a few places, the schools even stay open into the evening to provide everything from educational to health services. While it is certainly important for schools and other institu-tions to join together to respond to the needs of families, such initiatives rarely challenge the media-inspired view of inner city youth as problems to fix rather than as part of a solution to what ails our communities.

McLaughlin and Heath also found that "effective programs often provide activities in nontraditional settings, at nontraditional hours and with nontra-ditional personnel, and pay little heed to orthodox boundaries of the service sector, bureaucratic compartments or professional parameters."[9] Certainly, most schools are bureaucratic and traditional in their hours, hiring practices, and professional boundaries. As a result, many young people experience their time in school as a constant process of being tested, sorted, and remediated. As teens put it, they feel "dissed" by teachers, rather than respected.

Building Community Within the Classroom

The projects described in this chapter offer teachers and students new ways of relating and the possibility of changing the social dynamics of classroom life. Rather than being viewed as the judge—the adult arbiter of school standards and rules—the teacher can take on the role of a group leader, helping guide the group in its collective effort to produce a result that meets a "real world" or community standard. Cheryl Almeida, a researcher doing an independent evaluation of the Cambridge Service Corps quotes a student she interviewed as explaining: "A lot of teachers put a distance between themselves and the kids. They do not treat them as individuals, more like balls thrown around . . . Coming into this class I realized that I could be a person and a student at the same time."[10]

Bringing community-focused projects into the school curriculum can also have a beneficial effect on the relationships among the students. Shortly after joining the Cambridge Service Corps, my son, Sam, offered this analysis: "If you compare it (Community Problem-Solving 101) to most classes in the high school, it's fantastic . . . I don't know everyone's name in most of my (other) classes, and I may not learn them before the end of the year. Some students show up to other classes once or twice a week and couldn't care less. Students sit through other classes not understanding a word of what's said and not bothering to ask."

While a major thing motivating many students (including Sam) to come to school is the chance to interact with peers, and possibly with caring adults, it is also true, especially in large urban schools, that socializing takes place in relatively small groups. The overall experience is one of anonymity and, in some cases, even hostility. There is a kind of absurdity in bringing together hundreds, even thousands, of teenagers and asking them to sit next to each other in rows all day, *not* relating. The situation becomes even more problematic, in urban high schools like Rindge or Oakland Tech, which bring together youth from dozens of different nations and ethnic groups. It is no wonder that many teachers dread hall and lunchroom duty. Released from the classroom, students literally bump up against each other, in friendly and not so friendly ways. Administrators at our school spend a great deal of their time dealing with the consequences of fights and other forms of antisocial behavior among the students.

To counteract this behavior, some high schools have turned to anti-violence programs, like mediation training. Others have instituted special times during the week for all students to meet in small groups, such as in the "Family Groups" in many Philadelphia high schools. All of these remain outside of the main curriculum. Changing the social dynamics of the classroom is at least part of the impetus behind the cooperative learning strategies that some schools have embraced. But for cooperative learning groups to work, students have to feel that what they are being asked to do (cooperatively) matters. If the main motivation is to receive a good "group grade," at least some students will opt out, angering their peers and, if anything, adding to an unfriendly atmosphere in the classroom. Community-oriented projects selected by students and based on real needs have a better chance of helping students bond around a larger sense of purpose.

It is, of course, not easy for a group of students (especially a diverse group) to work together on a community project. For one thing, they are not used to the idea that other people in the class are truly depending on them. As one student revealed in an interview with Almeida: "At first I couldn't get how it worked: if you don't do this than the next person won't be able to do that and the next person . . . my attitude was always, 'Take this class, work hard and get an A,' or 'Forget it. I'll take the zero.' That attitude doesn't work in this class. You have to be more responsible . . . (there is) too much at stake. If you say you're going to do something, you have to be committed. People depend on it."

If the project itself makes sense and matters to them, and if the class takes time to work on team skills, the results can be dramatic. In their reflection papers, nearly every student in the Cambridge Service Corps comments on how much it means to them to work on something with peers who they might not otherwise have known or understood. Although their initial motivation to join the Corps had to do with a desire to make a contribution to a larger community, students have found it equally important to become a community within the class.

Another factor in changing classroom dynamics is that community projects bring students into relationships with a wider group of interested and interesting adults. The negativity and resistance many teenagers express towards adults (especially teachers) sometimes makes us forget how much youth do want to be in situations where they can work alongside adults and feel respected for their contributions. An important feature of many community projects is that youth are brought into close contact with a variety of adults working on issues in the community. "It is a powerful stimulation to the young to share in all enterprise worthy to involve the efforts of the older and better established members of the community," wrote William Kilpatrick, a colleague and disciple of Dewey's, " . . . There is a dignity about such that stirs youth as perhaps nothing else can."[11]

One can find echoes of this sentiment in the following words, written by Yaheisa Daniel just after completing a senior project in which she and three of her peers, coached by law students at Northeastern University, ran a successful workshop series on immigrant rights for over a hundred high school students:

> "The first workshop was really an experience that I will never forget. At the beginning of the workshop I was afraid. I did not even know how to control myself. I was the first one in the panel and I felt that I had to give the best impression to the public . . . When we finished with the presentations I felt so excited. It was a day that I will always remember. I did something very important for my friends and they supported me to do it. I define this workshop as a great experience in my life."

NOTES

1. National Center on Effective Secondary Schools, *Resource Bulletin* 7 (Madison: School of Education, University of Wisconsin, Spring 1990), 1.

2. Thomas Jefferson, *Notes on Virginia* (Paris, 1783), 268–275.

3. John Dewey, *Democracy and Education,* 318.

4. Israel Scheffler, "Reflections on Vocational Education," in V.A. Howard and Israel Scheffler, *Work, Education and Leadership: Essays in the Philosophy of Education* (New York: Peter Lang, 1995), 45.

5. Neil Postman, *The End of Education: Redefining the Value of School* (New York: Alfred A. Knopf, 1995), 4.

6. Shirley Brice Heath and Milbrey W. McLaughlin, eds., *Identity and Inner City Youth: Beyond Ethnicity and Gender* (New York: Teachers College Press, 1993) 4.

7. Heath and McLaughlin, *Identity and Inner City Youth,* 60.

8. Heath and McLaughlin, *Identity and Inner City Youth,* 59.

9. Heath and McLaughlin, *Identity and Inner City Youth,* 62.

10. Cheryl Almeida, "Evaluation: Vocational Integration with Academics Project," Rindge School of Technical Arts, unpublished manuscript.

11. William Heard Kilpatrick, "Introduction: Principles of Community Learning," in Samuel Everett, *The Community School* (New York: D. Appleton-Century Co., 1938), 15.

3

Connecting School and Work

Most fifteen year olds have little or no idea of what they want to "be." This, in itself, is not a problem. As most of us have heard by now, the average American can expect to change jobs five or six times in a lifetime; several of these switches might involve entering whole new careers or fields. More problematic is the passivity and helplessness that sets in when students can see no connection between their interests and efforts as adolescents and their future lives.

When students are asked to envision their lives in ten years—a question sometimes posed as a creative writing exercise—most will head straight into fantasy territory—imagining successful businesses, or careers in the NBA, as well as the accoutrements of success, like cars and beautiful houses. Students respond to researchers' queries about their career plans in a similar way: "Maybe I'll be an athlete, maybe I'll be a neurosurgeon, maybe I'll be a model," is how Charles Bidwell, principal investigator of the Sloan Study of Youth and Social Development, characterizes typical student responses in his comprehensive longitudinal exploration of how young people develop ideas about careers and work.[1]

Teenagers seem to have little knowledge about the careers that interest them. The problem is that they have almost no opportunities to talk seriously with adults, or one another, about how the present and future can connect—about how present interests can provide clues as to possible careers or life-styles, or how choices made in high school might affect options down the road. Particularly in cities and rural areas where unemployment and underemployment are becoming ever more common, young people lack even the most rudimentary knowledge of the world of adult work. If they hear about work at all, it is likely to be as a demeaning rather than a satisfying or fulfilling experience.

Certainly school proceeds with little or no reference to the world of work. Students take course after course with no idea about how any of this knowledge is used by real people in the real world; with no description of the actual jobs that people might do where any of these skills or knowledge might come in handy. The only students who could offer real information about career fields in the Sloan study cited above were the small number taking part in school-sponsored internship programs.

Students are caught in a terribly confusing situation. Their own experience teaches them that there is almost a total bifurcation between school and work. The jobs they hold draw on little if anything they have learned in school. Looking around them they see that the high school drop-outs or "squeak-bys" are doing basically the same (not well) as those who worked harder, graduated, and maybe even tried a semester or two at a community college. It should not surprise us that when we push them to go to college, they ask: "What's school got to do with it?"

They are right that many jobs are being deskilled (or eliminated altogether) and hence require few if any skills. But, at the same time, "good jobs" (defined, most simply, as jobs offering a living wage and a career ladder) increasingly demand both traditional school skills, such as reading, writing, and mathematics, and an array of personal and social competencies, such as self-management and initiative, communicating well and the ability to participative effectively in a team. An increasing number of these jobs are in technical areas—e.g., waste management, facilities management, hospital technician—that require at least two years beyond high school, and specifically the ability to problem-solve, use mathematics on the job, and adapt to changing technologies. The high school curriculum, as it is currently defined, does not necessarily help students develop such competencies, nor does it help them understand the changing nature of work, or more specifically, how they might find a work identity that brings meaning, as well as income, to their lives.

Tapping the Learning Potential of Work

Many teachers have experienced the pleasant surprise of seeing a student who seems perpetually tired and withdrawn in class looking active and alert as he rings up a sale behind the counter at the local convenience store. For at least the last fifty years, this contrast has fueled an impetus among some American educators to find a way to tap the learning potential of work. Until recently, the result of these efforts could be seen mainly in "cooperative education" programs—work placements arranged and supervised by the school, during part of the school day. Throughout the 1980s and early 1990s, such programs attracted around 400,000 students each year, for the most part remaining a small, marginalized part of a school district's offerings, with little or no connection to the academic program.[2]

In the past decade or so, the level of interest in such school and work arrangements began to grow, fed by escalating concerns about the economic competitiveness of the United States labor force and the long floundering period experienced by American youth between finishing school and establishing a career. In 1995, the term "school-to-work" entered the national vocabulary when Congress debated and then President Clinton signed the School To Work Opportunities Act. Although funded at a relatively modest level, and deliberately designed with a "sunset clause" that terminates the legislation early in the next century, the Act has had the effect of sparking interest in new combinations of learning and work. In the past several years, school-to-work initiatives have become part of the educational landscape in many local communities and school districts.

This development has not been without opposition from academic educators and parents, many of whom view school-to-work programs as a diversion from the important role of high school in preparing young people for college. Countering this charge, supporters argue that these programs can be excellent preparation for both college and future careers, especially—but certainly not exclusively—for the significant percentage of youth who are only going through the motions in school, and failing to develop the competencies or dispositions they will need for a successful transition into adulthood.

The challenge in school-to-work programs is to create something that does not look like school, as teenagers now know it, or like work, as most of them experience it. Teenagers need organized opportunities to explore and "try on" different work identities, while also learning fundamental concepts and skills that prepare them for college and careers. These are compelling, if difficult, tasks, judging from the growing number of programs that are attempting to tackle them. The first section of this chapter introduces the promise of workplaces as a context for student learning, through the eyes of high school students fortunate enough to experience productive combinations of learning and work. The programs described in the second and third sections of the chapter represent two different, and complementary approaches to creating such combinations.

One strategy is to establish internships or youth apprenticeships in which students spend significant amounts of time (either during the school day/year or after school and in the summer) in work placements that have been designed by employers and teachers to maximize the learning potential of the work experience. Focusing on this type of intensive work-based learning program, this part of the chapter considers how learning plans and projects—jointly negotiated by students, teachers, and worksite supervisors—serve to connect the work students do in their placements to academic content and skills.

The third section of this chapter revisits a question introduced in chapter 1: How can schoolwork become more like real work? Here the focus is on incorporating work-based problems and issues into the classroom, with business partners working alongside teachers and students on projects that bridge between the knowledge and skills fostered by academic and work settings. Three different types of work-like experiences are described: senior projects, field studies, and career explorations.

The field study approach is similar to some of the community development projects described in chapter 2, only here the focus is on creating projects that are real to the workplace—both in terms of tackling a real work problem and in establishing a community of practice such as one might find in a high performance workplace. Finally, this chapter ends by exploring some of the common themes emerging from both of these strategies for combining school and work.

Two Strategies for Work-Based Learning Projects

STRATEGY ONE: INTERNSHIP PROJECTS: WORK-BASED INVESTIGATION DIRECTED AT ADDRESSING A REAL PROBLEM AND CULMINATING IN STUDENT EXHIBITIONS AND PRESENTATIONS.

A. Defining Characteristics

- Students as workers
- Substantial academic component
- Collaboration of teachers and worksite personnel

B. Major Challenges

- Developing high quality work placements

- Finding enough support/time for students to complete independent work
- Negotiating a balance of academic, personal, and work agendas

STRATEGY TWO: FIELD STUDIES: CLASSROOM AND FIELD-BASED INVESTIGATION OF A COMPLEX, REAL WORLD PROBLEM, CULMINATING IN STUDENT EXHIBITIONS AND PRESENTATIONS.

A. Defining Characteristics

- Students as consultants to workplace/community group
- Substantial fieldwork component
- Industry/community experts act as coaches

B. Major Challenges

- Finding 'real enough' problems
- Logistics of field-work

I. NEW COMBINATIONS OF LEARNING AND WORK

"Something You Never Learn at School"

> During freshman and sophomore year, I didn't pay attention in class because I really did not care. I care now because this is something I really want to do. When you are interested in the work that you are doing, you will go the extra step. You will want to do a good job and you will not be bored as you would if you were in a classroom listening to the teacher speak. When that happens you just can't wait for the bell to ring . . . The program is not just about being released from school, but more about learning because you want to learn.

Rohit Rana shared these views in an article he wrote during his junior year at Cambridge Rindge and Latin School, about three months after he had entered a career internship program in facilities management, co-sponsored by Rindge and Harvard University. His article, appropriately titled, "A Turning Point," appeared in a newsletter that he and fellow interns put together as part of the language arts component of their integrated program of school and workplace learning.

When students respond to open-ended questions about what was best or most surprising about their school-to-work programs, most—like Rohit—make unsolicited comparisons between their time at work and their time in school.

Sometimes those comparisons are implicit, like the student who responded to the question of what surprised her most about her internship experience by saying simply, "I went every day." Often, they are quite (and embarrassingly) explicit. At one public event, a student intern thanked his mentors at work by enthusiastically explaining: "People there really respect each other." And then he added, with equal emphasis: "That's something you never learn at school!"

It is hard not to feel a bit hurt and puzzled by such remarks. Certainly, in most schools there are many adults who care about and respect their students. Teachers and administrators are, in a sense, paid to care. Schools are supposed to be settings where knowledge passes from one generation to the next, and where young people receive guidance from adults in developing their minds and their characters. In contrast, the emphasis at the workplace is on being productive at a set of defined tasks; the expectation is that people care more about getting the job done. Why, then, do students often feel more cared for and respected at their work placements than at school?

The answer is by no means obvious. But this paradox becomes somewhat easier to understand when one listens carefully to what students have to say. My own search has led me to analyze written and oral comments from numerous students, as well as to review interview data collected by others. Relationships with people at work emerges as a central theme: "People at work were so friendly." "My supervisor really cares about me." "It's just like, you know, I feel like I'm part of a team."[3]

These relationships "ranked high among the factors influencing the overall work experience," concludes Felicia Hayes, who conducted interviews with students as part of a multi-site documentation and evaluation of *Working to Learn* (Margaret Vickers, the director of the project, describes it in chapter 4).[4] Hayes notes that the longer students spent working within a particular setting, the more positive the impact of adult colleagues. She also found students to be emphatic that the approach in their work-based learning experiences was more fun, made more sense, and motivated them more than the usual school fare.

In the same sentence students might comment on the serious responsibilities of work, ("you have to perform at work") and yet how enjoyable it was ("you have something to look forward to"). Even the direct instruction at work seemed preferable to school. As one student told Hayes: "At Children's Hospital, there's visuals, a real person talking to you. . . ." Hayes concluded that students enjoyed the pace, delivery, and volume of information they received at work, which they contrasted to school, where teachers dispense discrete bits of information in a sequential order that may make no sense to students.[5]

Workplaces vs. Classrooms	
Workplace	*Classroom*
Clear purpose/need to know	Why do I have to learn this?
Real problems and audiences	Contrived assignments, for teacher only
One-on-one mentoring	25/30-1 student/teacher ratio
Working alongside adults	Evaluated by adults
Multiple uses of technology	Limited access to technology

The comments students make point to several features of internships or apprenticeships that make them very different from a typical classroom context. In the workplace: 1) Students experience a stronger need to know and to find out; 2) Students work alongside adults who coach them in the skills necessary to become more productive and valued employees; and 3) Students begin to understand real world expectations and what is involved in accomplished performance. In contrast, at school, students see a number of different teachers each day (usually for short periods) each of whom gives assignments and sets tasks that the student may perceive as having no value beyond competence in school. As part of their role, teachers assess whether the students measure up to a standard that may seem arbitrary or ill-defined to the students. As a result, students may be left feeling that "he doesn't care about me; he just wants me to do his assignments and study for his tests."

In 1994, Jobs for the Future (JFF) conducted a survey of over one hundred students in ten of the pioneering school-to-work programs across the country: 75 percent said they formed special relationships with adults in the workplace.[6] A majority also reported that their involvement in the program made them feel better about high school, and indicated that their work-based learning experiences were of high quality and rich in both learning and relationships. Only 3 percent found it boring at their placement, and over 50 percent said that at least half of their time at the worksite was spent learning new skills. These findings are consistent with earlier research comparing the quality of jobs that typically employ teens, and work experiences offered in school-supervised programs. Youth in the latter rated their jobs higher in terms of: 1) providing opportunities to learn a variety of new things; 2) using reading and writing and other school skills; and 3) getting to know adults on the job.[7]

The point of this analysis is not to romanticize work or to suggest that the solution to underachievement in schools is to put kids into the labor market more quickly. The work situations described so positively by young people are far from the typical "youth job" of flipping burgers or bagging groceries. Most teenagers have as much experience doing meaningless (and mentor-less) work as they have doing meaningless assignments in school. In fact, one of the problems facing school-to-work programs is the skepticism among potential students (and their parents) who suspect they will probably be dumped into jobs that require nothing but menial labor or mechanical skills.

At first, some students in school-to-work programs are suspicious of the teacher's assurance that the schoolwork they are doing—even if it is as hands-on as doing family medical histories or taking pulse readings of peers—will have any connection to what will be expected of them at the work placement. In explaining her resistance to seeing such a connection, one student explained that she simply never had to *know* anything in a job. Jobs weren't like that. She joined the program because it meant freedom from school and money to spend, not because she expected the job to be any different from those she had experienced on her own.

Discovering that College Matters

The positive features of work-based learning experiences also help to explain an unforeseen outcome that has emerged from school-to-work programs. Although the impetus behind setting up such programs has often been a desire to create a better school-to-work transition for seemingly non-college bound students (and, in some cases, students at high risk of dropping out), districts are finding that the vast majority of students coming out of these programs are heading to college.

In fact, this paradoxical phenomenon was brought home in the spring of 1994 when Rindge was invited to send interns and teachers to the signing of the School To Work Opportunities Act in Washington, D.C. At first, the invitation included a request for one of our students to speak at the event. When we submitted the name of a student, with a short description of the project she had completed in her environmental engineering internship, the information received an enthusiastic reception from the staff of the U.S. Labor Department, who were coordinating the event. But when they spoke with the student and found she was intending to go to college the next year, they selected a young man from another program. Their explanation was that it was important to dramatize the way in which this legislation can help the "forgotten half" of high school students who are not going on to college. Lost in this decision was the very important fact that this young woman had developed her college plans and aspirations while in the internship program.

Evidence from around the country documents that school-to-work programs help students to find their way into higher education, as they develop more ambitious career goals. Ninety percent of the students surveyed in the 1994 JFF study had plans to enroll in a two or four year college; an additional five percent planned to attend a vocational training program. This survey is consistent with other data from programs that have kept track of their graduates. These programs report college-going rates between 77 and 84 percent, even though many began with a majority of students who did not consider themselves to be college-bound.[8] "It is possible to achieve the goals of dropout prevention and college preparation at the same time, in the same program," concludes David Stern, Director of the National Center for Research in Vocational Education (NCRVE) and primary author of a number of studies of career academies in California, Philadelphia, and elsewhere.[9]

It makes sense that these programs would function as drop-out prevention. Students who do not like or do well in traditional classrooms have an opportunity to spend significant amounts of time in a very different setting, where they can feel better about themselves, demonstrate competencies, and receive school credit. One student, whose attendance record in school almost led to her application for an internship being rejected, provided a detailed explanation of how the process worked for her, in a speech she gave to a conference of Massachusetts educators: "You know how it is with teenagers," she began, pausing for effect. "We think we know everything. And school doesn't really do anything to change that. But at Polaroid I saw that there were things I didn't know and skills I needed to learn. And when I got back to school I realized I could pick up a lot of those things back there."

It still seems surprising that so many of these students then decide to go on to post-secondary education. The answer, again, may lie within the relationships students form with adults. Recently, at a luncheon for Cambridge employers, Janis Cruz, a student in the Rindge financial services internship program, described her own journey from someone who could not wait to graduate from high school to someone looking forward to college:

> I observed the people that I work with, and noticed that all of them were intelligent, successful, and happy. I knew they didn't get there by chance or just by walking in and asking for their positions . . . I don't want to be one of those people who gets up in the morning and dreads going to work. I want a job that I will get up each morning and on my way there think about what my day will be like and what I can accomplish, and when I leave be proud of what I have done for the day.

Because of discussions with people at the bank where she was working, Janis had come to associate good jobs with going on to further education.

> It really meant a lot to me when they (co-workers) took an interest in me. And they did not treat me like a child. They spoke to me as a peer, which

75

pushed me to think, speak, and react as a mature adult. Hearing from the people I work with and respect that college is important and how making goals and sticking to them matters has meant so much to me. Enough to make the girl who swore more school was a waste of time and that she would not go, actually look forward to going!

A number of students interviewed by Hayes recounted similar journeys. They also talked about how new clarity about their future goals led them to become more serious about school. As one student put it: the work "kind of focused me to do better in school, because I know what I want to do now."

II. MAKING WORKPLACES INTO LEARNING ENVIRONMENTS: LEARNING PLANS AND INTERNSHIP PROJECTS

Competencies for School and Work

To ensure that work is a positive educational experience for young people, the School To Work Opportunities Act calls for institutional and structural linkages between schools and workplaces. According to the Act, school-to-work programs comprise three major components: school-based activities, work-based activities, and connecting activities. The intent is to encourage schools and employers to find ways to set common learning goals, developing pedagogical strategies and activities that make the separate experiences of school and work into a more coherent whole.

Schools and districts have responded with a number of different models of work-based learning—including, for example, programs that place high school seniors in full-day six to eight week paid internships; that place juniors and seniors for half-days throughout the school year; that focus mainly on summer or after-school placements; or that rely on students finding their own placements (paid or unpaid) for some portion of their senior year. The important thing is not which specific model is in use, but whether the strategy, structures, and supports are in place to maximize the learning potential of the placement.

It should be noted, however, that most traditional vocational programs do not meet this criterion, despite the current trend in some states and districts to re-label such programs using school-to-work terminology. Nor would it be accurate to count most cooperative education students, who are allowed to leave the school building early to go to work. In such programs, it is typically left up to the student to integrate academic skills learned in one set of classrooms with vocational skills learned in shops and on the job; and it is left to the student to bridge between the disparate cultures of the school and the workplace.

Opportunities to develop important knowledge and skills are no more assured in school-to-work programs than they are in classrooms. It is important to identify the competencies to be fostered and to make these a central focus of the program. All of the school and work combinations discussed here involve a commitment of employers and school faculty to collaborate with one another and with students on setting clear learning goals and on designing and assessing student projects that further these goals.

The idea of establishing school-business collaborations for the purpose of improving academic performance and career prospects is not a new one. But what is called for now is qualitatively different. In the early 1980s, when *A Nation at Risk* galvanized attention to the crisis in United States schools, some employers and business organizations began to enter into partnerships with local school districts. Typically, employers would send out people from their human resources team to run workshops for high school students on job readiness skills or to participate in job fairs in the schools. Some also donated computers or other equipment.

In Boston, the schools and local employers took an additional step, developing an agreement that became a national model of a more intense form of collaboration. In the Boston Compact, the employers promised summer jobs or jobs after graduation to a certain percentage of high school students, if the school district could prove it was doing its job of preparing students, through such indicators as average daily attendance and standardized test scores. The theory behind such an agreement is that students would learn in school, and then apply this knowledge at work.

The best school-to-work agreements are based on a different theory— one that recognizes that the most productive education is to learn and work simultaneously, and that jobs can provide important learning experiences for students. This calls for a commitment on the part of both schools and employers to move away from business as usual and to redefine their missions. In Boston, this new type of school-to-career commitment (Boston employers prefer and use this term, rather than "school-to-work") is typified by Protech, a collaboration of the public schools, seventy-five employers, and the Private Industry Council (an intermediary organization that played a key role in forging the Boston Compact).

The 650 young people enrolled in Protech are not only eligible for summer and after-school jobs in an area of career interest, but are also in high school or college programs that allow them to focus on a combination of academic and technical subjects related to that career interest. At Brighton High School, for example, there is an academy-type structure (ninth through twelfth grade) for health careers and another for careers in finance.

Within these clusters, students take courses together, and the faculty meet as a team to plan ways to make the learning relevant to the broad career area. As part of the experience, Protech students participate in job rotations and explorations. By the summer of their junior year, if they are in good academic standing, they enter paid internships with participating employers, such as the New England Medical Center.

As an active intermediary, the Private Industry Council (PIC) uses several strategies to try to ensure the quality of the work placements, and to encourage close collaboration between employers and school people. First, there are monthly meetings of each grouping of employers (besides health and finance, these include utilities, business, environmental, and retail), which are usually also attended by teachers from participating schools. Keith Westrich, the director of Protech believes that these conversations among the adults are absolutely essential to the quality of the program. "We can't look to students for solutions that adults haven't figured out," he notes. "Some people start out coming because they're told to come by their boss. Through giving regular input, and having time to reflect, they develop ownership. . . . The meetings change the way adults think about children."

One result of such conversations is the development and piloting of a work-based learning plan that outlines hoped for outcomes of the school-to-career experience. These outcomes have been defined as eleven competencies that young people will need in order to excel, either in the modern workplace or in institutions of higher learning.

Eleven Competencies for Work-Based Learning (Project Protech)

1. Communicate and understand ideas and information
2. Collect, analyze, and organize information
3. Identify and solve problems
4. Understand and work within complex systems
5. Use mathematical ideas and techniques
6. Use technology
7. Initiate and complete entire activities
8. Act professionally
9. Interact with others
10. Learn and teach on an ongoing basis
11. Take responsibility for career and life choices

These competencies obviously go beyond a simple listing of specific skills employees are expected to have or develop on the job. It is similar to lists that have been generated by the New Standards Project, the Cornell Youth and Work Program, and the U.S. Department of Labor Secretary's Commission for Achieving Necessary Skills (SCANS). Stating the outcomes in such broad terms helps to clarify the educative function of the school-to-work placements, creating a platform for employer involvement in students' learning.

Using the eleven competencies as the starting point, several Boston employers and schools have begun to play specific roles in the development of a learning plan. The worksite supervisor is expected to provide a job description for the student's position, and to list specific tasks and objectives for the student. This is where the employer can specify any specialized knowledge or expertise that they want students to develop. The supervisor then looks to see how these relate to the eleven competencies, perhaps modifying the objectives in order to further reinforce certain competencies. On the school side, teachers identify particular content or domain knowledge and skills they are expecting students to learn. Teachers review these curricular objectives in light of the competencies, modifying where necessary to help the student develop these competencies.

While learning plans are still at the planning and piloting stage, school-to-work reformers are hopeful that such plans will prove to be a very useful tool in putting key competencies at the front and center of both school and work. At the very least, the plan encourages adults to make a conscious connection between the two settings. Westrich sees it as a "tool that drives a conversation about goals." It can also be a way to, as Westrich puts it, "engage students as the conscience for their own education." As the process unfolds, the student has a list of the competencies, indicating where and how s/he will work on each. The process heightens students' awareness of what they are learning and also helps them to see if there are particular aspects of the learning that need further development.

Eventually, the learning plans experiment will encompass assessment issues as well. Cooperating employers and teachers are supposed to agree on levels of mastery for each broad competency which then become a guide for teachers in the assessment and grading of students. In addition to typical workplace evaluations and school grades, students will be asked to provide work samples, projects, and/or presentations that demonstrate their progress in developing each of the competencies.

Internship Projects: High Skills and High Adaptability

One of the most powerful ways for students to work on the broad-based competencies listed by Protech and to make connections between the work at their site and their subjects in school is through doing projects. "To succeed in the twenty-first century, workers must be highly skilled and highly adaptable, both specialized and cross-trained," observe Mary Agnes Hamilton and Stephen F. Hamilton, whose Cornell Youth and Work Program has received national recognition as a pioneering apprenticeship program for youth.[10] Like colleagues directing other promising programs, they recommend that students undertake major projects as part of their internship experience.

Looking back over the five-year Cornell demonstration program, the Hamiltons conclude that projects are a key to involving students in aspects of work beyond the daily assignments and to fostering a deeper and broader understanding of workplace issues. Their research also reveals that students find work-based learning projects to be more substantial academically than some of the projects assigned in school. "Normally, English class and projects, I can whip through them and get them done in a week," notes one apprentice in an interview. In contrast, he notes that the work project: "I am working on every day in school. I spend my lunch time in the library . . . always working on it."[11]

Projects are also a central feature of Rindge internship programs, where the topics are jointly negotiated by interns, the internship seminar teacher, and the work supervisor. From the beginning of the year, students and supervisors know that the student is expected to carry out at least one major piece of independent work that relates to ongoing activities at the worksite and that will help the student develop new knowledge and skills. Although we have been committed to this assignment for five years, it is only in the last twelve months that we have really come to understand—and hence been able to articulate to teachers and workplace mentors—what we mean by an intellectually rigorous work-based project, and what it takes to encourage and support such work. Perhaps the best way to begin explaining what we have learned is to share two exemplars of this type of work.

Billy: Intern at Polaroid Corporation

Billy Penrose did a project in which he assisted his supervisor at Polaroid in documenting the company's compliance with the 1990 Clean Air Act, as required annually by the Department of Environmental Protection (DEP). Billy's job was to figure out how many Volatile Organic Compounds

(VOC's) Polaroid was emitting into the air by comparing the amount of chemicals ordered to the amount of chemicals in the waste drum.

To calculate the amount in the waste drum, he had to take the percent of a particular chemical listed on the label, multiple that by the drum volume, and then multiply that by the specific gravity of the chemical and by the weight of water. After calculating averages of all the emissions levels of the different chemicals, he put them on a graph. In the report he wrote for school, he not only described this process, but also explained why such calculations would eventually lead to an accurate method of calculating emissions.

In carrying out this project, Billy had to enter and analyze data using an Excel spreadsheet database, carry out hazardous waste composition analysis, and analyze and write up his findings. In order to include background material in his report, Billy interviewed his supervisor as to the reasons for this particular method of monitoring and the role of the DEP in monitoring environmental regulations. Finally, he prepared a series of presentation boards to display his graphs and findings, and made a public presentation to his peers, teachers, all of the participating supervisors at Polaroid, and school administrators.

Billy's project impressed everyone at the presentation. Most importantly, he impressed and surprised himself: "There are representations for each chemical to shorten the name so that it will fit on the graph . . . I had to remember all of these abbreviations in order to be quick at the data entry process. I never thought even for a second that I would remember any of them, but I remembered about 85–90% of them, and that has helped increase my working speed by approximately 60% and that is a big difference." In his paper, Billy indicated how much he now cared about the work and how much pride he had developed in himself as a result of his successes. The pride extended to the company as well: "We are doing an excellent job at maintaining low pollution levels," he concluded in his report.

Allison: Cambridge-Lesley Careers in Education

For her placement, Allison Reid-Cunningham worked two mornings a week in a preschool classroom in Cambridge—one of a small number of classrooms that fully integrate typical learners with those with special needs and handicapping conditions. The other three mornings she attended a humanities seminar at Lesley College (co-taught by a high school teacher and a college professor). Not surprisingly, the longer she spent in the preschool classroom, the more interested Allison became in the issues raised by this type of special education inclusion model. When it came time to select a topic for her project, Allison recalled: "I knew exactly what I wanted to research. I wanted to find out more about what professionals and experts had to say about inclusion."

Allison began by reading a book and several articles about the topic, which she found in the Lesley College library, with the help of her seminar teacher. Then, since she preferred "to learn by talking to people" she developed a questionnaire and identified numerous people she wanted to interview. They included teachers in integrated as well as self-contained special needs classrooms, parents of children enrolled in integrated programs, and professors at Harvard University and Lesley College. Allison documented and synthesized this research in a fully footnoted paper with an extensive bibliography.

Her research notes also became the basis for her identification of five major issues to highlight through an audio-visual presentation. She used slides that she had taken in the classroom, and the voices of the people she had interviewed to illustrate these issues in a twenty-minute slide-tape show. Throughout this process, she was supported by a mentor with expertise in the field of early childhood education, and by her seminar teacher. Her final presentation was shared with a panel that included her mentor, her parent, her seminar teacher, and the teacher of the inclusive preschool classroom.

Allison concluded in her report: "This project is important to me because people often challenge me when I say that I believe in inclusion. They say that I have not had enough experience, or that inclusion works only very rarely. Prior to researching this topic, I had very few arguments to refute these statements. Now I can cite research and vast personal experience to prove my points."

A Seminar at the Worksite

Students need support to be successful in carrying out complex projects at the worksite. When Rindge launched its first school-to-work programs over five years ago, we decided to create an integrative seminar to connect classroom and worksite learning. This seminar takes place in the work setting, but is run by a high school teacher. In a typical week, students might spend three mornings at the worksite, working alongside an adult who has signed on to be their mentor/supervisor, and two mornings in a conference room, participating in a seminar with other students in the program. In the afternoons, they are back at school taking a variety of courses. By holding the

seminar at a worksite, we try to ensure contact between the teacher and supervisors, and make it easier for people at the worksite to bring their expertise and views into the seminar.

The students in the seminar are all part of the same program (e.g., financial services, health sciences) but they are not necessarily all doing similar jobs, nor are they even working at the same site. For example, in the
financial services program, five different banks and credit unions provide
placements. Students at one bank might be working as tellers, and, at another, be helping out the loan officer. The seminar meets for several months
at each of the various cooperating institutions, thus giving students the opportunity to spend time at each of the worksites of their peers. This arrangement also suits the banks, which would not want to tie up a conference
room for several hours a week all year long.

The curriculum of the seminar centers around the experiences students
are having in the worksites, helping them to construct meaning from those
experiences through close examination of relationships and events at work
and by connecting their particular experiences to those of their peers and
to broader themes of the humanities (such as identity, affiliation, and the relationship of the individual to the community). We have found that the
more students understand the purposes of the organization, the more sense
they can make out of their particular activities and projects. The work logs
students keep often contain clues as to what interests them at their worksites (which can point the way towards a project topic), as well as difficulties they are having. (See chapter 5: Hands-On Humanities for a more
detailed consideration of meaning-making at work.)

Five Essential Elements of Career Internship Programs

- Concrete context for learning—the workplace
- Reflective context for learning—the integrative seminar
- One-on-one relationship for students with adult mentors
- Projects linking the seminar, the workplace, and academic disci-
  plines—negotiated among student, teacher, and supervisor
- Exhibitions and presentations of student work

The seminar also provides a supportive setting for learning the skills
necessary for project work. These include cognitive and social skills that are
essential to success in a career and in college. Before doing their final projects, students develop and present "mini-projects" during the first half of the

year. These usually take the form of case studies that investigate an aspect of the work the students are doing in their placements. The parameters for the mini-project are similar to those for the final project, but the stakes are lower and the supports much more direct. For example, early in the process, the teacher might offer lessons on how to use graphic organizers and how to use flow diagrams to describe a complex system. Because the project is likely to center on a description and analysis of work tasks, the supervisor also may take an active role in helping the student to shape it.

As the presentation day nears, the teacher provides detailed instruction on presentation skills, perhaps bringing in one of the supervisors to share a presentation that s/he has made recently. Seminar time is set aside for rehearsing and providing feedback to one another. The presentation takes place only in front of peers and direct supervisors, without the added burden of performing before corporate vice-presidents or school department heads. This ensures that all of the students have had at least one experience presenting a project before they get to the more formal exhibition of their final projects.

For the final projects, students are expected to prepare written reports, as well as oral presentations, in which they describe both the process and product of their efforts. Encouraged to draw directly from their site logs and journal entries, students are expected to tell the story of how they went about doing the project, from getting the initial idea to preparing for the presentation. They are also expected to inform the assembled supervisors and peers about the concepts, ideas, and knowledge they gained from doing the project. Most of the presentations include graphic or audio-visual displays, as well as a written and oral report.

The presentation is more than simply an opportunity to showcase the work. Knowing how to do a good job of presenting one's work to peers and supervisors is in itself a valuable skill. Even more importantly, the feedback that students get, from their peers as well as their supervisors, has a very important motivating effect on them. Often, students seem more interested in the comments and responses supervisors make than in the grade they will receive from the teacher.

Whenever we describe our internships, a number of people ask questions about how assessment issues are handled. Actually the process is quite straightforward, and, we have found, very similar in different schools. First, the supervisors evaluate the interns, using forms similar to those for other employees. In our case, the seminar teacher then reviews this document, along with other work completed by the students. The final project is presented to a panel of supervisors and teachers (the student sometimes invites a teacher with whom s/he has a close relationship, or a teacher whose disciplinary expertise is in the area of the project, e.g., the electrical teacher, in the case of a technical project, or a science teacher if the project is in environmental engineering). The project is given a final grade by the seminar teacher, in consultation with the student. Students are aware from the beginning that the work has to measure up to a real world standard which, ultimately, appears to be as motivating to them as the knowledge that it will receive a grade.

Developing Academic and Technical Competencies on the Job

One of the most impressive things about many internship projects is the level of proficiency students demonstrate in using the tools and technologies of the workplace. Nevertheless, it remains very hard for teachers to accept that skills can be acquired in the process of applying them. Countless times I have heard teachers say things like: "It's fine to send kids out for a real world experience, but make sure they have gotten all their aca-demics first." Or, "How can you be thinking of sending Karen to work in an office at Harvard real estate? She barely knows how to do word-processing." The assumption is that before confronting situations where they might need to use a skill, students need to learn such skills in classes.

It is amazing how prevalent this belief remains, even though every teacher knows dozens of cases in which students have not acquired the knowledge and skills courses are intended to teach. For example, during the first year of CityWorks, teachers complained repeatedly that the students could not do accurate measurements. Several insisted on stopping the model-building to teach lessons on how to use a ruler—something, all felt, that the elementary schools should have, but clearly did not teach. Students responded by groaning, "This is baby stuff. We did this in fifth grade!" It took a while, but the team finally realized that our best bet was to find ways to support students in using rulers *as* they built their models, until they were making accurate measurements on their own.

No matter how hard high schools try to keep up with advancing technologies, students are more likely to encounter and master sophisticated hardware, software, and other new tools in the workplace. In the research that Mary Agnes Hamilton and Steve Hamilton conducted of their demonstration program, they found clear evidence of the youth gaining technical competence, which they define to include "not only mastering increasingly complex procedures, but also understanding fundamental principles and concepts underlying them, increasing capacity for analytical judgement and becoming computer literate." As an illustration they quote one of the students: "I was basically 'Miss Accounts Payable' while the lady I work with was on maternity leave because I knew what was going on. . . . It makes me feel important that I am doing something that's beneficial to the company. I'm not just there to file."[12]

Asked to specify what they have learned from their internships, most students will begin by describing the technical competence they are developing. In an assessment of his experience, one Rindge student recently offered the following accounting of new skills he had acquired:

> I'm learning new computer skills which will be very helpful in business. I've learned how to make a spreadsheet and how to use that information to find a new vendor. I learned how to compare vendors and am more aware of how they are selected . . . I've also learned a lot of skills in terms of being aware of how offices are managed and learning the different jobs that people have.

We have found that it is not uncommon for students in an office setting to learn four or five new applications (from spreadsheets to multi-media presentation software) within the first few months on the job. Those working in more technical jobs might learn various aspects of control technologies or the laboratory skills involved in such technical tasks as testing water for impurities or taking a blood sample.

One of the unfortunate effects of the wall that often exists between the school and the larger community is that it cuts off access to important resources. In an attempt to prepare students for an increasingly technological society, many schools have made technological proficiency into a graduate requirement. Too often, this comes down to students taking the 1990s version of a typing course. At best, they learn to use a keyboard, often on old equipment and with outdated software.

Ironically, these same high school computer courses are recognized as having value for all students, whatever their destination, while technical learning that takes place at work is more likely to be viewed as training for a particular occupation, and hence potentially narrowing a student's future options. The specific tasks may not be transferrable. But, insofar as students become comfortable with using a variety of technical resources, and gain experience in design, problem solving, and experimental protocols, they are learning skills that will serve them well in many future workplace or educational settings.

School Seminars: Supporting Individual Internships

The particular model of a worksite seminar used by Rindge works well when a number of students work for the same company or organization or within an industry with related worksites (e.g., banks). Outside of a major urban area, schools may have to rely mainly on small firms, each of which can only take on one or two interns. For example, Noble High School, in a rural area of southern Maine, has a career internship program for juniors and seniors in which students play a major role in developing their own work placements and projects.

Meeting together in a seminar for several hours each week, students learn to do research into various career possibilities, develop sites for job shadowing and career exploration, develop a learning plan, and come up with topics for quarterly projects. Like the Rindge students, they are required to keep journals, which become the basis for reflective conversations, and also help point them to possible topics for their projects. In a visit to the seminar, I heard students describe internships in an animal hospital, police department, sheriff's department, doctor's office, physical therapy department of a local hospital, bakery, law office, local elementary school computer lab, and a fire and rescue EMT team. For every ten or so students, an academic teacher serves as an advisor, helping to negotiate the learning plan, reading the students' journal, meeting with the students quarterly for a skills conference, and generally supporting their work on the projects.

Each quarter, students do a project related to the work at the site and/or their interest in the career area of their internship. The first quarter project derives from the essential question: "What does it mean to be a(n) _____?" Students are given a structure for conducting an in-depth study of a career that interests them. In the next three quarters they are expected to develop projects related to their internship site, addressing a question or issue of importance to the site and incorporating academic competencies. For example, the student working with the fire and rescue team is doing a public relations project. It addresses the need of the team to let others in the community know about their work, as well as the student's need to work on writing and oral communication skills.

Schools, such as Noble, with career internship programs based on individually-determined placements, find that an important strategy for strengthening connections between projects students do at work and the academic agenda of school is to design ways for teachers to spend time visiting the partnering employer(s) at the workplace. Some companies now provide week-long externships for teachers in the summer, giving them an opportunity to experience first-hand the activities and problems students might be observing or tackling at the worksite. Short of this kind of hands-on experience, teachers can learn a lot from spending even a few hours observing and interviewing people at the workplace.

One way to make the most of such a visit is to use an interview protocol, such as the "Learning Site Analysis Form," developed by the Northwestern Regional Education Laboratory (NWREL).[13] This tool includes a series of questions designed to capture information about the skills required by specific jobs, the characteristics that define the workplace, and potential applications of academic subjects at work. "The interview can be a springboard for project ideas that are founded on real demands and expectations of the job and workplace," explains Dio Morales, one of the developers of the protocol.

It can also be an opportunity to discuss one of the most risk-taking aspects of internship programs for teachers and worksite supervisors: their involvement in something akin to a role reversal. When students are in their work placements, the supervisor takes on more of the tasks of direct instruction, helping the student to learn particular skills, habits, and areas of knowledge needed on the job—showing the student, for example, how to use computer applications or carry out certain technical procedures.

At the same time, the teacher has to assume more of a supervisory role, making sure the student has the support s/he needs to complete academic and work tasks, and helping the student to reflect on and make sense of the experience. This arrangement leaves teachers free to do a different type of teaching: they help students to articulate what they are learning, coach them on project-doing skills, and hopefully, connect what they are learning to academic domains. It is interesting to note that although finding this new role somewhat challenging, teachers who have worked with internship projects are usually quite impressed by and pleased with the work students do.

Finding Projects that Matter

Whatever internship model a school adopts, the problem remains of how best to help students craft good projects. Initially, in the Rindge internships, we assumed that the project should be primarily determined by the work supervisor, with some modifications from the seminar teacher and the student. We soon realized that requiring the project to grow directly out of needs of the workplace is not necessarily enough to make a project engaging and worthwhile. With the intent of making the projects more academically relevant and intellectually demanding, the school began to take a stronger hand in shaping the projects. But, again, the results were not entirely satisfactory.

Especially in the more technical internships, much of the work began to resemble science fair projects. For example, a number of seniors chose to build models demonstrating technical principles from their work. One student constructed a working model of forced hot water heating controlled by a computer; another constructed a similar model of a refrigeration system. In both cases, their supervisors generously allowed them the time and materials to do these projects and provided the instruction necessary to make them come out well. The problem was that these projects neither emerged from a deep interest of the student's, nor did they make a real contribution to the worksite. They were, in short, contrived—albeit well-executed.

I have heard similar stories from friends in other school systems who, in trying to enhance the learning potential of the worksite, found they were turning the experience into what kids find least appealing about school. The way in which worksheets and certain school assignments can turn a potentially engaging experience into an alienating one was brought home to me recently in a seminar on work-based learning, in which a teacher at the Bridge School in Chelsea, Massachusetts, shared projects that several of his students had completed as part of an internship experience.

Bridge School is a program that attempts to motivate at-risk students by a combined experience of work and learning. Each student has a placement in a local business or agency for part of every school day. To obtain academic credit for their time on the job, they must complete an internship project. Aware of their students' previous difficulties with meeting even minimal expectations in school, the staff have taken pains to make the work requirements very clear. Like the examples we saw at the seminar, every project had to include such elements as a drawing of the physical plant, an interview with someone at the site, and a written discussion of a piece of art that expresses something about this occupational area.

We all enjoyed reading through the booklets students had made. The work looked great, and we were suitably impressed. Surprisingly, the teacher seemed less enthusiastic, describing a hot debate at his school as to whether to discontinue the project altogether. Despite the fact that the projects generally look good in the end, he explained, students and staff alike have come to dread the tedium of completing this set of requirements. Getting students through the experience was a lot like the proverbial pulling of teeth.

Although it was tempting to chalk this up to the resistance of a group of at-risk students, another incident had occurred recently that challenged this explanation. One of the students was fired from his job. Upset and furious, the student rejected the idea of moving immediately to another placement. Instead, after some discussion with the teacher about what workers do in such situations, he talked with a union member who represents adult workers at his site, and decided to pursue his right to a hearing. To prepare, he read the materials provided by the union, and, with the teacher's help, wrote up his case and presented it. Having set his own assignment, this student was willing to put in the type of persistent effort and to work on all of the skills that the internship project had been designed to (but rarely did) call forth.

It is just such a situation that William Kilpatrick, a colleague of John Dewey's, must have had in mind in 1938 when he wrote: "It is an inherent feature of purposeful activity that we begin with the interests of the pupil. We begin there because there is nowhere else to begin, if we are to get (as we must) self-activity from the child."[14] Kilpatrick took care to explain that this does not mean teachers should be satisfied with where the student's interests are at the beginning of a project. Rather, a teacher should help the student choose the "best" of the initial interests, and then allow these interests to grow as the student tries to reach his goals and finds it advantageous to make use of ideas, approaches, and information that might otherwise be of little interest or value to him.

Only some interns (e.g., Billy) are given actual work assignments that are of deep interest to them and have the potential for leading to intellectually rigorous investigation. Others, as was the case for Allison, may need help in creating their own assignment, for example, by undertaking an investigation that will help them better understand what is happening at their worksite and may enhance their performance there. The Cornell Youth and Work Program offers a useful document for apprentices and their advisors to guide them in thinking about what makes a good topic and how to frame an issue.

What Makes a Good Topic[15]

- Focuses on something that is important in the workplace
- Is researchable, that is, the apprentice can find information about it
  —information accessible to apprentice through inquiry in the workplace as well as in conventional places, e.g., library
  —confidentiality can be maintained if required
  —costs, time, and expertise required for research are within reason
- Connects with other aspects of the occupation (not isolated or self-contained)
- Apprentice cares about the topic
- Stimulates curiosity and questions that guide research
- Teaches the apprentice something new

If students keep journals or work-logs, these are a wonderful source to mine for potential topics. One of the advantages of the intensive seminar approach used at Rindge is that there are multiple oportunities for ongoing conversations with peers, the seminar teacher, and employers. Ideas for topics often emerge from such conversations. In both the Rindge and Cornell programs, students also receive the explicit message that internship projects should be of direct benefit to others. In a sense, colleagues and supervisors at the worksite are the natural beneficiaries of the intern's work, especially if the project makes a real contribution by influencing what happens in the workplace. We have found that the most successful projects done by our interns make just such a contribution (e.g., Billy's project, previously described).

While it may not always be feasible for a young intern to make a such direct contribution, there are other potential beneficiaries beyond staff at the worksite. In a list of examples, the Hamiltons suggest that the intended audiences of a project completed by a healthcare intern might include patients and their families or a grade school health or science class, as well as more work-based audiences such as staff or volunteers in the department. The point is for the project to include real products directed at real audiences.

When we first started supporting workplace projects, we were not aware of how important it was to provide students with such clear criteria. With the benefit of hindsight, I now can see that many projects our students completed in the past had much greater learning potential than we helped them to realize. For example, last year one student made a very competent (and well-received) fifteen-minute video of her worksite as part of her final project. Her intent was to celebrate what a great team her co-workers were and to capture some of the feeling of collaboration. Although people greatly enjoyed it, the video made no real contribution to the site, nor did it greatly enhance her skills (except in video editing).

With a little more direction from us, she could have delved more deeply into the topic of teamwork, perhaps through studying the growing literature on high performance workplaces, and through interviewing an organizational consultant. This research would have then suggested some essential features of teamwork that she could have used to organize her observations (and video footage) from her workplace. The result would have been a more thoughtful, and thought-provoking piece, that could have been of use to the team or the human resources department in orienting new employees.

The criterion of doing something that benefits others would also have enriched the learning experience of the students who built models for their senior projects. The central problem with the models was that once the work was completed and presented, it made no real contribution to the site, nor to anyone else. It is almost embarrassing now to realize how easy and sensible it would have been to arrange for the students to use their models as a basis for a lesson they could have taught in a science course at the high school or at a neighboring elementary school.

III. MAKING SCHOOLWORK MORE LIKE REAL WORK: SENIOR PROJECTS, FIELD STUDIES, AND CAREER EXPLORATION

Letting Seniors Define Projects

After several years of hearing from graduates of the Rindge internship programs how important these experiences had been in preparing them for the work or study they have undertaken since, we asked ourselves a new question: What if we gave all seniors in the high school the opportunity to do a major, independent project, offering them the same type of support available to students in the internship program? Would they get the same benefits from the experience? Could the principles and structures of work-based learning be used to support projects not related to a particular work setting? Given the difficulties of arranging enough internships, this is an important question for schools.

With a planning group consisting of the vice principal of the high school and several curriculum coordinators, we looked into the experience of several other high schools that had initiated senior projects, and decided to pilot our own version, making the program as similar in structure as possible to the internship project. As in the internships, seniors doing projects would be in a seminar where regular routines for reflection would be established (e.g., journals, peer reviews, etc.); and, in addition to a seminar teacher, they would have one or more mentors who were experts in the domains of the project. The project would culminate both in a written paper and in a presentation to a panel, which would include their mentors and others with expertise in the field.

Guidelines for Panelists

- *Purpose:* Has the student made clear his/her purpose for doing this project, particularly in terms of its personal and social relevance?

- *Findings:* Has the student arrived at a coherent set of findings, described how the work connects to other work within this field, and identified new questions to pursue?

- *Reflection:* Has the student told the story of the project and analyzed what s/he learned about learning, and assessed his/her own strengths and weaknesses?

> • *Communication:* Is the work presented in a way that highlights its strengths and is observant of conventions of written and oral communication?

The main difference between senior projects and internship projects was that it would be up to the student to provide his/her own "concrete context for learning." In some cases this might be a workplace, but it did not have to be. Whatever the context, the goal was for students to find a way to take some steps on the journey from novice to expert in their chosen field.

For most students electing to participate in the pilot year, the concrete context was the school itself: they chose to do projects that would make a direct contribution to their immediate community—whether through doing workshops for particular students, as was the case for the students who researched immigrant rights, or through preparing a report and recommendations to the elected school committee as to how to address the underachievement of African-American students.

For several others, the context grew out of their commitment to artistic expression and performance; for example, the spring dance concert provided the perfect exhibition space for a student who wanted to choreograph and perform an original piece. A few students had to invent their own contexts. Perhaps the most original was developed by a student doing a project on women and self-portraiture. She invited a dozen women to do self-portraits and then bring these to a brunch at her house, where she videotaped their discussion of the meaning of self-portraiture in their lives as women and artists.

While finding their own "concrete contexts" for learning did not prove to be very difficult for the students, some had difficulty (as some interns always do) in formulating a topic, within their broad area of interest, that was both important to them and feasible as a project. Perhaps the best example of this was the student who started out with the idea of creating a curriculum on twentieth-century art—certainly too broad an undertaking for a semester-long project. After much probing, the seminar teacher was able to discover that underlying this big idea was the student's anger that the curriculum in her high school art courses included very few women artists. At that point, it became clear that she could focus on researching and developing a curriculum profiling certain women artists.

For the planning team, this young woman's struggles, even more than the projects that flowed easily to fruition, was the justification for our efforts. It was all too easy to imagine this student going off to college, facing her first big paper, and choosing a topic as vast as twentieth century art. After staying up all night, she would more than likely produce a classic freshman essay so unfocused and unclear as to occasion a low grade and perhaps negative comments from the instructor. It is hard for students to recover their belief in their academic abilities after such an experience.

This difficulty was not surprising, considering that most of the seniors had little or no experience in independent learning. Because this was a pilot year, we interviewed students who participated, asking each of them what in their high school careers prepared them for this type of project. Most stared blankly at us and responded with "I can't think of anything." A few recalled a big project they had worked on in the fourth or fifth grade.

By requiring students to write a reflection paper, where they were to tell the story of how their project developed, as well as a more traditional research or inquiry paper, we hoped to make them more cognizant of what it took to find a compelling topic within a broad area of interest and, more generally, to force them to articulate what they had learned about the process of doing independent work. Nearly all the students commented directly on both the difficulties and satisfactions of the experience. As one student put it: "I have learned far beyond the subject matter of my project. I believe it has simultaneously been one of the best and most frustrating learning experiences of my high school career."

Graduation by Exhibition

In building support for senior projects at Rindge, we derived inspiration and information from the Paul M. Hodgson Vocational Technical High School in New Castle County, Delaware. Since 1990, the "Senior Project" has been a centerpiece of the Hodgson staff's efforts to create a fully integrated academic and vocational program and to raise the intellectual level of student work. Until just over a decade ago, Hodgson was a "share-time" vocational-technical high school, with students taking academic classes back at their "home schools." When Hodgson created its own academic program, the perception lingered that this was a place for kids who "couldn't make it in the academic world." This began to change in 1989, when Steven Godowsky became principal and encouraged the faculty to adopt the set of educational reform principles of the Coalition of Essential Schools, particularly the concept of assessment by exhibition.

Like Rindge, Hodgson could draw on its history and expertise as a vocational-technical school where the repertoire of teaching methodologies include performance-based assessment and projects that prompt students to produce real products for their own use and for others. To honor both the vocational and academic traditions, faculty members at Hodgson designed their Senior Project, with equal weight to each of three "P's"—a paper, a product, and an oral presentation. Each student is expected to write an extensive (twenty pages) occupationally based research paper that expands his/her knowledge about a vocational area, to design and construct a product related to the vocational program, and to make a public, formal oral presentation to a panel of adults.

The first piloting took place in 1990. By 1994, the Hodgson Senior Project was featured as an exemplar of authentic assessment and accountability in a study conducted by Jacqueline Ancess and Linda Darling-Hammond of the National Center for Restructuring Education, Schools, and Teaching (NCREST).[16] In reviewing students' Senior Projects, the researchers noted how much the work improved from the first to the second and third cohorts of students. By the time of their study, they were deeply impressed by the consistency with which students took integrative approaches to their topics, looking at them through several disciplinary lenses and from a number of vantage points.

Ancess and Darling-Hammond cited a paper on "Medical Malpractice" as an example of this type of work. The paper includes actual case studies of malpractice suits, as well as legal considerations of relevance to a medical assistant, such as breach of duty, contributory negligence, and comparative negligence. The young author makes appropriate use of mathematical tools in a series of graphs and charts to illustrate the dramatic annual increases in malpractice claims and insurance premiums, and finally, delivers a scientific and medical explanation of one area of frequent malpractice complaints—laparoscopic surgery.[17] In project after project, the researchers found a sophisticated treatment of science topics and extensive uses of mathematics. They also noted the students' consistent ability to weigh and balance the pros and cons of different technologies or approaches to a problem.

One of the important things about the Senior Project at Hodgson is that the faculty has found a way to make the projects work-like without necessarily being work-based. While students focus on an occupational area, they are not necessarily doing projects arising from a co-op, internship, or apprenticeship experience. Nevertheless, the projects are structured in a way that emulates some of the best characteristics of learning-rich work environments. Each student selects a Project Committee that serves as a resource during the entire project. The Committee must include a faculty advisor of the student's own choosing, an English teacher, and a teacher from the student's vocational program. In addition, many students include a representative from industry or business, a co-op employer, or a former student who has been through this process before. Although students do a great deal of work on these projects independently, it is a specific focus of time in their vocational/shop periods and their fall English course.

This design reflects many of the key features of work-based learning, and in that sense, meets the standard of "real enough" (see chapter 1). The student selects a topic of personal interest, the Project Committee serves the function of a community of practice, and the advisor acts as a mentor, guiding the student's work throughout the process. Students also have the opportunity to interview people in the field and to explore their topic with real tools and materials, from standard medical texts on oncology used by a student doing a project on the "Diagnosis and Nursing Care of Patients with Frontal Brain Tumors," to fine woodworking tools used by a student researching the craft of bed-making and building an eighteenth-century pencil-post bed.

Of course, one cannot just expect students to do a wonderful independent project—magically and on cue—in their senior year. In their study of Hodgson Senior Projects, Ancess and Darling-Hammond noted the extent to which the Senior Project had affected the faculty and curriculum of grades nine through twelve. Seeing the positive effects on students (e.g., higher rates of homework completion, higher grades, increased competence in writing, and increased commitment to completing a task), faculty members became increasingly willing to consider changes in their curricular and teaching practices. Among the changes noted by the researchers: faculty are "increasingly likely to direct students to find their own answers to questions . . . to ask probing questions and create inquiry-oriented classroom activities, rather than simply to lecture."[18]

In the creation of new learning opportunities for students, faculty began by analyzing the skills and knowledge students would need to meet the demands of the Senior Project—a good example of the "backward planning" model designed by Joe MacDonald for the Coalition of Essential Schools, and brought to Hodgson by Godowsky. The result has been the incorporation of more research skills, more projects, and more public presentations long before students reach senior year.

Field Studies: Kids As Consultants

How can schools ensure that students enter their senior year prepared to carry out sophisticated projects with substantial field components? One way to prepare students is to involve them in field studies in which they serve as consultants to local organizations and businesses. This involves the school forming partnerships with work organizations that are willing to work collaboratively on designing projects that are real (or real enough) to the students and the employer, and that fulfill the requirements of academic work students are expected to complete.

In Boston, for example, the CVS corporation has been working closely with Fenway Middle College High School for several years. In one recent jointly sponsored project, eleventh graders from the school conducted a market analysis to determine where to locate a new CVS pharmacy and retail outlet in Roxbury, a predominately African-American section of Boston. While other Boston neighborhoods had several CVS outlets, there were none in Roxbury. The students were given the opportunity to propose a site. Although fully aware that the company would probably not rely only on their calculations in making a monetary decision as to where to locate a store, the students still felt involved in a real problem. By bringing this type of problem to a group of high school students, CVS was moving beyond treating these young people as workers or potential workers, to viewing them as project consultants.

Organized into small work teams supported by experts from various departments within the CVS organization, students analyzed demographic and economic data to determine market demand for a CVS pharmacy in different neighborhoods. Students also worked with CVS staff to identify and evaluate several possible locations for the new store. This involved visits to sites to analyze first-hand the pros and cons of possible locations. Students worked with architects on design options for the new store and worked with accountants on financing plans. In addition to providing experts to coach and mentor students on various aspects of the project, CVS also offered students several opportunities to shadow employees in corporate headquarters as well as the retail stores. This helped students gain a more complete understanding of the business.

This project was also supported by the students' mathematics and humanities classes. In math, they learned to use statistical methods to organize and analyze the demographic data they had collected. They also used mathematics to develop and analyze financing options and likely return on investment. Students practiced and sharpened their writing skills through the preparation of a report summarizing their findings and recommendations, and developed public speaking skills through presentations of their findings to CVS executives.

Like the internship projects described earlier, field studies allow students to forge a working relationship with adults who have expertise in a particular kind of inquiry or problem solving and who instruct or coach them in the knowledge, skills, and dispositions required by the project. If the role of the project in internship programs is to connect work-based activities and issues to academic subject matter and skills, the role of the project in a classsroom is to connect academic learning to activities, issues, and expertise available at the workplace. The fieldwork students do may not actually affect a major corporate decision, but they go through all of the stages of the work that an actual consultant would complete—from research of various sorts to a final presentation—and they receive coaching not only from their teachers, but also from others with expertise in the key tasks. In this way, schoolwork becomes more relevant and more like real work.

Finding Pathways

At Rindge, in addition to connecting academic courses to work-related problems and tasks, we have also found it useful to set up a special "hybrid" setting that combines features of classrooms and workplaces. Neither a traditional academic class nor a shop, Pathways, like CityWorks, reinforces the skills of project-doing. The class also gets students out into a variety of workplaces and gives them an opportunity to "try on" a number of different work identities.

In designing Pathways, we looked closely at the job readiness and job skills programs that some schools offer (usually for students who are doing very poorly in school and hence are highly at risk). Through workbook exercises, lectures, and some role-playing, students in these programs are expected to learn how to dress, how to put together a resume, how to fill out an application, and how to present themselves in interviews. While we agreed that these are all very important skills, we also recognized that they cannot be taught effectively in a decontextualized way, to kids who are already turned off to school. Many students have a very low tolerance for worksheets, even when the questions are directed at helping them to articulate their own values; and even when the workbook activities are supplemented with a few speakers or role-plays. Worksheets read "school," and school, in their view, is contrived and disconnected from "real life."

What makes Pathways unique is that the year is built around a series of job shadowing experiences. Over the course of the year, each student, on average, goes out on four different job shadows. Each quarter of the year, students hear from a panel of adults from the workplaces offering shadowing opportunities that term. They then select the workplaces that sound interesting to them, and spend three or four hours at the site in the company of an adult who works there. Although each job shadow only lasts for about three hours, it becomes the focal point of a great many other activities.

To prepare for their shadowing experiences, students do preliminary research about the types of career(s) that they will observe (they usually make use of the career resource center in the school, or the public library next door). Based on this information, they come up with a list of questions to ask at the site. Before going out, students have to verify the appointment through a phone call to the worksite, have their parents approve a trans-portation plan (students go on their own to the job shadow), and get per-mission from teachers to miss their classes for the day. After the shadow, students are expected to write a thank-you note and, combining the earlier research with what they learned on site, to prepare a job shadow report.

We originally assumed that students would be very excited about going out on the job shadows and perhaps less excited about doing all of the ar-ranging and writing—that the shadow would be the "carrot" that would carry them through. In some cases, that has been true—especially if the stu-dent has a degree of self-confidence and the job shadow itself seems par-ticularly intriguing (e.g., going out in a squad car with the police, spending the morning at the local hiphop radio station). To our surprise, we have found that in an equal number of cases, students are very anxious about the job shadow, and avoid doing the required preparation because they are frightened to go.

We have spent a lot of time trying to figure out exactly what scares them. For some, it seems to be the idea of spending time with a stranger ("he probably doesn't even want me to come"); for others there is a fear of not fitting in or of having to change in order to fit in ("I'm not going to get all dressed up and shit."); sometimes it is just plain discomfort with taking public transportation into an unfamiliar part of town ("there's drunks and homeless people on that subway"). These issues have become the basis for interesting discussions in the class; the very process of surfacing their anxi-eties has helped students to participate.

Can spending half a day at each of three or four different worksites re-ally have much value to a student? This is a question people often ask about the Pathways program. It was also one of our major questions in starting the program. The answer we have arrived at is that work-based learning, even at the modest level of job shadowing, results in students' making real con-nections with adults and learning a great deal about the way these adults think about and approach their work.

One Pathways student, Jennifer, ended her job shadowing report about her day with a photographer with the following comment: "After a long day of picture-taking it was time for me to get on the train and go home. When I was on the train back I recapped my day with Ms. Devereau and came to the conclusion that someday I might want to be a photographer and I might want to be a host to a kid who wants to follow into the footsteps of photography." She concluded: "It taught me a lot about cameras and about the art of photography. I really had a good time and I really learned a lot from Ms. Devereau."

Clearly, this student felt a real bond with the woman she shadowed. She had never met a photographer before, much less a woman who ran a photography business. In fact, it is evident in many of the job shadow reports that the student and the host went beyond a superficial exchange of information. In his job shadow report about the assignment editor in the news department of a local television station, Marco wrote: "Tom doesn't just produce the news; he has to make it more appealing so people won't change the channel . . . Tom would be very excited if he knew that I like watching his news. . . . Since a group of us went to go visit WBZ we are more likely to watch WBZ news because we now know many people that work there."

Students seem to discover the extent to which workplaces are also places where learning and thinking go on: "He showed us a room where they kept tapes up to 1984. They keep it because it helps them figure out what mistakes were done in the past and how they can improve it. . . . He has a computer which lists all the subjects to write about and which ones he wants to use, change, or fix up." Even when students shadow someone whose job is not that attractive, they seem to get something valuable from the experience. After shadowing a mail person at the local post office, Alfredo wrote: "All of the people that work there said to me stay in school, do good in school, and go to college so I wouldn't end up working in a place like that."

Although central to Pathways, the job shadowing sequence is by no means the entire curriculum. In addition, students take on several substantial projects during the year. For example, this past year, one month-long Pathways project involved starting and running a mini-enterprise. After doing some market research, each different section of Pathways developed its own entrepreneurial venture. Students could make something to sell, or they could order a ready-made product, if they modified it before selling it. Within the class, students had to figure out how to accomplish all of the tasks involved, from product design to marketing.

In the most successful of these ventures, one class ordered colored beads which they then combined into flags for students to wear around their necks. In the multicultural environment of Rindge, where students come from over forty different nations, such flag-pendants quickly became a sought-after item. Within days, orders were coming in much more quickly than the capacity (or desire) of the students to manufacture more flags. Over a period of a week, the class made a profit of fifty dollars. More importantly, they learned some important lessons of supply and demand, and even had to consider the ethical question of whether to keep manufacturing an item that, in at least one instance, seemed to exacerbate tensions between two students from different countries.

A third major strand of the course consists of a combination of job readiness skills, career awareness activities, and readings and discussions about work. For the skills and awareness aspect of the course, we rely on commercially available materials that address various aspects of work preparation, including: workplace skills, career exploration, and job search. The Pathways class never spends too many days in a row on such activities. Rather, the teacher mixes them with reading and discussing newspaper articles (from features on local entrepreneurs to analyses of trends in the job market) or excerpts from books that focus on how people develop careers and the struggles they have had making a life and making a living. Sources range from the oral histories in Studs Terkel's *Working* to selections from the *Autobiography of Malcolm X.*

IV. DEVELOPING COMMON CRITERIA FOR REAL WORK AND SCHOOLWORK

Field studies and job shadowing offer a less intense worksite experience than does an internship or apprenticeship. Learning activities that occur as part of an actual work placement carry particular advantages that, for the most part, cannot be replicated inside the school.

What Work Placements Offer

- An authentic context for complex problem solving in which students must deal with real-time constraints and pressures

- A place for reality-testing about different work settings and career options which casual observation (e.g., job shadowing) can't provide

- The chance to learn how to navigate the modern workplace and demonstrate their capabilities to adults who can help them get ahead

---

Although other forms of work-centered learning (i.e., senior projects, "consultantcies," field studies, and job shadowing) cannot be an alternative to work experience, they can offer an important complement to it, and one that is potentially available to larger numbers of students, including young people in the earlier years of high school (or before). Convinced of the value of work as a context for learning important skills and as a motivating factor that can help to reengage young people with their studies, a number of school districts are becoming quite creative at identifying and supporting new combinations of work-based or work-related learning, and at convincing local employers to participate in these hybrids.

For example, nine "career pathway teams" of Boston teachers and employers have come together in workshop sessions jointly sponsored by the district, the Private Industry Council, and Jobs for the Future. With the help of Michelle Swanson, founder of the ComAcad (see chapter 1), the teams explored different mergers of learning in workplace and classroom settings. At the end of three days, they had developed the outlines of specific work and learning projects to pilot during the spring semester.

In addition to such efforts in Boston, a number of school teams in the Milwaukee public schools have embarked on a similar process, joining together with teams in Boston and several other districts in a new Quality Work-Centered Learning Network, based at Jobs for the Future. One of the goals of this effort is to examine the quality of student work emerging both from field studies and internship projects in order to try to throw more light on questions like: "How real is real enough? How substantial does the involvement of work partners need to be? What school structures and supports need to be in place for students and for teachers?"

Because work placements and field studies are so different from business as usual in the schools, it is important to articulate a set of criteria that define their essential and unifying dimensions and lay the groundwork for establishing quality standards. The list in the box below represents an initial attempt by the Quality Work-Based Learning Network to clarify the ways in which learning-rich work placements and field studies are similar to one another, as well as the ways they differ from many other learning activities.

Dimensions of Work-Related Learning

1. Experiences are structured around learning goals, agreed to by students, teachers, and outside partners, that assist students in reaching standards and graduation requirements of the district.

---

2. Students carry out projects that are grounded in real world problems, take effort and persistence over time, and result in the creation of something that matters to them and has an external audience.

3. Students receive ongoing coaching and expert advice on projects and other work tasks from employers and community partners. By learning to use strategies and tools that mirror those used by experts in the field, students develop a sense of what is involved in accomplished adult performance and begin to internalize a set of real world standards.

4. Students develop a greater awareness of career opportunities in the field and deepen their understanding of the educational requirements of these careers.

5. Students develop their ability to use disciplinary methods of inquiry (e.g., to think like a scientist) and enhance their ability to tackle complex questions and carry out independent investigations.

6. Students are able to demonstrate their achievements through multiple assessments, including: self-assessment, specific performance assessments (e.g., oral proficiency exam) and exhibitions.[19]

The Search for Intellectual Rigor

Although each of the programs described here has set its own particular criteria for internship projects or senior projects, they all share a vision of adult achievement that is, in a sense, the ultimate standard by which students, faculty, and work mentors assess the students' work. Interestingly, adult accomplishment is also the starting point used by Fred Newmann and Gary Wehlage in their book, *Successful School Restructuring,* as they try to answer the broad question of "how do we know when students have learned to use their minds well—rigorously and creatively?"[20]

Looking at the intellectual qualities involved in complex professional accomplishments, they note a bridge designer draws on established knowledge in a variety of fields (including engineering, architecture, various natural sciences, and mathematics), produces new conceptions of design and construction in order to address the unique problems and special conditions of a particular setting, and finally, uses this knowledge to make something of utilitarian and aesthetic value. The researchers propose that authentic student achievement should meet the same criteria: the student should construct knowledge through disciplined inquiry to produce discourse, products, and performances that have meaning beyond success in school.

Based on these criteria, they developed a set of standards that can be used to gauge the intellectual quality and authenticity of the pedagogy of the classroom and the work students do. Analyzing the mathematics or social studies work of 2,100 students from classes with high, medium, and low levels of authentic pedagogy, the researchers found that in classrooms where the pedagogy scored high, students also scored significantly higher on a performance scale designed to measure the intellectual quality of student work.

Newmann and Wehlage's study focused on 130 academic classrooms in public schools that had previously been identified as having made "significant progress in restructuring." It became clear to them that: "the tools of school restructuring do not assure a schoolwide focus on learning of high intellectual quality or authentic teaching."[21] It is striking the extent to which the student projects and performances described in this chapter—emerging from programs with a vocational focus—embody the expectation that all students can and should do rigorous intellectual work, and how close they come to meeting the standards of quality outlined by the researchers.

Beyond Social Class Sorting

Too often, combinations of work and learning are perceived as only being for those having "academic difficulties." Despite the efforts of programs like those cited in this chapter to create rigorous, high-quality work-centered and work-based learning experiences and despite the high college-going rate from pioneering internships and youth apprenticeships, there continues to be a social class bias in who enters, or is channeled into school-to-work programs. Rather than being seen as a central part of school restructuring or as a primary vehicle for teaching the knowledge and skills that all students will need, these initiatives are viewed as the latest solution to the ever-growing problem of what to do with the non-college bound.

Perhaps part of the problem lies in the term itself: "school-to-work" gives the impression that the reforms are merely about a smoother transition into the labor market for those who are not intending to go to college. In an attempt to deal with the tracking issue, reformers have tried to change the name to "school-to-career." So far, this has proved equally problematic, since it perpetuates the view that these programs are about preparing students for a particular career (singular) rather than empowering them with skills and competencies required by a broad range of potentially rewarding careers (plural).

Used in a high school context, either "school-to-work" or "school-to-career" seems to single out that population within the school who do not have college plans. Certainly this is a large and important group of students. Although the percentage of students entering post-secondary education is rising, it is still true that about 40 percent do not go on to college after high school, and the majority who do go on do not complete a college degree. Many of these students were ill-served by their years in high school—receiving weak preparation for post-secondary education, few opportunities to explore potentially rewarding careers, and little exposure to the skills required in an increasingly technical labor market.

When students graduate from high school they enter a labor market that is very unwelcoming to them. Between the ages of eighteen and twenty-seven, they hold, on average, six different jobs and experience four or five periods of unemployment. Even if and when they settle into more permanent employment, they have increasingly more limited chances to earn a decent wage. Between 1979 and 1993 the earnings gap between graduates of high school and four-year colleges increased dramatically.[22]

Improving the quality of education for this group of students is an important goal. But any attempt to tailor programs to the "non-college-bound" seems destined to failure. In the history of educational reform, one can find numerous examples of good intentions towards "low-ability" or "high-risk" students leading ultimately to lowered expectations and watered down, dead-end programs. Students who fail to do well in an academic milieu are denied the opportunity to do anything that requires them to be thinkers or problem solvers. Instead, they are "remediated"—which means they are asked to accumulate even more bits of knowledge and subskills. In the name of addressing their deficits, anything that might be of interest—that might capture their attention or imagination—has, in effect, been removed from their curriculum.

One could reasonably argue that college-bound students do not have as immediate a need for these programs as those not planning on college. If spaces in school-to-work programs are limited, why encourage the participation of those who function well in the normal routines of school? One answer has to do with the sorting function of schools. Ultimately, the presence of students with good high school records is of vital importance in keeping the focus of teachers and program designers on high-quality, rigorous intellectual pursuits and in ensuring that school-to-work programs also help prepare students for post-secondary learning experiences.

A second, more important answer, is that linking classroom learning with workplace learning offers the promise of a better, more powerful education for a broad range of students. This is the implication of the research conducted by Newmann and Wehlage, as well as the work of Lauren Resnick and other cognitive scientists. These scholars point out the disjuncture between the conditions of learning in the classroom (where students are expected to do most of their work alone, come up with a single right answer, and perform without access to tools or technology) and the characteristics of modern workplaces (where communities of practice use materials and technologies to identify and evaluate multiple solutions to problems). It is time to reconsider the dominant methods and strategies of teaching and learning in light of this gap.

NOTES

1. Lynn Olson, "The Career Game," *Education Week,* October 2, 1996, 31–33.

2. David Stern et al, *School to Work: Research on Programs in the United States,* The Stanford Series on Education and Public Policy, no. 17, (London: The Falmer Press, 1995), 22.

3. Direct quotations from students are from interviews conducted by Felicia Hayes in the spring of 1995, shared with the author by Margaret Vickers, the Director of *Working to Learn* and a chapter author in this volume.

4. Felicia Hayes, "Findings," unpublished manuscript, December 7, 1995.

5. Hayes, 8.

6. Hilary Kopp and Richard Kazis, *Promising Practices: A Study of Ten School-to-Career Programs,* (Boston: Jobs for the Future, 1994), 10.

7. Stern et al, *School to Work,* 20

8. Kopp and Kazis, *Promising Practices,* 8

9. David Stern, Marilyn Raby, and Charles Dayton, *Career Academies: Partnerships for Reconstructing American High Schools* (San Francisco: Jossey-Bass, 1992), 70.

10. Mary Agnes Hamilton and Stephen F. Hamilton, *Learning Well at Work: Choices for Quality* (National School-to-Work Opportunities Office, 1997), 15.

11. Hamilton and Hamilton, *Learning Well at Work,* 21.

12. Hamilton and Hamilton, *Learning Well at Work,* 11.

13. "Learning Site Analysis Form," *Connections: Linking Work and Learning* (Portland, OR: Northwest Regional Education Laboratory, 1997).

14. Kilpatrick, "Introduction: Principles of Community Learning," in Society for Curriculum Study, ed. Samuel Everett, *The Community School* (New York: D. Appleton-Century Co., 1938), 13.

15. Cornell Youth and Work Program, http://www.human.cornell.edu/youthwork/

16. Jacqueline Ancess and Linda Darling-Hammond, "The Senior Project: Authentic Assessment at Hodgson Vocational/Technical High School," (New York: NCREST, Teachers College 1994), 16–19.

17. Ancess and Darling-Hammond, "The Senior Project," 16.

18. Ancess and Darling-Hammond, "The Senior Project," 22.

19. The author developed this list in her capacity as director of the Quality Work-Based Learning Network of Jobs for the Future.

20. Fred M. Newmann and Gary G. Wehlage, *Successful School Restructuring: A Report to the Public and Educators by the Center on Organization and Restructuring of Schools,* (Madison, WI: University of Wisconsin-Madison, 1995), 8.

21. Newmann and Wehlage, *Successful School Restructuring,* 28.

22. Richard J. Murnane and Frank Levy, *Teaching the New Basic Skills: Principles for Educating Children to Thrive in a Changing Economy* (New York: The Free Press, 1996), 3.

4

Working to Learn

Building Science Understandings

Through Work-Based Learning

Margaret Vickers

Each year, tenth-grade life science students at Noble High School in rural Maine spend several weeks doing organism counts and chemical tests on the local rivers and reservoirs. This five-week unit usually takes the form of a whole-class project, and the particular problem the class focuses on varies from year to year. For example, last year, teacher Scott Eddleman's students decided they wanted to work out why their favorite swimming hole on the Salmon Falls river clogs up with algae every spring. The students collected samples from various points in the river, visited the sewage treatment plant, consulted with local water-testing professionals, and finally called a town meeting at which they presented their conclusions and made recommendations for more stringent treatment of the sewage effluent that enters Salmon Falls above the swimming hole.

I. STORIES FROM THE FIELD

Noble High School is one of a growing number of schools that are connecting science and work-based learning through the *Working to Learn* project. The project began three years ago, when a small group of science teachers, scientists, and curriculum writers received their first grant from the Pew Charitable Trusts. Now in its second phase, the goal is to help adults from workplaces and the community form partnerships with high school science and mathematics teachers. Under this arrangement, teachers and workplace experts join together in providing learning experiences for students, and students engage in learning activities at work as well as at school.

Teachers who follow the *Working to Learn* approach are committed to developing whole-class or individual projects that bridge classroom and workplace or community settings. Instead of starting with abstract principles of science and adding applications as an afterthought, teachers like Eddleman begin with problems that arise at work or in the community, and introduce the scientific and mathematical ideas needed to identify and test possible solutions to those problems. Students use these ideas as they develop and complete a substantial project. Some projects, like the Salmon Falls study, engage the whole class, but students may also do projects individually or in smaller groups.

The *Working to Learn* approach is sometimes called "backward-mapping," because the first task in every unit is to provide first-hand experiences through which students attempt to solve real-world problems that interest them. The idea is to begin with the experience, and end up with subject-matter knowledge, rather than the other way around. While the problems selected for study should be interesting to students, relevance is not the only criterion. In addition, each problem should be complex and multifaceted enough to support extended reflection.

Many different frames of inquiry can be used to reflect on complex workplace and community problems. In schools where the teachers work in teams, student projects sometimes involve a multidisciplinary approach. But if too many disciplinary threads are woven into a single project, it becomes difficult to sustain coherence or achieve conceptual depth. The focus of the *Working to Learn* units is on engaging students in solving the problems raised by the projects, using scientific concepts and scientific habits of mind, together with relevant mathematical and technological skills. At the end of every project, students are expected to report their findings to an audience that includes both specialists and non-specialists. Every student project includes a requirement for clear oral, written, and graphical communication.

To date, the *Working to Learn* project has developed three units: "Water Testing and Aquatic Ecology," "Heating, Ventilating, Air Conditioning, and Heat Flow (HVAC)," and " Cardiovascular Diagnosis Physiology." All three begin with suggested workplace experiences designed to kindle the student's interest in related science concepts. For example, in the unit on water testing and aquatic ecology students learn how to assess the quality of the town water supply and also come to understand the essentials of aquatic ecology. In the unit on heating, ventilating, and air conditioning, students learn how HVAC systems work and also learn about the physics of heat transfer, liquid flow, and thermostatic control. The cardiovascular unit introduces some common diagnostic techniques for finding out if something is wrong with a patient's heart, lungs, or blood and uses these to provide students with a basic understanding of the anatomy and physiology of the cardiovascular system.

An overarching goal of *Working to Learn* is to create connections between science as it is used at work and science as it is presented in documents like the *AAAS Benchmarks* and the *National Science Education Standards*. This is not easy to do. As explained later in this chapter, science subject matter has traditionally been organized around the "big ideas" or abstract principles of the discipline, like the principle of conservation of energy. Such principles summarize an enormous amount of information, but students often find it hard to see how these ideas relate to everyday human needs.

Consider what typically happens in a conventional physics lesson when heat flow is discussed. The question most often used to structure a traditional science lesson on this topic is: How is heat transmitted? Through workbook exercises and classroom discussion, students are commonly taught to give an answer such as the following one.

Heat is transmitted through:

- conduction,
- convection, and
- radiation.

In most classrooms there will probably be a handful of students who will memorize such information in order to please the teacher and get a good grade. These students may give the right answers on tests, but are unlikely to know how to use the concepts they have studied in practical settings.[1] Both the desire to learn and the ability to retain conceptual knowledge demand a special kind of engagement—we call it a "need-to-know" mentality.

Last year I was observing an anatomy and physiology class at the Fenway school in Boston, where the teacher, Ms. Kennedy, had students in pairs and was teaching them to take each other's pulse rates. One of the students, Loretta, was carrying out this task with obvious reluctance and was quick to speak her mind. "Why do we need to do this? What's it for?" she demanded to know. Ms. Kennedy explained that learning to take pulse rates was an important skill, and that when Loretta started her internship at The Childrens' Hospital next week, she would need to know how to do it. Loretta simply did not believe her. "I want to go to Childrens' Hospital because I want a job," she declared, "But I don't want this stuff!" Even though this was a relatively "hands-on" lesson, Loretta could not believe there would be a connection between the "stuff" teachers make you do in science, and what goes on in a real job. Such a connection had never been there before. As far as she knew, most jobs involved simple routines, like preparing fast food, or mindless labor, like pushing a broom.

It took direct experience to change Loretta's ideas about the connections between work and learning. When she settled into her internship in the EKG department at The Childrens' Hospital she learned, for example, that casual jobs are different from career-oriented work. She had experienced quite a few part-time jobs, but she only thought about them while she was at the worksite. "Being an intern at The Childrens' is different," she explained. Now she thinks about her hospital job in the evenings, plans her work for the next day, and focuses on problems she needs to solve. Her attitude to school has changed too. For her end-of-semester exhibition, she explained to her classmates how you could use EKGs to find out if something is wrong with your heart, illustrating her talk by handing out some of the EKG charts she had collected during her work at the hospital.

Instead of having to arrange internships or site visits, it would, of course, be easier to deal with students like Loretta by simply starting class lessons with verbal scenarios that describe the connections between school and work. A class lesson might simply begin like this: "Today our topic is heat flow. Have you ever had a headache because you were in a stuffy room? What do you think we could do about this?" The teacher then goes on to explain to his students that as soon as you understand the principles of heat flow, you will know how to solve these problems.

In our experience, students are rarely convinced by such talk; they respond much better when they are invited to plan and carry out investigations, and they are proud when the results they obtain lead to actual changes. One *Working to Learn* unit invites groups of students to investigate why people get headaches when they work in particular classrooms in their school, or in particular offices in nearby buildings. This unit works best if the teacher can form a partnership with a qualified heating, ventilating and air-conditioning technician. The technician's task is to show the students how to carry out air quality measurements and guide them as they find out how each component of the system works and how the parts relate to each other. Once they have some understanding of the building's

HVAC system, the technician supports them as they troubleshoot and come up with suggestions about ways of improving the system. As the students gain these experiences, the science teacher plays a complementary role, encouraging them to reflect on what they are learning about air quality and heat flow, and involving them in laboratory experiments that allow them to make sense of the key principles involved.

The differences between this type of science curriculum and the conventional approach are more than skin deep. When students are invited to make sense of real-world issues, there is a greater emphasis on science in action, and less emphasis on abstract science. In contrast to traditional school science, curricula that start with workplace and community experiences are much more interdisciplinary, and stress closer links between the different branches of science, and between science and technology. As students learn to analyze and solve workplace problems, they often need to be introduced to techniques and concepts that are used by professionals. Most of these techniques are rarely taught in school science. For example, water quality tests such as those used for ascertaining the level of nitrate or dissolved oxygen are rarely performed in high school science courses and even if they are, the broader implications of the factors being tested are not usually addressed.

In developing the water-testing unit, we carried out worksite investigations and found that one of the competencies for a general foreman at a water treatment plant is: "Ability to perform water quality tests: Dissolved oxygen, turbidity, pH and chlorine, and general knowledge of the significance of these tests so that further actions may be suggested." If a student involved in a water-testing internship learned to perform and interpret these water tests at work, then reflected on the results in a school ecology course, she would achieve the required workplace competency but would also come to appreciate the complex interactions among living organisms and their physical environment in a river ecosystem.

Working to Learn curricula place a high priority on involving workplace supervisors as *partners* in the learning process. While this is a distinctive feature of our approach to science learning, in one sense our work is just a new and fledgling member of a broader family of "contextually-oriented" science and mathematics courses. These courses aim to integrate the sciences more closely with each other and with relevant aspects of mathematics and technology education; they situate learning in the context of community or work-based problems; they emphasize higher-order thinking and problem solving; and most of them involve extended student projects.

Several science and mathematics courses that share these characteristics have emerged over the last ten years, with some models showing a greater degree of contextualization than others. The American Chemical Society's (ACS) *Chemistry in the Community* is an issues-based course that requires interdisciplinary connections, and now boasts an enrollment of 250,000 students. The ACS is now taking workplace links further with its new *SciTeKS* modules, which actually incorporate workplace simulations. The *Science Education for Public Understanding Program* has developed several units that promote the use of scientific principles, processes, and evidence in public decision-making. North Carolina's *Teaching and Learning Cross-Country Mathematics* is a pre-calculus course based on mathematical modeling of real-world phenomena. Full descriptions of this program and others like it are available in *Changing the Subject,* a book which provides twenty-three case studies of recent innovations in science, mathematics, and technology education.

The vision for high school science and mathematics emerging from such examples is quite different from the framework that has governed these subjects in the past. Radical plans for innovation in any subject-matter area raise deep anxieties among teachers, parents, and students, and these anxieties are quite understandable. Parents worry that the innovators want to throw standards to the winds. If something you as a parent learned to do at school—especially something hard like long division—is eliminated because it is easier to use a calculator, what does this mean for your child?

If an integrated subject called "Science at Work" is introduced at the school, should your child take it, or should she take the traditional physics class? Teachers, parents, and students all worry that grades in non-traditional subjects will be rejected by college admissions staff. If science and mathematics are going to be taught differently in the future—if these subjects are going to become more inclusive—then deeply held attitudes such as these will have to change.

II. SCIENCE IN SCHOOL: CHANGING THE SUBJECT

Historically, within the scientific disciplines, there has been a tendency to value abstract thought above practical problem solving, and pure research has usually been considered superior to applied research. It is hardly surprising, therefore, that one of the assumptions held by many math and science teachers is that solving decontextualized calculus problems is more difficult than repairing a broken engine or making a kite. In short, the "best" students are thought to be those who enjoy scientific knowledge as an end in itself, rather than seeing it as a basis for designing artifacts or understanding the real world.

It is easy to be tyrannized by this view of science; after all, many parents, teachers, and even scientists consider it to be "the truth." The full story of the history of science is longer and more complex than can be told here, but it is not necessary to go very far back in time in order to discover that most of the inventions that have shaped the modern world resulted from the work of practical men, rather than the work of scientists. In fact, my reading of the history of science reveals a dynamic, complex interaction between abstract theorizing on the one hand and the inventions of new devices and the improvement of systems on the other.

Writing on the history of technology, Clinchy pointed out that Daimler's internal combustion engine, the Wright brother's airplane, Edison's light bulb, and the radio of De Forest and Armstrong were all produced by "extraordinary tinkerers rather than university savants." Despite the fact that they were largely divorced from academe, the influence of these inventors on the cultural and economic life of their societies was substantial.[2] As Clinchy noted:

> . . . a close examination of the process of historical change in the West from medieval times through the Renaissance and the Industrial Revolution and on into quite recent history makes it clear that technological innovation has brought about most of the great social, economic, and cultural transformations in Western society. Until the advent of World War II and the scientific/political alliance that produced nuclear weapons, as well as nuclear energy and the digital computer, the crucial inventions that have most changed our lives did not emerge from the disconnected world of university-based scholars but from the everyday life of the workaday world.[3]

While the tinkerers of the late nineteenth and early twentieth centuries were making tangible contributions to everyday life, university-based scientists managed to secure a privileged position for themselves in the academic world, forcing practical science to the margins. Thus, the value academia now places on "pure science" arose late in the nineteenth century, as a result of a series of political struggles between scientists on the one hand, and practical men—the technicians and engineers—on the other. (Women were largely excluded from these struggles.)

The outcome of this historical struggle has obvious implications for how different kinds of knowledge came to be valued by the universities, and ultimately, by the schools. Commenting on the relationship between science and technology, historian David Layton wrote:

> The educational message systems of curriculum, pedagogy and assessment were used increasingly in the second half of the nineteenth century to define and promote 'pure science' as a dominant category detached from

practical contexts. . . . The important point is that . . . 'abstract theory' secured the high ground, as well as high status, while 'practice' was seen as demeaning and lacking in prestige.[4]

These developments in academia meant that by the early twentieth century, educators had already begun to define science and mathematics as abstract disciplines.

The second element of this story focuses on the world of work. As the twentieth century began, new developments were taking place that would place a decisive wedge between the industrial sector's managers and designers and the practical men and women who worked on the factory floor. In 1913, the first assembly lines were installed in Henry Ford's Chicago plant. The technologies of mass production promulgated by Ford and Taylor spread rapidly to other industries, greatly boosting America's prosperity for decades to come. Before the invention of mass production, artisans and craftsmen not only designed carriages, but also built them. In the Taylorized workplace, a new hierarchy was put in place: thinking, designing, and managing became the prerogative of a select elite, while the vast majority of workers carried out routine operations on the process line.[5]

As this system of production grew, the message sent to schools was that the economy did not need large numbers of young people to be highly proficient in science and mathematics. While a small, highly qualified elite would be needed, the vast majority of students would never be required to use higher order math and science skills at work.

The dominance of abstract science continued in the 1950s when it received an additional boost from the emergence of cold war politics. Nearly every science and mathematics teacher who is still in the workforce and almost all the curriculum materials now in use were strongly influenced by the enormous influx of federal funds for science and mathematics education that followed in the wake of the Soviet Union's successful launch of Sputnik in 1957. Cold war anxieties motivated the first wide-scale attempts by the federal government to influence what American schools taught and how they taught it, and groups such as the Biological Sciences Curriculum Study (BSCS), the Physical Sciences Study Committee (PSSC), and the School Mathematics Study Group came into existence. They generated a raft of instructional materials that continue to influence the science and mathematics curricula of America's schools to the present day.

One of the defining moments of this era took place at Woods Hole, Massachusetts, in September 1959, when thirty-five scientists, educators, and scholars met for a ten-day conference sponsored by the National Academy of Sciences. Jerome Bruner had been invited to help the conference define some guiding principles for curriculum development. What he wrote there was so influential that it is worth repeating. Bruner's argument helped to define one of the major strands of thought about the purposes of the academic curriculum, serving as an elegant restatement of the 1828 Yale Report on "faculty psychology."[6] Essentially, the idea behind faculty psychology is that the mind is like a muscle: it needs to be exercised, and to do this, challenging subjects like calculus or physics are best (in 1828, the same argument was used to sustain the then-dominant position of Latin, Greek, and the Classics).

Bruner's argument went something like this. The things we learn in school should take us somewhere in adult life: in particular, school learning should make us better at solving new problems and more efficient in our performance in life and at work. To this end, Bruner argued, the most powerful things we can learn in school are the big ideas or fundamental principles of a discipline, because if we understand these we can make intelligent inferences about a wide range of phenomena. Whereas training in specific skills only equips a person to carry out specific operations in situations that are similar to the one in which the training occurred, an education in the fundamental principles of a discipline leads to continuity of learning, because it allows the individual to transfer these principles to new situations. This type of transfer is dependent on mastery of the structure of a discipline. It follows from this that curricula must be designed in a way that is true to the underlying structure of its subject matter.[7]

The influence of this argument is evident, for example, in how college preparatory chemistry is currently taught. Rather than beginning with a study of natural and man-made materials and how they are used, or with the roles scientists can play in safeguarding our environment, in classic chemistry courses one begins by attempting to explain the chemical properties of the elements in terms of the atomic structures of those elements. A "good student" is one who can explain the regularities of the Periodic Table in terms of the way in which successive electron shells are filled as the atomic number increases. Abstract structural reasoning like this comes first, and "applications," if they are introduced at all, come at the end, after an understanding of the "fundamentals" has been established.

To produce courses that reflect the structure of the subject, Bruner argued, we must "enlist the aid of our most able scholars and scientists in designing curricula for our primary and secondary schools." It is no coincidence that the PSSC Physics project, the "new math" movement, and numerous other curriculum reforms of the 1960s and 1970s strongly reflected the theoretical orientations of the university-based subject-matter experts of that era. It is also no coincidence that courses like *Chemistry in the Community,* courses that begin with the applications and end with the theory, have had to work so hard to establish a legitimate place in the high school science curriculum.

At present, fewer than one in four high school students complete a full four-year science sequence. For both personal and economic reasons, this is an undesirable state of affairs. Science education can qualify individuals for good jobs in a wide range of occupations; it also helps prepare individuals to be informed and active participants in civic life. Higher-order skills such as thinking, problem solving, and reasoning that modern workplaces demand are an integral part of the development of scientific literacy. In the past, such skills were part of the elite curriculum, but in the future, they must be part of *everyone's* curriculum.

Science Education, Technology Education, and Sophisticated Uses of Simple Mathematics

Over the last two decades, there has been a steady but incremental shift in what our nation wants from its workforce. In earlier decades, the education system was called upon to develop a small but outstanding cadre of scientists and engineers. This elite occupied the highest positions in Taylor's hierarchical workforce. Those who labored at the lower levels of this hierarchy were not expected to be highly educated. Economists today paint a different picture, claiming that the nation's economic well-being now depends upon our ability to develop in all workers the skills that were once reserved for the elite.[8]

Largely spurred by this new economic context, many groups have put forward compelling arguments in favor of scientific literacy for all. The case is made, for example, by the National Center for Improving Science Education in *The High Stakes of High School Science,*[9] and by the American Association for the Advancement of Science in *Science for all Americans.*[10] Reports such as these show that while the policy of "science for all" has widespread support, there are many obstacles to overcome if we are to implement it on a substantial scale.

This chapter has already referred to some of these obstacles. Foremost among them is that the subject matter of science has been constructed in a way that attenuates or even nullifies the many connections that exist between science and technology. Yet, today's students live in a world designed by humans, a world in which the impact of technology cannot be ignored. We are surrounded by objects and systems that shape the way we interact with the world: from microwave ovens, calculators, computers, sports equipment, VCRs, and stereo sound equipment, to the more exotic technologies in the daily news such as genetic engineering, organ transplants, magnetic resonance imaging, rocket launches and space stations, and the internet. Technology is an important part of human culture and, as such it should be studied and experienced by all as part of general education.

In their recent book, *Technology Education in the Classroom: Understanding the Designed World,* Senta Raizen and her colleagues propose that technology education as a field of study should become a part of the K-12 curriculum.[11] As the book explains, most school subjects depend almost exclusively on cognitive skills. Technology education departs from this tradition. It goes beyond the academic orientation of the "pure sciences," which tend to ignore the man-made world in which students live. In technology education courses, students are typically involved in designing, building, and evaluating real artifacts; they are also encouraged to develop a critical awareness of the many effects technology has on everyday life.

In a typical technology education project, students are asked to think about an everyday problem from several perspectives, and to design and build an artifact that represents one possible solution to that problem. Another common technology education activity takes the form of product evaluations, such as the one described here:

> Go to a large hardware store and look for jar openers. Some are fixed to the wall, with rubber teeth to grip the lid. Some are small and portable. Some involve levers, to give a mechanical advantage in moving a stiff lid. Another jar opener is just a rubber ring, and there is even a small sheet of latex. The latex helps you grip the lid, but offers no mechanical advantage. The prices range from 50 cents (for a latex sheet) to $15 (for the one you fix to the wall). Which one is the best?

Even a deceptively simple problem like this one has many solutions, depending on who the jar opener is for, whether the cost matters, whether it needs to be portable, and so on. A typical feature of projects like these is that there is no single right answer, and because of this, technology education programs will always put the student in the driver's seat.

Over the past five years, most states have introduced new curriculum frameworks for science. Reflecting the growing interest in technology education, some states have created curriculum frameworks that align science standards with technology education standards: the New York science and technology framework provides a particularly well thought-out example of this approach. When science courses and technology education courses are aligned, both are enlivened, and students can develop a more coherent understanding of the complementary roles science and technology play in the designed world.

Unfortunately, however, many schools continue to teach science as abstract theory and add applications as an afterthought. Abstract principles may be important to the structure of the discipline, but methods of instruction that present these theories as entities in their own right without reference to the individual's lived experience are relatively ineffective. There is now a substantial body of cognitive research indicating that decontextualized learning does not last.

Contrary to what Bruner believed, when fundamental principles are learned in isolation, they are rarely invoked in real-life settings.[12] Rather than being transferred to new contexts, the ideas students learn in school are often forgotten, or simply remain inert. It is not altogether accurate to say that classroom learning is decontextualized. Rather, the classroom is a context that has its own characteristics; it is a context which does not resemble any of the situations students are likely to encounter in the world outside. In school, the principles and processes required to solve particular problems are usually evoked by seeing those problems in their customary pencil-and-paper formats. As a result, these skills remain attached to the school context, so that when a related problem is encountered in a real-world setting, the problem-solving processes that are required by the situation do not readily come to mind.[13]

One of the underlying assumptions of traditional science and mathematics education is that the curriculum should be structured around the general principles of the discipline. It is also assumed, however, that students will only master these principles through the practice of isolated sub-tasks. Students who are not immediately successful are often required to engage in repetitive practice until their teacher is satisfied that they are ready for the next step. Raizen argues that this practice has its origins in skills training, and that it entails, " . . . decomposing any competency to its smallest parts and teaching each part separately, on the assumption that, if each sub-skill has been learned, all the sub-skills can be put together and the competency will have been acquired." She further explains that:

> . . . it has been a standard practice in education and training programs to develop lists of needed skills or competencies. These are then related through some posited hierarchical structure which is decomposed into sub-skills to be taught one at a time until mastery is obtained, whereupon the next sub-skill in the hierarchy is taken up. The isolated sub-skills, often freed of any context, have become reified as individual "building blocks" of expertise to be used as the basis for instruction. . . . Yet, this

decomposition and decontextualized teaching of skill hierarchies is seldom effective either in educating for general purposes or in training for work.[14]

Scientific and mathematical literacy involves a great deal more than a knowledge of isolated facts or a facility with isolated skills. Both demand higher-order processes, such as carrying out a scientific investigation, using evidence to inform decision making, employing mathematical strategies to identify alternative solutions to problems, and carrying out tests or simulations to determine whether the proposed solutions work as they are supposed to. As the complexity of most people's jobs increases, we are reaching the point where skills like this are routinely required of clerks, finance assistants, and technicians. For example:

> A financial assistant in a major HMO has been asked to make projections about changes in payments that might be expected if one of the firm's corporate accounts was altered in a particular way. The company wants to increase co-payments and broaden the scope of coverage, all without changing premiums. The assistant calls up a standard spreadsheet template that covers all the HMO group policies, and locates cells where projection calculations are made. He will need to study these cells to be sure he understands how their formulas now work, then modify them to reflect the proposed changes, and finally run several test cases to be sure that his changes accomplish what he intended.[15]

This example was provided by mathematics educators Susan Forman and Lynn Steen, who have collected a great deal of information about the uses of mathematics in the modern workplace. In an article that contrasts school mathematics with mathematics at work, they come to the conclusion that high school mathematics courses generally focus on exposing students to increasingly sophisticated mathematics (culminating in calculus), whereas at work people are increasingly being called upon to make sophisticated use of relatively simple mathematics. As they see it:

> Mathematics in context is, typically, very concrete, but not necessarily very straightforward. Problems arising from real situations generally can be solved in a variety of ways, and do not necessarily have unique "correct" answers. . . . Mathematics at work typically involves real data with realistic measurements expressed in common units. The technical skills required to deal with these data are relatively elementary—measurement, arithmetic, geometry, formulas, simple trigonometry. The problem-solving strategies, however, often require a cognitive sophistication that few students acquire from current school mathematics: planning and executing a multi-step strategy; consideration of tolerances and variability; anticipation and estimation of relevant factors not immediately evident in the data; careful checking to assure accuracy.[16]

Can We Achieve Scientific Literacy for All Americans?

In order to achieve widespread mathematical and scientific literacy in this country, mathematics at school should resemble mathematics at work, and science at school should resemble science at work. We urgently need new courses that overcome the lack of connection between these two worlds. But this will require changing the place science and mathematics currently occupy in the structure of the comprehensive high school.

Approximately seventy-five years ago, in a context of rapidly increasing secondary school enrollments, and the extension of mass education from elementary school to high school, educators had to decide what kind of curriculum would serve everyone. The decision they made was to introduce a diversified program of studies adapted to the supposed 'needs' of different students. This decision led to the now-familiar tracking system; it also meant that the high schools had to decide how to allocate students to these tracks.

Ever since then, high school science and mathematics have been "exclusive" rather than "inclusive" subjects. In most high schools, only a minority of students are expected to master these subjects at an advanced level. In addition, they have tended to play a "gatekeeper" role, in the sense that level of performance in these subjects is used to determine who will be in which track. A student's performance in algebra at the middle school level, for example, often determines what track he or she will follow later on. Teachers of science and mathematics pride themselves on their rigorous approach to their disciplines, and many are accustomed to assuming that only a self-selected minority will ever enroll in calculus and physics, the capstone subjects of the four-year sequence.

In most comprehensive high schools, there are well-established practices that exclude all but a small minority of students from these senior-level courses. Course sequences, for example, operate as a series of successively higher hurdles which students must vault over to complete the race to college. In science, students proceed from the lower hurdles put in their path by earth and life science courses to the higher ones of college-prep chemistry and physics. In mathematics, it has been customary to sort students during the middle school years into two tracks: a short "terminal" track is offered to those deemed unlikely to go to college while the full four-year math curriculum is reserved for the "college-bound." Because college requirements dominate, calculus has become a rite of passage for those aspiring to professional qualifications. The hurdle race is one that relatively few students actually complete, and even among those who do, only a relatively small percentage are well prepared and eager to major in science and mathematics at the college level.

In an attempt to lower the hurdles, most schools organize science and mathematics programs around some form of ability grouping. In her 1994 *Profile* of the science and mathematics education community, Iris Weiss found that while 75 percent of teachers believe that "virtually all students can be taught to think scientifically or mathematically," most high school teachers think it is preferable to sort students by ability level. Seven out of ten high school science and mathematics teachers surveyed said that students learn science and math best when grouped with students of similar abilities.

The effect of this ability grouping, however, has not been to encourage more students to stay in the race. Weiss also found that teachers of so-called "low-ability classes" are more likely than those teaching "high-ability classes" to rely on textbooks and assign worksheet problems and are *less* likely to engage students in hands-on science activities or reasoning about mathematical problem solving. In low-ability classes, the emphasis is on preparing students to take multiple choice tests, and little time is spent on developing deeper understandings. Because these students are considered to be slow at science, the material they are given is often broken down into tiny steps, so they rarely sense the thrill of grasping the big picture. It is not surprising that many students respond to the low expectations of the traditional regimen by rejecting future studies in mathematical, scientific, and technical disciplines.

If science education is to make the contribution it ought to make to developing higher-order thinking skills in *all* students, then we will need new courses, new approaches to teaching and learning, new methods of assessment, and new forms of high school organization. This is, in effect, systemic reform: it demands coordinated and more-or-less simultaneous change in several aspects of a high school's educational program at once. We need new courses that begin with concrete experience and introduce problems that are more like those individuals will face in their everyday lives: problems that demand a sustained effort of understanding, with answers that are not guaranteed or known in advance.

We need new approaches to teaching and learning, because as Iris Weiss found, the practice of having students fill their class time by doing worksheets is still widespread, especially in relation to students who are not considered to be college-bound. This book suggests many strategies for engaging students in extended projects, in work that gives them the experience of being productive, that encourages them to generate ideas and products that can change their world. Extended science projects of this kind involve "doing" science, not just knowing it. In many respects, this is a radical position, since it implies that the process of scientific thinking is more important than simply knowing scientific facts and concepts.[17] It also implies a need for new methods of assessment to ensure that students who carry out extended project work have their achievements recognized and rewarded in appropriate ways. Finally, we need to "undo" tracking, finding other, more effective and equitable ways to meet students' needs and support their continued learning.

Many of the arguments put forward here were first advocated by John Dewey many years ago. Writing about the science teacher, he wrote, "His problem is that of inducing a vital and personal experiencing . . . what concerns him, as a teacher, is the ways in which that subject may become a part of experience."[18] Writing about science as a subject, he argued that "the logically formulated material of a science or branch of learning . . . is no substitute for the having of individual experiences."[19]

Although Dewey is often remembered as championing a form of education that builds on individual experience, a closer reading of his work shows that his real goal was more complex. In describing Dewey's work, Willis suggested that his aim was to bring "subject matter, individual and society into a new, flexible and dynamic relationship in terms of how each contributes to the development of experience."[20] One of Dewey's disappointments was that progressive educators tended to neglect the contributions that the disciplines can make to enriching and structuring individual experience. In *Experience and Education,* he noted that "the weakest point in progressive schools is the matter of selection and organization of intellectual subject matter. . . ." Later in the same book he reiterated this point by asserting that while "the organized subject-matter of the adult and the specialist cannot provide the starting point, it represents the goal toward which education should continually move."[21]

This chapter has argued that we need to go beyond the legacy of the past, and that we should provide a challenging program of science and technology education for all high school students. It has described several courses and programs that suggest how this might be done, and has provided a brief overview of recent cognitive research which supports the view that students are likely to learn better if they are actively engaged in *doing* science in real-world contexts. Ideally, learning should begin with experiences in the workplace or in the community, but the quality of the experiences students receive should not be compromised. While students need direct connections with practitioners whose work provides motivation, meaning, and context for project activities, they also need the support of their classroom teachers as they systematize their thinking and learn to use the intellectual tools of science, mathematics, and technology to make sense of their experience.

In today's workforce, decision making and quality control are becoming part of job expectations at all levels, from the production floor to the executive suite. Frontline workers are expected to read graphs, interpret data, troubleshoot problems and suggest solutions. Unskilled blue collar workers, who until the 1970s comprised over half the workforce, are now a declining minority. The real growth in employment opportunities (even for those without baccalaureate degrees) are in fields where some form of mathematical or technical competency is needed.

Thus, the pressures for a more even distribution of scientific and mathematical knowledge are both societal and personal. The societal argument links national economic growth with a broader educational base, and the personal argument links promising careers with better qualifications. As Lynn Steen and Susan Forman argue, the desire for high-quality jobs will require increasing levels of mathematical literacy, primarily because of the widespread impact of computers. The same motivation holds true for science literacy. Good jobs increasingly depend on the kind of thinking, problem-solving, and reasoning skills developed by a study of sciences, and, in addition, domain-specific scientific knowledge is important in many workplaces.

Lauren Resnick wrote, "Although it is not new to include thinking, problem solving and reasoning in *someone's* school curriculum, it is new to include it in *everyone's* curriculum. . . . It is a new challenge to develop educational programs that assume that all individuals, not just an elite, can become competent thinkers."[22] Reformed high school science programs that are inclusive, integrated, and project-based are essential if we hope to achieve this goal.

NOTES

1. John Brown, Allan Collins, and Paul Duguid, "Situated Cognition and the Culture of Learning," *Educational Researcher*, 18:1 (1989), 32–42. Lauren Resnick, "Learning In School and Out," *Educational Researcher*, 16:9 (1987), 13–20.

2. Paul Black and Marvin Atkin (Eds), *Changing the Subject: Innovations in Science, Mathematics and Technology Education*. New York: Routledge/OECD, 1996.

3. Evans Clinchy, "Higher Education: The Albatross Around the Neck of Our Public Schools." *Phi Delta Kappan* 75 (1994): 745–51.

4. Evans Clinchy, "Higher Education," 746.

5. David Layton. "Science Education and Praxis: The Relation of School Science to Practical Action," *Studies in Science Education* 19 (1991), 48.

6. Bernard Doray, *From Taylorism to Fordism: A Rational Madness* (London: Free Association Books, 1988).

7. George Willis, et al. *The American Curriculum: A Documentary History*. (Connecticut: Praeger, 1994).

8. Willis (op cit.). Chap. 31 reproduces excerpts from Bruner's report to the Woods Hole conference.

9. Robert Reich, *The Work of Nations: Preparing Ourselves for 21st Century Capitalism*. (New York: Vintage Press, 1992) Richard Murnane and Frank Levy. *Teaching the New Basic Skills: Principles for Educating Children to Thrive in a Changing Economy*. (New York: The Free Press, 1996.)

10. National Center for Improving Science Education, *The High Stakes of High School Science*. (Washington, DC: NCISE, 1991.)

11. American Association for the Advancement of Science, *Science for all Americans*. (Washington, DC: AAAS, 1993.)

12. Senta Raizen, Peter Sellwood, Ron Todd and Margaret Vickers, *Technology Education in the Classroom: Understanding the Design World*. (San Francisco: Jossey Bass, 1995.)

13. Lauren Resnick, "Learning In School and Out." *Educational Researcher,* 16:9, 1987, 13–20. Senta Raizen. "Learning and work: The research base. In L. McFarland & M. Vickers, *Vocational Education and Training for Youth: Toward Coherent Policy and Practice*. (Paris: Organization for Economic Cooperation and Development, 1994.)

14. Senta Raizen, "Learning and work." John Brown, Allan Collins, and Paul Duguid, (1989) "Situated Cognition and the Culture of Learning," 32–42.

15. Senta Raizen, "Learning and work," 82.

16. Susan Forman and Lynn Steen, "Mathematics for Life and Work." In I. Carl (Ed), *Prospects for School Mathematics: Seventy-Five Years of Progress*. (Reston, VA: National Council of Teachers of Mathematics, 1995), 219–241.

17. Susan Forman and Lynn Steen (1994). "Mathematics for Life and Work," 221.

18. Forman and Steen (op cit.) make the same argument for mathematics education.

19. Dewey, cited in Willis, et al., *The American Curriculum: A Documentary History,* 127.

20. Dewey, cited in Willis, et al., 126.

21. Willis, et al., *The American Curriculum: A Documentary History,* 124.

22. John Dewey. *Experience and Education.* (New York: McMillan, 1938) 95 and 103.

23. Lauren Resnick. *Education and Learning to Think.* (Washington, D.C., National Academy Press, 1987) 7.

5

Hands On, Heads Up

Uncovering the Humanities in Work-Based Learning Programs[1]

Robert C. Riordan

In a large urban medical center a group of educators and business leaders are getting a first-hand look at a high school health careers program. Students in this program rotate through several stations, including medical records, the lab, admissions, food services, and nursing. Their aspirations range from entry-level jobs to medical school and beyond. Back at school they take anatomy and physiology and other career-related courses.

In the lab the visitors meet Hector, a student intern assigned to assist in a variety of tasks, from reading blood tests to writing up results to monitoring the inventory. The visitors ask Hector what he's learning about blood chemistry and lab procedures, what his career plans are, and how he compares his experience in this program to that of regular school. They want to know what he is learning from his program mentor and his supervisor. They nod as he describes his surprise and delight at the way adults in the workplace value his work. They smile as he discusses his new sense of purpose and his new appreciation of the relevance of schoolwork.

The questions about academics relate mainly to math, science, and business. Hector answers them thoughtfully. However, there is a whole area that remains untouched by the visitors' questions, simply because it does not occur to them to ask. What Hector is really thinking about much of the time is how it feels to work in a place where people are dying. How do individuals face death? How do families, hospital personnel, and the institution deal with the impending loss of loved ones, patients, clients?

These are issues for the humanities, in a worksite unexpectedly as rich in humanities content as in "technical" content. Hector's reflections about dying could lead to a range of authors and texts from Tolstoy to Willa Cather, Jonathan Edwards to Jack Kevorkian, or Jessica Mitford to the *Tibetan Book of the Dead*. Such thoughts could also be the starting point for explorations of bioethics, the social organization of the hospital, medical technology, and the quality of life. Moreover, worksites like Hector's are equally rich in opportunities for students to practice the skills involved in observation, description, inquiry, reflection, speculation, and presentation. Knowing how to engage in such processes, students are ready for lifelong explorations of such issues.

This chapter considers the potential of internships like Hector's as a context for exploring the humanities. The first section describes two internship programs which incorporate seminars built around humanities themes. These accounts are followed by a discussion of six principles for "hands-on humanities." A third section focuses on the role of writing and reflection in school-to-work programs. The fourth and final section considers hands-on humanities in the light of new curriculum standards, ending with a discussion of the role the humanities can play in broadening and deepening school-to-work reforms.

I. HANDS ON HUMANITIES AT THE
CAMBRIDGE RINDGE AND LATIN SCHOOL

I have been involved in school-to-work activities in Cambridge, Massachusetts as a high school English teacher, a program designer and internship seminar leader, and most recently as the K-12 English language arts coordinator for the system. In these successive roles I have crossed back and forth between the vocational and academic wings of the school, working with a wide variety of mainstream, bilingual and special needs students. In the end I have discovered that it is as important to bring hands-on pedagogy to the humanities as it is to strengthen humanities content in the vocational area. Even this misstates the issue, however: it's not about importing content or pedagogy from one area to another, but rather about merging these areas and conceiving of work with adolescents in newly integrated ways, beyond disciplinary divisions.

The Cambridge-Polaroid Technical Internship Program

My interest in the notion of hands-on humanities began several years ago, when I was director of the school-wide writing center at the Cambridge

Rindge and Latin School (CRLS). I noticed that while some of the vocational students might have trouble completing English assignments, they would write more fluently when asked to describe how to put together a circuit board. This wasn't really a surprise, since I had long been aware that it's easier for any of us to write about things we know. I also knew that these students needed more practice than they were getting—lots more—if they were to grow as writers and thinkers.

At about this time Larry Rosenstock, who was leading occupational education in Cambridge in new directions, asked me to help design a program for students who would be working in the building and maintenance division at the Polaroid Corporation. At the time, Polaroid maintained thirteen buildings in Cambridge, as well as plants in nearby Waltham and Needham. For Jim Hawkins, the Director of Technical Services, this was a workforce development and diversification effort; he wanted to encourage young men and women of color to enter the trades. For us, it was a chance to integrate academic and vocational education. Students would come from the mainstream of CRLS as well as from the Rindge School of Technical Arts. The challenge we set ourselves was to develop an academically respectable technical internship program, with a strong humanities component. The first task was to develop a daily seminar for the students on site at Polaroid, for English and social studies credit, where the experience of the workplace would become the text of the course, and students would explore that text through writing, projects, and conversations with Polaroid employees.

In the Cambridge-Polaroid Technical Internship Program, students kept journals, interviewed peers and supervisors, published a newsletter with photos, text, and graphics, constructed portfolios of their work, and developed projects for an exhibition at the end of the year. My Polaroid counterpart, the supervisor of the carpentry shop, arranged for Polaroid personnel to visit the seminar twice a week to talk about their work and their lives. The supervisor of the heating, ventilation and air conditioning shop (HVAC) informed the students that he would no longer be able to use fluorocarbons next year. He was back in school, learning the properties of the new refrigerant. The fire safety chief told how his shipboard fire fighting experience in the navy had qualified him for his present job, even though he had no idea as a young sailor that he would ever work in fire safety. Hedrick Smith, author of *The New Russians* (and subsequently, *Rethinking America*), came to interview the students about the program; knowing that Polaroid was starting a factory in Russia, the students ended up interviewing him about the lives of Russian teenagers. Jim Hawkins arranged for the students to present their work at his weekly staff meetings.

Early on it became clear that we were tapping a rich array of humanities issues as well as specific site issues. Students' early reflections about the workplace focused on the reception they were getting from adults, the process of learning the formal and informal rules of the organization, and the problems they were encountering as young newcomers: Can I do this work? Will the adults here like me? Will I get a fair shake? Must I leave my friends in school behind? The journal entry below addresses some of these issues and, most notably, indicates an already blossoming developing relationship with a mentor:

> On my first day to work, I walked to Marie Brown's office in the Control Center. I was introduced to Christine Cedrone (Administrative Secretary), Deborah Scott (Senior Clerk), and Maria de Chaves (Administrative Specialist).
>
> I worked with Marie, my supervisor, for the first day. We went through the Control Center Technical Internship Program book. We did this after she and I worked out a first draft budget of my income and my debts. After we did that I know about how much money I would have for me to spend. First we figured out about how much a week I made after taxes were taken out. Second, we figured out my monthly pay. Then, the four months were totaled up to give me an approximate figure.
>
> As the day went on, Marie and I talked about her only daughter that she is very proud of. Marie adopted Gina when Gina was one week old. Later, Marie was interrupted by a phone call from Gina. "Speak of the devil."
>
> We talked about a lot of things including writing down questions and making lists of what I need to spend my money on.
>
> The first day was scary and overwhelming because I had never worked in Polaroid. I didn't know what to expect and there was a lot of information I needed to learn.
> —*Cambridge-Polaroid Technical Internship Program Newsletter,* April 1991

By the end, students were addressing more complex versions of these issues: What is quality work? What am I learning? What is the connection between this work and my life? What is real? Where am I going?

What Work Means to Each of Us

Work to me is breaking a sweat when doing a job. A way of life. A need in society. Without work there will be no money, and I see it like this: money talks.

—Lorraine Acuna

I believe that work is a way to survive in this world, because you need a roof to sleep under, you need food, clothes, and everything nowadays costs something. Just surviving takes a lot of work.

—Javier Montero

To me work is a way of expressing yourself because everyone does things differently so it gives you a chance to do things your own way, in some cases.

—Calvin Dunne

Work to me is a way to make a living and support a family. Work is something you do every day that you will benefit from and also someone else benefits from your work. To me work should be something you love to do. Sometimes if your job is something you love to do it becomes more than a job, it becomes a way of life.

—Joe Amaral

I see work as a means of independence. When you work you earn money. With every passing day you mature and adjust into the real world. To some it starts off slow and some very rapidly. Work makes you discover who you are.

—Ken Cruz

—*Cambridge-Polaroid Technical Internship Program Newsletter,* May 1992

Eventually, journals, projects, and conversations with co-workers were also the source of numerous topics touching on broad societal themes and issues from the environmental responsibility of a manufacturing company to gender roles and racism in the workplace, and from the technological revolution to the generation gap. Throughout, the goal was to use students' work experience as a basis for developing an integrated approach to the humanities in a technical setting.

From the beginning, we aspired to provide much more than job training. Our partners at Polaroid agreed with this approach. Together, we assumed that all of the students should become lifelong learners, with the skills to thrive in any post-secondary environment, including college. As we progressed, we were confident that the seminar and the work experience could serve as the prototype for structured, supported school-to-work internships, rich in humanities themes and processes.

The Cambridge-Lesley Careers in Education Program

The following September we started a second internship program: the Cambridge-Lesley Careers in Education Program, designed to encourage high school students, particularly students of color and students from low-income families, to pursue careers in education. Cambridge-Lesley students spend two full mornings per week working as teacher aides in elementary school classrooms, grades K-3. The other three mornings they attend a seminar at Lesley College, co-taught by a Lesley professor and a Cambridge teacher. Here they share observations from their site logs, hear presentations from their cooperating teachers and other education professionals, develop classroom projects, construct portfolios, and prepare public exhibitions of their work.

As in the Cambridge-Polaroid program, the basic "text" of these seminars is the field experience. Here, too, students gain access to this text by talking and writing about it in a multitude of forms, for a variety of purposes and audiences. They keep worksite logs, reading logs, and personal journals. They write lists, flow charts, chronologies, narratives, fantasies, interviews, dialogues, instructions, letters, and reports. They write to record observations of worksites, to reflect on significant learning experiences, to think through problems, to articulate learning and project goals, and to share experiences with other participants.

Consistent with the precepts of good writing instruction, every piece of writing has a use—or multiple uses. The accumulated shorter writings constitute a resource bank for larger products: a report, a presentation script, a newsletter, an autobiography, a resume. The writing advances the overall purpose of the seminar, which is to provide a context for students to reflect on their work and their lives. In the end, the work and the reflection come together in a public exhibition of students' work. For final projects, students have designed curriculum units on topics ranging from the neighborhood to blueberry muffins, researched issues such as the inclusion of special needs students and the meaning of friendship among young children, produced plays with their students about racism and other hot topics, and developed original games for reinforcing basic skills.

In the Cambridge-Lesley seminar, the first issues to emerge in students' site logs had to do with entry and classroom management. Do I belong here? Will the children—and the teacher—accept me? How can I get Johnnie to join the circle? These questions broadened and deepened over time to encompass issues of identity, stereotyping, and change. Can I be a teacher and still be me? Do children come to school already determined by their home environments? Can they change? Can we help them change? Should we try? Our hope was that in their work with children, students could broaden their sense of possibility both for the children and for themselves, moving from superficial interpretations of children's behavior to deeper understandings of human development.

In the second year of this program, as the theme of identity emerged, I noticed that some of the students were labeling the children in the classrooms where they worked. At the same time we were reading sections of *The Autobiography of Malcolm X*. We saw Malcolm fashioning his life, changing, owning the change, moving beyond labels—particularly the racist label and the carpenter's future his eighth-grade teacher prescribed for him. Although students understood the pernicious effect of labeling in Malcolm's life, several of them continued to talk about the children in their own classrooms as the "troublemaker," or "bad kid." In an effort to look at this, we did an exercise on stereotyping, where students wore labels without knowing what their own labels communicated to others (e.g., "You think I'm stupid"). In the ensuing discussion, Juanita talked about a class at the high school, where she would arrive first and go stand by the window and look out. When her friends came in they would all join her, and then when it was time to start the class, the teacher would say, "Juanita, sit down."

"So what did you do?" I asked.

Juanita replied, "I sucked my teeth and sat down."

"Juanita," I said, "Don't you see that you're in a cycle here? She singles you out as a troublemaker, and when she does, you suck your teeth, and when you suck your teeth she thinks you've got an attitude."

"Yeah, but she shouldn't be picking on me like that."

That led us into a discussion of how it is the teacher's responsibility to break that kind of cycle. In Juanita's case, in her elementary classroom, that meant finding a way to go beyond seeing Jose as only a "troublemaker." Several days later, she reported that she had observed Jose being "good," putting his arm around a classmate who was crying—and had pointed that out to him.

Somewhere in this ongoing discussion, at my wife's suggestion, I brought in Edgar Lee Masters' poem, "Aner Clute," about the effect of labeling and stereotyping. Several lines in particular caught the attention of my students. Masters' narrator, a townswoman-turned-prostitue, poses the question: "Suppose a boy steals an apple/ From the grocery store/ And they all begin to call him a thief." Several lines later, she concludes: "It's the way the people regard the theft of the apple/ That makes the boy what he is."

The poem became something of a touchstone in the months that followed. Someone, often Juanita, would say, "Yeah, just like that poem we read." And later, in her semester self-evaluation, she testified to the possibility of change: "This past summer and this year I have grown up a lot. I know that I can be who I want to be, and that I do not have to be what others label me as. I'm not going to give up, and I know you won't give up on me."

Jocelyn's Project: The Possibility of Change

Change became a major theme for all of us at Cambridge-Lesley that year—identity, stereotyping, and change. But the sense of the possibility of change didn't come so much from books. Interestingly, there was often a striking disjunction between what the students saw in the books and poems they were reading and what they said about the "real world" of their classrooms. They could say how Malcolm X changed, for example, and how he owned the change himself. They had absorbed the academic content, so to speak. But asked if the children they were working with could change, they would say, "No. They come to school the way they are, and they're not gonna change. There's nothing the school can do about it." One student, Jocelyn, took it further: "I'm not gonna change, either. If you don't like my attitude, that's your problem."

But Jocelyn had already encountered a problem in her classroom that needed changing. The teacher's aide, whom Jocelyn had known since she herself was a kindergartner in that room, turned over the attendance to her one day, saying, "They have funny names, and I can't really tell them apart." This, in reference to the African-American children in the room. Jocelyn was stunned. She wrote up the incident in her log and brought it to the seminar. We discussed options. My Lesley College colleague asked Jocelyn whether she felt angry? "No," said Jocelyn, "just sad." "What makes you sad?" "I'm just sad that Mrs. Y hasn't kept up with the times."

In the end, Jocelyn took this issue on as a project—not directly, but more broadly, by focusing on the possibility of change in her kindergartners. She herself had long been a marginal student—bright, but lacking academic confidence and not interested in school. Now, in her work with children, Jocelyn began to reconsider her earlier declaration about change. She and her cooperating kindergarten teacher (who had been Jocelyn's kindergarten teacher) identified four children who were not being read to at home. For her major project, Jocelyn decided to read to these children one-on-one and observe and record their behavior. She chose the books in consultation with her cooperating teacher, the Lesley professor, and the Lesley College librarian. Each time she read to the children, she recorded her observations in her site log. Finally, she prepared an exhibition and presented her project to an audience of teachers, parents, administrators, peers, and others.

Jocelyn called her project, "Ma, Look! I Can Read!" In her final presentation, she began by holding up an old book called *Ten Little Niggers*. "I couldn't read this to the children, " she said. "You'll see why." She read a portion of the text, explaining, "This is how black children were portrayed in children's books back in the 1960s and before." Then she displayed one of the books she had selected to read with the children: *Mufaro's Beautiful Daughter*, an African tale.[2] "I love this book!" she exclaimed. "It's beautiful! . . . The women in it are pretty. . . . The children can see themselves and familiar things in it. . . . I just love this book!"

Jocelyn proceeded to read her observations about her sessions with the children, as recorded in her site log. One child was fidgety and distracted when they sat next to each other on the stairway, but was very attentive when sitting on Jocelyn's lap. Another child brightened up at the section about Haitians in *Everybody Cooks Rice*. A third child made a connection when Jocelyn read to her in Spanish.

Journal Excerpts: "Ma, Look! I Can Read!"

March 16, Latoya: I read *Corn Rows*. She told me that she loves corn rows and braids. With Latoya, I found that she was not holding much interest when she was sitting on the stairs, but when she sat on my lap, she started paying attention.

March 25, Tisha: I read *Everybody Cooks Rice*. She loved it and related to it because a part of the book talks about Haitians, and how they eat rice. She went on and told me about what her family eats. The project has brought us closer together, and now she always wants to be around me.

April 19, Janitza: I read *Que Bibo?* She read along with me in Spanish, and we had fun, and she liked the fact that I read to her in her native language, Spanish.

Summing up at the end, Jocelyn said, "I've found that reading is a fundamental part of learning. To take one child's experience, for example, before I started reading to her, she was not very nice to me or to a lot of the children. But now after the reading, she hugs me, wants to be around me, and is a lot nicer to the other children. Now, I know I cannot take full credit for this change, but I hope that I have played a role in it."

In the question period that followed, a first grade teacher in the audience offered a spontaneous, real-world assessment from an expert in the field: "Thank you for telling us right at the beginning how much the books meant to you, and why. Apart from all the things you noted in your observations about how much kids get from being read to in such a meaningful and close way, you're modeling, you're showing them your feelings about the books, and your doing this . . . gives them a world, and it's a beautiful act of teaching that you've just described."

Inspired by her kindergartners, Jocelyn also wrote and illustrated a book for them, called *Tomorrow*. In it, she writes from the perspective of a child whose parents are divorced. Daddy has promised to take her on a Sunday outing, but he calls to say he won't be coming. The child is disappointed and sad, but then Mommy offers to take her on an outing, where she can pick out what she wants to buy. The story ends as it began, the child exclaiming, "Tomorrow is going to be a special day!"

In Jocelyn's description of the changes she observed in the children, the subtext is about her own change, from a disaffected, alienated student to a young woman with a mission. She went from wondering about her kids and saying *she* wouldn't change (even knowing that Malcolm changed), to seeing kids change and changing herself, in ways that we could see. In the process, she performed deep, hands-on humanities work, creating a caring environment in a place where the classroom aide had trouble telling the children apart. Jocelyn could have been in someone's high school classroom ignoring *Silas Marner,* but instead she made a connection with kids and with children's literature, developed an aesthetic response, and wrote herself and her kids a children's story which not so coincidentally addressed an issue in her real life. This is not to say that no one should read *Silas Marner,* but rather that the internship experience provided Jocelyn with a better context than the classroom for entering the humanities conversation as a fully engaged participant.

In the intersection between hands-on work and personal narrative qua children's story, Jocelyn's work touches much broader themes. Valerie Smith writes:

> The slave narratives and the protagonist-narrators of certain twentieth-century novels by Afro-American writers affirm and legitimize their psychological autonomy by telling the stories of their own lives. . . . The paradox [is] that by fictionalizing one's life, one bestows a quality of authenticity on it. . . . The processes of plot construction, characterization,

and designation of beginnings and endings—in short the processes of authorship—provide the narrators with a measure of authority unknown to them in either real or fictional life.[3]

In other words, in telling our stories, we invent ourselves—selves that are at once real and ideal, mediated by the audience and by the context of our lives. This means that even more important than the texts that teachers select are the texts that students create. In high school classrooms—and in school-to-work programs, whether in education, health careers, or the building trades—it is *processes of authorship,* more than acts of consumption, that constitute the vital substance of the humanities curriculum.

This approach to the humanities, with students entering the conversation as authors, embodies John Dewey's maxim that understanding derives from activity. Here, the curriculum flows from the project, instead of the other way around, and so the curriculum is fluid rather than fixed, and the teacher is deeply involved in its construction. In the Cambridge-Lesley program that year this process of construction began with high school students reflecting on real work in the world—writing site descriptions and autobiographical fragments, exploring violence and racism in the community and the media, and later examining children's toys and the text on cereal boxes. The themes grew out of student journals and conversations about issues at their work sites and in their lives. The selection of specific texts came out of conversations, not only with the students, but also with my Lesley College co-teacher, our various guests in the Cambridge-Lesley seminar, my colleagues in a seminar at Harvard, the cooperating elementary teachers, my wife, and my friends and colleagues at CRLS. I was deeply immersed in a planning backwards process about an essential question of change which applied to me as a teacher, too. Could my students change? Could I reinvent myself as a teacher? As my students were engaged in inquiry and projects, so was I.

II. RETHINKING CURRICULUM AND PEDAGOGY: DESIGN PRINCIPLES

Jocelyn's work attests to the feasibility and the power of linking humanities and work in a hands-on approach. She was dealing directly with deep humanities issues in her field placement: issues of child-rearing, gender, the uses of technology, the role of the media in shaping contemporary values, racism, and, most important, the possibility of change. Within her project, her choice of books is marked by a profound understanding of what is important in multicultural education. In an article on cultural equity, Henry Louis Gates, Jr. discusses three rationales for multicultural education: representation, relevance, and aesthetics. According to Gates, the first two are weak rationales; it is the third—the aesthetic rationale—which really counts.[4] Jocelyn recognized this distinction instinctively and concretely in her project presentation when she held up the beautifully illustrated African tale and exclaimed, "I just love this book!" Her level of discourse may be different from Gates', but the understanding is deeply rooted in her workplace experience. The elementary classroom and the seminar together gave Jocelyn a context for working on change and developing a deep understanding of essential questions in the humanities.

Six Principles for Hands-On Humanities

1. Situate students in the world beyond school.
2. Treat students' experience as a primary text.
3. Create contexts for shared reflection.
4. Practice academic and workplace skills in an adult milieu.
5. Help students encounter the world through publication, presentation, and exhibition.
6. Think of the teacher as inquirer and clinician.

The work of Jocelyn and other students suggests several design principles for a more hands-on approach to the humanities. These principles call into question current classroom practices and point toward new ways of thinking about the humanities in schools.

1. *Situate students in the world beyond school.* Speaking at the Harvard Graduate School of Education to a group of student teachers, Jocelyn said, "I used to have a lot of trouble getting up to go to school. Lots of times I just didn't make it. But now I've got something to go to, because when I go in my classroom I've got all these kids coming up and giving me hugs." Reason enough, not only to go to school, but to tackle real intellectual problems. And it was through her involvement with children in the present that she became invested in her future, and the pedagogy became a pedagogy of hope.

A corollary of this principle is that student projects should make a contribution to the workplace or community. Respect in the workplace is accorded to craft and contribution. Perhaps many students do not feel respected at school (see the discussion in chapter 3) because their schoolwork doesn't seem worthy of respect: not for those who do it, not for those who assign it. By helping students develop work worth doing, teachers themselves gain no small measure of self-respect.

2. *Treat students' experience as a primary text.* In work-based learning, the experience in the workplace is a "text" to be read and understood like any other text. This "reading" is the key connecting activity between school, the workplace, and students' lives. As students share their accounts and interpretations in the seminar, they encounter other accounts and perspectives. This collection of shared experiential texts leads to other texts in, about, and beyond the workplace. Ultimately students come to realize that events in the workplace, and human events anywhere, are to be interpreted for their action implications. As they design projects, they begin to do more than "read" their experience: they shape it. This is why autobiographical writing is so important: it describes and contextualizes the shaping.

Although students are constructing identities as they plan and execute projects, they are not always aware that this is so. Autobiographical writing sharpens that awareness. Not that students must write a new autobiography every year, but it is crucial that they engage in structured reflection on the meaning of their lives and work in the world. This is fundamental humanities work, based on one of the oldest precepts in the humanities: Socrates' "the unexamined life is not worth living."

Cambridge-Lesley Careers in Education Program
Autobiographical Fragment: Identity Moments

In the seminar we have talked a lot about who we are, from the "three things" we brought in to some of our achievements and to the labels and roles we have assumed in school. We have also taken a look at other characters or persons: Aner Clute in *Spoon River Anthology,* Malcolm X in his junior high school classroom, in Roxbury, in Harlem, in prison, and on the national and world scene.

For the next fifteen minutes or so, write about an event or situation in your life which has had an important influence on your sense of who you are. Here are some choices:

CHOOSE ONE!

1. A time when you stood up for something you believed in
2. A time when your view of the world—or yourself—changed
3. A time when you felt really free
4. A time when you broke the rules
5. A time you felt proud to be who you are
6. (Make up your own!)

> Write as quickly and freely as you can, in whatever form you wish. Don't worry about grammar or spelling for now: keep the pen moving forward. Include as much detail as you can: remember where this event or situation occurred, who was there, what people said and did, what you said and did, how you felt at the time, and how you feel now, remembering this event or situation.
>
> These writings will be typed up and shared with the class, with your permission. They will be useful for your autobiographical paper, due later this term.
>
> —*Adapted from Herrmann and Tabor, "Experiments & Experiences in Writing," unpublished curriculum manuscript.*

There is a further connection here. When we invite our students to write autobiography—or, more broadly, personal narrative—we are inviting them to join with us in exploring and defining, not only their lives, but also the literary landscape in which they live. As they make writer's choices, ask questions, and express their emerging values for an audience of peers, they touch the great and fundamental themes that are embedded in the texts we bring into the classroom. In this way, personal narrative always faces outward to the world of real persons and enduring human issues.

Looking outward evokes biography as well as autobiography. In particular, student interviews with worksite personnel give them a look at possible lives, afford practice in interview skills, and allow discussions of historiography.

3. *Create contexts for shared reflection.* Schools need to establish contexts where, through writing and shared reflection, students can discover the meaning of their work. Some schools, such as Central Park East Secondary School in New York, create this context by means of journals and student portfolios, mediated through teacher-advisors and advisory groups. In the Cambridge-Lesley program, this reflective context takes the form of a seminar at Lesley College, meeting for two hours, three mornings a week. The seminar provides what Paulo Freire refers to as a "theoretical context" for students, accompanying the more "concrete" context of their fieldwork.[5] As such, the seminar pushes the work of action and reflection: act in the concrete setting, reflect and plan in the theoretical setting. The overall aim is that the learner, whether teacher or student, should come to understand that his or her thoughts and words actually matter; they can move audiences and transform the world.

There is another reason for the seminar: it provides a place where school and worksite personnel can share the responsibility for teaching and learning. A school-to-work program, properly speaking, breaks the mold. It is a social action project, calling for schools to be like high performance workplaces and workplaces to be twenty-first-century learning environments. Such a project in itself is a matter for reflection by all participants, who invariably find that they need to reinvent themselves in new roles.

Hands-on Humanities:
Integrative Processes for Active Learning

- Observation and Reflection
- Journals/Learning Logs
- Conversation
- Inquiry
- Projects
- Portfolio
- Presentation/Publication/Exhibition

---

4. *Practice academic and workplace skills in an adult milieu.* Beyond academic and vocational curriculum and students, there is a further integration in work-based learning: that of adolescents into the adult world. The current practice in schools is to segregate adolescents by age-cohort, with adults serving an inevitable and often unwanted custodial function. Work-based learning puts adults and adolescents side by side, working together, applying academic and workplace skills on the job. In the process, students hone their skills and develop relationships. They also get a first-hand look at possible lives, as witness the interview below, written by a student for the Cambridge-Polaroid Technical Internship Program Newsletter (April 1991).

Joe Davis
by Fritz Rodene

Joe Davis is fifty-seven years old and a great guy. He is currently the supervisor of the electrical shop at Polaroid. He really cares about us students being here and getting this experience.

He'd probably do anything to get us on the right path. I remember that when I met him the first things he told me were "In order to succeed you have to care," "Prepare yourself with an education," and "You have to decide right from wrong."

One year after high school Joe joined the Navy. Right after boot camp Joe took his GCT test to help him decide which career to go in. After taking the test he chose to go into the electrical field.

While in the Navy Joe visited over twenty different countries. Some of the many countries he visited were Iran, Cuba, and South Africa.

After the Navy, Joe came to the outside world. He worked for A.W. Ashton in Somerville for eight and one-half years. Then afterwards he applied for a job at Polaroid. He got accepted.

Joe started working at Polaroid on November 11, 1965. He worked as an electrical journeyman under the supervision of Dave Green who has since passed away. Joe has been an electrician for over thirty years. Over the years Joe has become a better worker by learning from his mistakes.

In the twenty-five years Joe has been working in Polaroid, he has not seen major changes in how the business gets done. He has noticed that world competition has influenced somewhat of a shift towards a more formal business working environment. Of course, over the years the corporation has gotten a whole lot bigger.

Joe enjoys being a supervisor. He says he enjoys working with a bunch of great guys. He learns from them and he tries to help them out. He says most of all he enjoys his responsibilities, and his job pays well.

The most important thing to Joe right now is to be financially set. He would like to retire at age sixty-two and every two years he'd like to go on an extended trip.

Adult-adolescent integration need not be restricted to the workplace; it can be imported to the school. At the Horizonte Training and Instruction Center in Salt Lake City, adults and adolescents sit side by side in classrooms. Started as an adult training center in the 1970s, Horizonte soon began working with adolescents who had dropped out or had been pushed out of the city's high schools, until now it is a full-fledged high school itself, as well as an adult training center. Not only does Horizonte send students to the adult workplace, it also conducts school in an adult learning place.

5. *Help students encounter the world through publication, presentation, and exhibition.* Her teachers and classmates might never have fully understood or appreciated Jocelyn's work without her presentation and exhibition. It was there that she truly assumed control of the learning, and where the integration of school and work bore fruit. But it was also important to her teachers for what it told them about Jocelyn and for what it suggested about the potential of the program. As a vision of what is possible, the exhibition becomes a spur to further planning, to make what is possible, likely.

6. *Think of the teacher as inquirer and clinician.* In hands-on humanities, the teacher functions not as the dispenser of all the great thoughts and ideas, but as a clinician who helps students recognize and explore the essential questions that emerge in their everyday observations and experiences. For example, students in a humanities class in the medical careers strand at Hoover High School in San Diego develop inquiry projects around their own questions such as, "Should assisted suicide be legal?" "Is circumcision advisable from the standpoint of health?" "Does heckling influence the performance of professional athletes?" Paying attention to questions such as these can help us as teachers, not only to choose more wisely the texts we bring to the classroom, but also to *see and hear our students better.* If we are interested in developing a highly skilled work force and an active, responsible citizenry, we need to better understand and appreciate the scope of our students' dreams and the depth of their work.

Getting out to workplaces helps teachers to do this work. There are a number of ways to accomplish this, some more intense than others: by leading a seminar on site, as I was able to do; by acting as workplace supervisors, as teachers at the Gateway Institute of Technology in St. Louis do; or by participating in summer workshops. The point is that it is difficult to be a guide without knowing the place, or at least entering it along with students. Schools and community partnerships need to provide time and training for teachers, including significant exposure to the workplace and to the ethnographic skills for assessing its learning potential.

It is not surprising that teachers with experience in another field, particularly those with clinical skills in fields like medicine, business, or communications, often become excellent teachers in school-to-work programs. Nurses and other clinical professionals, whose work involves observation, recording, and reflection, are naturals for this kind of teaching, in which the teacher's process of inquiry and conversation mirrors that of the students. In fact, states which wish to implement school-to-work on a systemic basis need to revisit their certification and pre-service requirements. Those candidates lacking significant workplace experience should get exposure, while those who come from the other jobs but lack educational background should receive training in hands-on pedagogy and in establishing contexts for reflection.

III. WRITING AND REFLECTION IN SCHOOL-TO-WORK PROGRAMS

Many students emerge from high school with limited writing skills. This is a frequent lament of colleges and workplaces alike. Despite the fears of some that sending students out to work will undermine the development of basic skills, in good work-based learning programs the rule-of-thumb is to write often, for many purposes and many audiences. In fact, such programs are often better situated than classrooms to provide contexts for writing, not mere pretexts.

With respect to form, the perspectives of school and workplace are markedly different. The five-paragraph essay, an artifact of schooling, is irrelevant for the workplace, where concerns are not so much with paragraph structure as with leaving enough white space on the page and providing clear, concise answers to critical questions. The criteria for good writing vary according to the purpose of the writing. A staff memo or a newsletter article must be spelled impeccably; in a student journal, a too-intense concern for spelling may inhibit getting the flow of thought onto paper.

Writing and Reflection: Some Reminders

1. Write often.
2. Write for a variety of purposes.
3. Write in many forms.
4. Write for a variety of audiences.
5. Share the writing as part of an ongoing conversation.
6. Teachers write and share their writing, too.
7. Start where students are; take a developmental view.
8. Respond to student writing as real and purposeful.

Here are some general reminders for those who would introduce or re-
fine writing in their school-to-work programs:

1. *Write often.* Students need to practice, and to see purposeful writing
as part of their daily routine. The journal is a reasonable means toward this
goal (see "The Shop Log/Journal," below). It also serves as a spur to conversation, a place to record important ideas, and a resource bank for project development. In assigning journals, it is important to strive for a balance
between freedom and structure. Some students prefer to write on their own
with minimal direction; others ask, "What am I supposed to write about?"
Suggestions for writing should be presented so as to accommodate these
varying student needs while addressing program goals for shared reflection.
Other routines can be laid over the daily journal routine, such as bi-weekly
journal summaries, end-of-term reflections, and the construction of indexes,
tables of contents, and lists of recurrent themes.

Technical Internship Program:
The Shop Log/Journal

As part of your work in this program, you are required to keep a shop
log. The log will be divided in two sections: work record and journal.
In the work record you will enter what you have done each day in the
shop, what tools you have used, and what problems you have encountered.

In the journal, you will write about some of the things you are observing and learning. For some of your journal entries, you will be given
specific topics to write about. For others, the topic will be up to you.

What to write
- reactions to the job, the seminar, things in general
- notes, observations, information
- reflections on your work
- descriptions of people, places, events, situations
- ideas or feelings to explore or remember

When to write
- at work, in the seminar
- at least three times a week; consistency makes a good journal
- early in the morning, late at night, any time of day
- when you face problems or decisions
- when you are wondering about important questions

How to write
- informally
- in your own voice
- quickly and freely, in any form you wish
- take chances

How much to write
- write long entries (a page or more) as often as you can to develop ideas fully

Remember that your site log is to be shared with the seminar teacher. You will be asked to share some of your journal entries with your peers, too.

Above all, remember that your journal will be a rich resource to you as you develop projects, autobiographical writings, and newsletter articles for this course.

—Cambridge-Polaroid Technical Internship Program
Adapted from Toby Fulwiler, University of Vermont

2. *Write for a variety of purposes.* We write to think, to remember, to discover, to create and communicate meaning—not merely to demonstrate competence, though becoming a better writer is a certain by-product of regular writing. Every writing has a use. Shorter writings may turn into larger products: autobiographical fragments may contribute to a longer autobiography, work log entries and interview notes may be used for newsletter articles, reflections on life and work may turn into portfolio entries. Writing should never be assigned as busy work.

Cambridge-Lesley Careers in Education Program
A Structured Journal Assignment:
First Day Observations

At some point during the morning, take ten or fifteen minutes to sit off to the side, observe, and write. Try to pick a time when everyone is busy. Relax and observe for a while before you start writing.

- Notice carefully what is going on: what people are doing. Try especially to notice details—small things such as arm movements, body positions, facial expressions, the way people stand or walk, the way people speak as well as what they say.

- Try also to sense the atmosphere. Is it warm? Cold? Friendly? Frantic? Organized? Purposeful? Casual? Serious? Humorous? What makes the atmosphere like that?

- How do you FEEL in this place? What reactions to it do you have? What does all this action remind you of? Make some comparisons.

Now write! Try to get down as many of your observations as you can, and include as many of your own personal reactions and feelings as possible.

We're working on sensory perceptions, and on *detail*. Try to put to work the exercises we've been doing in class on paying attention to your senses and tuning into detail.

—Adapted from Herrmann and Tabor, "Experiments & Experiences in Writing," unpublished curriculum manuscript.

3. *Write in many forms.* The workplace calls for forms of writing rarely, if ever, introduced in schoolwork, including memos, inventories, orders, requests for information, newsletter articles, incident reports, and training manuals. But since we aim for more than mastery of "business English," the range should extend beyond these, to include everything from free-writing exercises to scripts, autobiographies, stories, and poems.

4. *Write for a variety of audiences.* One of the great advantages of work-based learning programs is that they provide authentic audiences for student work: workplace colleagues, supervisors, clients, and the general public. The teachers, college professors, and parents who viewed the exhibitions of Jocelyn and her peers, and the company-wide personnel who received the Cambridge-Polaroid newsletter, lent an air of interest and support that both inspired and validated the work. Our students enjoyed such contact and such validation throughout their internships.

5. *Share the writing as part of an ongoing conversation.* The idea is to turn writing into talk, and talk into writing. Here, the principle of writing to learn links with the principle of learning together, as students discover each other's responses to common situations, thereby seeing new possibilities for their own writing. Such conversations don't materialize out of thin air, however. They require training and practice, with plenty of teacher modeling.

6. *Teachers write and share their writing, too.* Nothing demystifies writing more quickly for students than to watch their teachers struggle to put words on paper. Nothing helps teachers understand student writing more

than to write for the same reasons as the students—to learn, to collect thoughts, to discover meaning, to communicate.

7. *Start where the students are, and take a long-term, developmental perspective.* Good writers develop over time. Good writing teachers try to convey the value of writing and equip their students with strategies for development over the long haul. It's pointless and pernicious to denigrate or disqualify students for what they "can't do." Even the most challenged student can write lists, questions, interview notes, and observations. And students will develop as writers when they see the results of regular writing and attend to what their peers are writing. The key is to ask for thoughtful products, honor students' present work, and let complexity and propriety flow from there, as students become more practiced and fluent.

8. *Respond to student writing as real and purposeful.* At a writing workshop for teachers, workplace supervisors, and students in the Cornell Youth and Work Program, a student wrote, "This is the first time I've ever had a conversation with an adult about writing where I wasn't being graded." Too often, writing in schools is treated as a competency test, with each "mistake" seen as a stain on the writer's character. Consider the effect of a teacher's rule that each run-on sentence will result in a ten-point deduction on the grade: we see short, simple sentences and a reluctance on the part of students to take chances, try new constructions, or attempt to express complex ideas.

A more productive approach is first to identify themes and issues in the writing, and help students figure out what it is that they want to say. It is often more useful to point out student strengths: "Here, this works, do more of this," rather than "Don't do that." When students are simply told what not to do, they still don't learn what to *do*. Finally, it makes sense to ask questions that might lead to more writing, expressing a reader's needs while leaving ownership with the writer.

At Rindge, shop teachers became good readers of student writing because they learned to respond out of their own expertise, rather than try to replicate their own experience of being corrected by English teachers. Students, too, can learn to point out strengths and ask salient questions, as has been shown in high school classrooms and writing centers across the country. (See "Peer Response to Writing: A Quick Sketch" below for a general response template.)

Again, the principle of hands-on humanities comes into play: we can take the same approach to student writing that we take to the work of professional writers in our reader response journals: What is this piece about? What moves me? How is the piece put together? What questions does it

150

raise? Students who learn to respond to writing in this way are picking up skills of reading and literary analysis.

Peer Response to Writing:
A Quick Sketch

1. Take notes, feedback. Concentrate on strengths. What words and phrases stand out? Use the author's words.

2. What themes and ideas come through? What is the piece about?

3. What are the strengths of this piece?

4. What questions do you have?
   - for elaboration ("Tell me more about . . . ")
   - for clarification ("What do you mean when you say . . . ")

5. What are your suggestions as the piece moves to the next draft?

IV. WORK-BASED LEARNING AND HUMANITIES STANDARDS

Work-based learning offers contextualized pathways to engagement in literature and history. When students are engaged in the world through internships or community service, the great concerns of the humanities arise: identity, affiliation, work, responsibility, truth, beauty, justice. Students see the importance of grappling with these issues, of deepening their understanding of how people and institutions deal with human events. But even here, work-based learning is far more than a pathway to literature, or a means to promote student engagement in the humanities classroom. Here Dewey is to the point: education is not preparation for life; education is life itself.

Current humanities conversations in the academy reflect both a divided intellectual community and a desire for synthesis. In one view, there is no single historical or philosophical truth, but rather a constellation of voices, heard and unheard, "privileged" and disenfranchised. This view is accompanied by a broadened notion of text, shifting ideas of the nature of authorship, and a new focus on the role of the reader in creating meaning. A second view maintains that there is a truth which we progressively uncover and that Western culture, for example, expresses universal human values and thus should be the bedrock source of curriculum content in the schools.

The controversy over national and state standards in language arts and social studies reflects this division: there are those who advocate for a curriculum based on specific, fixed content for all, while others instead advocate common structures and processes for emerging voices. Nonetheless, for high school humanities, there is general agreement (among teachers, if not among all policymakers) that the aim is to honor a wide variety of voices and perspectives in our explorations of history and literature. Moreover, virtually all national and state standards efforts, not only in social studies and language arts, but also in math and science, insist on "contextualized" learning, whereby students develop skills and understanding by doing real work for real purposes and audiences.

Although scholars and teachers tend not to realize it, school-to-work aligns well with these notions. How natural it seems, for example, for students in the workplace to write to construct and convey meaning for a variety of purposes and audiences—one of the linchpin language arts standards. Moreover, in their project work and reflections, these students, perhaps more explicitly than their school-bound peers, are actively engaged in the business of the humanities: to articulate the self and encounter the world; to acknowledge difference, yet find common ground.

In most schools, programs linking school to work still occupy a marginal position. Teachers, curriculum leaders, and policy makers pay little if any attention to the potential of workplace learning for all students. For example, work-based learning is barely mentioned at the conventions and in the publications of the National Council of Teachers of English. Perhaps it hasn't occurred to many language arts professionals that work-based learning offers a rich context for the essential language arts activities: reading, writing, speaking, listening, viewing, and presenting. Perhaps they understand school-to-work as a program for children other than those they serve. If this is so, then current notions of school-to-work and language arts instruction are inadequate; to say the two are incompatible or unrelated trivializes both and does justice to neither.

Nevertheless, there is a growing public awareness that the demands of the job market have outpaced the schools, and that schools and communities need to conceive of education differently. In the past few years educators and business leaders have been reconsidering basic assumptions about schools and workplaces, teaching and learning. What is worth knowing? How do learners construct an understanding of something? How do we know what they are learning? Whose responsibility is it to strengthen the link between school and career? What new roles and configurations are necessary?

If we ask what adolescents—at work, school, or play—are really working on, and if we have the patience to pursue the question, we begin to understand that they are constructing their lives. This view takes us far beyond the simple provision of a work placement accompanied by instruction in basic skills. School-to-work programs require that teachers see their roles differently and take new clinical approaches. They call into question a fundamental structural principle of American education—the separation of hands and minds. Work-based learning can broaden the content and the notion of text, provide entry into virtually any text, and give students more purchase on the adult world than is available in school.

The pedagogy discussed in this chapter is not new. Work-based and constructivist pieces of pedagogical reform have emerged independently of and prior to current school-to-work notions: writing process reforms, project-based learning, cooperative learning, oral history, community service learning, authentic assessment, and multicultural teaching. The point is that these methods and stances are valid and important in classrooms, but lacking real world contexts, they too can seem contrived. We still labor under the misconception that the classroom is the best or only place for learning. We would do well to listen again to Dewey's insistence on occupation as a context, not for career preparation, but for learning.

This insistence on context is no trivial matter, for it entails shifting the physical and conceptual center of secondary education out of the academy. School-to-work reform calls for schools and workplaces to mediate a new process of entry into the adult world. This task is much broader than job training, and schools can not do it alone. Workplaces and other contexts for action, reflection, and exhibition invite the learner—and the teacher—to make connections and articulate the learning. This fundamental work of uncovering the humanities in work-based learning brings school-to-work into the mainstream of education reform, where it belongs. This is a project for adults and students together, worthy of our deepest commitment and illuminative of our best hopes for the future.

NOTES

1. An earlier and much shorter version of this chapter appeared in *Teaching the Humanities: The Journal of the American Council of Learned Societies Elementary and Secondary Schools Teacher Curriculum Development Project,* Vol. 1, No. 1, Summer 1995.

2. John Steptoe, *Mufaro's Beautiful Daughters* (New York: Lothrop, Lee and Shepard Books, 1987).

3. Valerie Smith, *Self-Discovery and Authority in Afro-American Narrative* (Cambridge, MA: Harvard University Press, 1987).

4. Henry Louis Gates, Jr., "Cultural Equity?" in *Humanities in the Schools,* American Council of Learned Societies Occasional Paper, No. 20, 1993.

5. See Paulo Freire, *Cultural Action for Freedom,* Harvard Educational Review, Monograph Series No. 1, 1970, 14 ff.

6

Lessons from the Field

The programs described in this book use community and workplace issues and contexts to involve students in more active and engaged learning than is typical of most high school classes. Because my goal has been to portray something that many people have not experienced, I have tended to focus on the "what" and the "why" rather than the "how." The danger of this approach is that the featured programs can appear to have sprung—unblemished, fully-developed, and unassailable—out of the minds of their founders. This is far from the case. Each of these programs has experienced (and continues to experience) false starts, mistakes, and moments of doubt, as well as criticisms from those who do not understand or agree with its approach. Furthermore, because these programs challenge so many assumptions about teaching and learning, all remain relatively fragile.

Perhaps one of the most important lesson to learn is that each group of innovators has to make the most of its own local circumstances, resources, history, and opportunities. Yet, it can still be useful to hear stories about how others have done just that. Drawing on such stories, this chapter explores some of the key design issues schools and districts face as they try to support and nurture community and work-focused projects. Achieving the conditions essential to this type of education may indeed mean overcoming some of the most sacred "givens" of a high school, from the way time is allotted to the definition of the teacher's role. The second part of the chapter reviews four major trends that are affecting the degree of acceptance of these changes in both the worlds of policy and practice: high school restructuring, the movement to raise school standards, economic developments, and finally, the movement to start new small schools.

I. DESIGN ISSUES FOR SCHOOLS

Recognizing Teachers as Learners

Linking schools more closely to work-based and community-oriented projects, in the ways proposed in this book, requires teachers to make some profound changes—in their relationship to the subject matter, the students, and the world outside of the school. Like corporations that are finding it necessary to "re-engineer" the way they do business, schools too need new ways to support teachers in making these changes. There are serious problems with where and how school districts currently invest the limited dollars they have for professional development.

For many teachers, the only team time supported by the district occurs in weekly or biweekly after-school department meetings, with perhaps some arrangement to "release" teachers for occasional workshops on specific methodologies that have been deemed important, usually by a central administrator. Even if time could be added (e.g., by building in one or two professional development days during the school year, or creating periodic "early release" days), there are still problems with simply offering a series of workshops, or formal occasions of learning, when teachers are brought together for training. The "training" model of professional development is designed, at best, to enhance the technical capacity of teachers to carry out a particular approach. Any of us who have ever attended or been brought in to run such sessions know how resistant teachers can be to such training.

Their reaction is not surprising, notes Judith Warren Little of the University of California, who has done extensive research on teacher development. As she succinctly puts it: "Questions of how are irretrievably tied to questions of whether and why."[1] In other words, the same argument about the importance of having a sense of purpose and meaning applies to teachers as well as to students. If teachers are going to buy into an educational reform strategy, they have to believe that it matters, that it will address real issues or problems they see, and, most importantly, that it will make a real difference to students.

On one level, it seems obvious that if teachers are treated as empty vessels to be filled with new wisdom, it will indeed be hard (if not impossible) to move them away from similar assumptions about their students. Just as it is a mistake to treat students "as if" they care, it is a mistake to treat teachers "as if" they already buy into a proposed reform. Moving towards more project-based, community-oriented instruction raises serious questions for teachers, particularly in how far to go in abandoning the traditional curriculum of discrete academic subjects and skill-oriented instruction. "Teachers," notes Little, "do not decide the worth of such trade-offs on the basis of workshops that instruct them on how to achieve curriculum integration."[2]

In my experience, teachers, like students, work really hard when they believe in what they are doing. And, like students, they deserve to know why they are being asked to do something; they need a frame of reference that makes sense to them. The hardest thing to overcome is a sense of cynicism and futility, bred from too many educational bandwagons. With each change of superintendent (and such changes can come often in urban districts) teachers find themselves expected to jump on still another of these wagons, with threats of accountability lurking in the background.

For teachers to be enthusiastic about a proposed change, they need to believe that there will be value added—for the students primarily, but also for themselves as professionals. This is a case that can be made for the reforms proposed here. But such belief does not come from someone like me trying to convince the teachers of its validity. Teachers start to believe in a new approach when they get the support and resources they need to work with that approach in the classroom, and when they get the time to reflect on the results with one another—in other words, when they get real opportunities to discover and to construct its value for themselves.

Training Model vs. Design Team Model	
Training Model	*Design Team Model*
Top down	Bottom up
Workshops *for* teachers	Meetings *of* teachers
Formal occasions for learning	Learning is ongoing
Teachers as recipients of knowledge	Teachers as researchers
Teachers as implementors	Teachers as initiators
Focus on techniques and skills	Create new norms of practice
Maintains "closed door"	Builds interdependence

The best strategy we found at Rindge for doing this was the creation of design teams of teachers. As was described in chapter 1, we began our reform efforts not by offering teachers training, but rather, by forming such a team. For the first year, the CityWorks design team—all twelve of the teachers leading studio groups—met on a daily basis. The meetings were critical to what we were trying to accomplish—giving us time to reflect on what had happened that day, to review, revise, and propose curriculum activities, and to look at the student work that was being generated. We talked, and sometimes fought our way to new practice. In order to create this common planning time, it was necessary to close the vocational shops for a class period each day, an unpopular move with both our teachers and counselors from other parts of the high school, who saw the shops as perfect electives for students with a free period. But the payoff was considerable.

Acutely aware of their own low status within the comprehensive high school, Rindge teachers were especially cynical. They had seen reforms and reformers come and go. What they had never experienced was a change effort in which they would be encouraged to use everything they knew and understood, not just about students, learning, and schools, but about the world outside of school, where they had developed considerable expertise as parents, community members, and, in many cases, as entrepreneurs and independent contractors. For many years, vocational teachers at Rindge had spent virtually all of their time at school teaching narrow technical skills that were occupationally specific. Most believed that this is what it meant to be a vocational teacher. State mandated curricula reinforced this notion. Vocational teachers received manuals for their shop areas listing duties and tasks that students in that area were expected to undertake. Little was left to the teacher's judgment.

We suspected that Rindge teachers were experiencing cognitive dissonance. Certainly the curriculum they were teaching at school left out much of what they knew to be important in their own work and lives outside of school. This was brought home to us early in our reform efforts in a conversation with a teacher who had taught carpentry at Rindge for many years. Like many vocational teachers, he was an independent contractor outside of school. He explained that he would very much like to turn his business over to his sons, both of whom were skilled carpenters. The problem was that neither son seemed to be good at most of the other tasks associated with running a successful contracting business, such as, making good estimates, writing contracts, dealing with clients and subcontractors, and getting variances from the local zoning board.

Talking with this teacher, we realized that he held within his own experiences the seeds of a new approach to practice. Even though he continued to teach carpentry as a set of subskills, he knew that his students, like his sons, needed a broader set of skills. The challenge for us was to create a professional culture which would encourage him and his colleagues to unearth the reasons behind their current practice, and to reconsider that practice in the light of changing economic and social realities.

What we did not realize at the time was how important the design team model would become throughout our ninth- through twelfth-grade program—not only as a source of ongoing innovation, but also as professional

development for teachers. Within a few years, five such teams were func-
tioning: in addition to CityWorks and Pathways, there is a team of technical
and science teachers collaborating on a new technology education program, and a team of academic and technical teachers creating a fully integrated ninth-grade program. The fifth team includes both teachers and
community partners involved in our eleventh- and twelfth-grade career internships (see chapter 3 for description of the internship programs). Teams
meet at least once a week to work on courses that are jointly taught by participants, and each is led by a teacher who is responsible for convening
weekly meetings, synthesizing ideas into curriculum plans, ordering materials, making contacts with outside resource people who provide additional
expertise, and generally helping everyone else to work productively. (See
"Changing Job Descriptions" below for more on teacher leaders.)

Finding Time for Teamwork

The particular design team model developed at Rindge may not be right or
possible for other schools. The important thing is for teachers to find time
together to take ownership of new ideas and approaches and discuss with
colleagues how to make such innovations work. In a recent study of sixteen
promising programs that link school and work, a team of researchers found
collegial groupings or "teacher learning communities" in all of the programs
studied. They concluded that such groupings were vital in enabling teachers to take risks and experiment.

Time for such communities to form and gel is not at all easy to find in
the normal school day. When asked what they will need to explore new approaches to teaching and learning, teachers will frequently bring up the
lack of time in their day. Most districts and union contracts specify only two
kinds of teacher time: instructional time or other forms of direct service to
students (typically 75–80 percent of the school day); and "prep periods." Although prep periods are theoretically a time when teachers could collaborate, they are usually not scheduled in such a way as to allow this to
happen. Nor are there incentives for teachers to use time in this way, rather
than correcting papers or taking a break between other duties.

How highly teachers value the opportunity to work collaboratively was
brought home to me again recently in a meeting with the health occupations career pathway team at East Boston High School in Boston, Massachusetts. These teachers had agreed to teach for five periods in a row each
day in order to have the last two periods of the day for common planning
time with their partners in the East Boston Neighborhood Health Center. Al-

though the teachers admitted to feeling drained by this schedule, they all felt it was worth the trade-off.

Regular time together as a team does not preclude the need for more intensive periods of design and planning work. Good projects are not easy to design; nor are they easy to assess. Complicating matters further, it is important to involve outside community and business partners in both of these aspects of project-based teaching and learning. Partners can play a critical role in design—offering ideas for "real enough" problems students might undertake. And, equally critical is their role in assessment, sharing their perspectives regarding real-world standards for the work, and working collaboratively with faculty to establish benchmarks that help students mark their progress towards those standards.

Most of the school teams that I have seen successfully incorporate project-based learning have benefited from the opportunity to spend three to five days together, during which time they experienced first-hand some of the elements of project-based learning and visited the worksite or community site of a partnering organization. In most cases (but not all) this time has been scheduled during the summer. The expectation is that by the end of the workshop, the team will have made a good start on designing a project that is grounded in community or work realities, and on setting criteria for assessment of student work that will result from the project. On the last day, they have a chance to experience the process of doing presentations and exhibitions, as they share the work they have done, preferably with other teams focusing on similar designs.

The basic elements of this workshop design have been used by a number of the networks working with school programs described in this book: including, the Hands and Minds Collaborative of the Center for Law and Education, the Urban School Initiative of the National Center for Research in Vocational Education, Working to Learn, and the Benchmark Communities Initiative of Jobs for the Future. In addition, some of the networks make consultants available to work with the teacher teams. The design team approach is not an argument against ever bringing in consultants or trainers to work with the group; teachers, like all learners, need new input and support from people with particular sets of expertise. The important thing is that the team choose which consultants and what kinds of workshops will be most useful to them. Hopefully, in most cases, the ones they select will "model the educational model" they are intending to use with students.

Summers are also a valuable time for teachers to do some experiential learning of their own. For example, an increasing number of communities have begun to arrange internships (ranging from one or two days to several months) for teachers at local businesses. Through the internships, teachers gain first-hand experience with the skills now required at the worksite, and, more specifically, assess the learning potential of various worksites where they may place students.

Some schools are also taking advantage of outdoor adventure opportunities, such as are available through Outward Bound. While white-river rafting may not be as directly relevant to work-based learning as summer business internships, teachers in these programs are reminded of the power of experiential learning and of what it is like to be a learner again—a novice taking the risk of doing something for which they are not fully prepared. This can be a useful metaphor in creating empathy for students, but also in preparing for some of the risks involved in changing one's own teaching practice.

Rewriting Job Descriptions

"Teachers and principals have been so long protected . . . they dread venturing into the cold world of the community outside."[3] This statement, written in 1938 by an educator advocating a more community-focused type of education, gives an indication of the longevity, and the depth of the chasm between school and the "real world." What seems increasingly clear in the schools, is that this "dread" stems, at least in part, from institutional realities that keep teachers focused on and confined to activities within the four walls of the school, and, usually, within the four walls of their own classrooms.

In such an environment, even small obstacles can seem insurmountable. For example, de Leeuw from the Oakland Health Academy cites the frustration both he and outside experts experience when he is trying to reach them by telephone. Like most teachers, he does not have easy access to a telephone during the school day, nor a reliable system for getting messages quickly. In our era of phone tag, it can take a teacher days, or even weeks, to reach a potential partner or mentor and explain why he is calling. Complicating matters further, many teachers do not live in the community in which they teach, and thus have relatively little contact with the issues, groups, or activists of the area.

There seem to be virtually no incentives and quite a few disincentives to "venturing out." To overcome such barriers, the schools described in previous chapters have developed new job descriptions and added new roles to the school community. "One thing that's been interesting as this school has evolved," notes Chuck Ericksen, referring to the Flambeau district high school in Wisconsin, "is that our roles have changed." For instance, Ericksen went from being the person brought in to deal with at-risk students to the "community education coordinator" with a broader set of outreach activities. As the Flambeau programs have grown, he has also succeeded in increasing the number of positions within the system with job descriptions that provide time to support community projects.

In a high school of just over seven-hundred students, there are four such positions, including the equivalent of two positions for coordinating "gifted and talented" initiatives, one technical coordinator to link students up to technical projects; and one school-to-work coordinator. In addition, there is a family-school coordinator to do home visits and run after-school activities. As Ericksen explains, having people in these flexible roles "allows for some real support for teachers when they take on projects." This seems like a lot of flexible positions for one rural district, especially one that is, as Ericksen puts it, "very frugal, very cost conscious." His explanation is that administrators and school board members alike "have seen the benefits to students of the community connections . . . they see things working; they hear stories." These observations have led to a willingness to invest in this new approach to educating the youth of the community.

The Flambeau strategy for creating school-community connections has been to enlarge or redefine existing roles that already have some flexibility, such as "gifted and talented" coordinator. Rindge has reduced the teaching load of a number of faculty members to create new flexible positions. In addition to the teacher who coordinates the CityWorks program, one teacher was given a reduced teaching load to serve as school-to-work coordinator, another to coordinate the technology education program, and a third to serve as the coordinator of the Cambridge Service Corps. Although part of their time is taken up in "non-teaching" duties and hence they see fewer students in a day than is called for in the "average teacher load" formula, what they do instead makes it possible for other teachers to offer a rich mixture of integrated and project-based instruction. They are vital to the overall productivity of a team.

They also can often bring in additional resources—either in the form of funding or volunteers. Both CityWorks and the Cambridge Service Corps have found an important source of help in local community organizations and youth programs whose missions explicitly include working with high school students. "Youth workers want to spend time in the high school—it's where the kids are for a good part of the day," explains John Shea, teacher of the community problem-solving course and coordinator of the Corps. The problem is that schools do not usually have anyone with time to reach out to those organizations, or to figure out how best to integrate what they have to offer. Because this is part of Shea's job description, he is able to bring in other people from the community.

The creation of such liaison positions can come from city and community sources as well as from the school. For example, Cambridge Community Services, a local nonprofit, has raised funds to hire several people who work with the school, providing additional support (e.g., college and career guidance) to students in school-to-work and community projects. In addition, several staff members from the city's Office of Workforce Development spend portions of their time helping to set up new internship opportunities for students. They see this as an important part of their overall mission of developing the future workforce of the city.

In general, our experience has been that the more you reach out to the community, the more people in the community will come to you with interesting ideas and sometimes even with useful resources. In the early years of CityWorks, the human resource director of the Polaroid Corporation decided to let an employee teach one period per day of CityWorks and to attend the team meetings. He saw this as a "perk" to offer employees working in the multi-craft environment of Polaroid, who might be interested in trying their hand at teaching, and we saw this as an ideal way to bring together the cultures of the school and the workplace. (A Rindge teacher also spent time at Polaroid each day, leading a lunchtime seminar of students doing internships there).

The CityWorks Walkabout and Teen Visions projects have also resulted in increasing community interest in the Rindge program as a whole. For example, after several years of students doing such projects, the director of Rindge received a call from Harvard University to find out whether our students could do research on pedestrian traffic near the school, which they could use to bolster their argument for the need for an overpass between two of their buildings. Other calls have brought donations of computers and offers of volunteer services (all of which are accepted, of course). Perhaps even more significantly, the fieldwork that students do in CityWorks functions as a natural outreach mechanism for finding community businesses and agencies that are willing to sponsor job shadowing opportunities for students in their tenth-grade year, or even longer-term internship placements for juniors and seniors.

Bringing Employers to the Table

I do not mean to minimize what it takes to set up partnerships between schools and outside organizations. All of the programs whose stories are told here expend considerable effort on establishing good relationships with partners. Convincing employers to create new paid internships for students can be especially difficult. The school's creation of new roles is one way to signal a seriousness about looking for collaboration, not just a donation. But the communities that have succeeded in getting broad participation from employers have also relied on the active intervention of an independent employer organization or intermediary, such as Boston's Private Industry Council.

In her book about school-to-work reforms, Lynn Olson, a reporter for *Education Week* writes about Boston as well as Tulsa, Oklahoma and Austin, Texas, each of which has an unusually large and strong internship or apprenticeship program. "What they have in common," explains Olson, "is a strong intermediary that can provide the link between educators and employers and a commitment to building a system. . . . The trick is finding which organization best represents employers in a community and getting it interested."[4] Not surprisingly, such interest is most likely to come from clear labor market needs—such as the need for a more racially diverse and technically competent workforce. The communities Olson writes about have been successful because the intermediaries have hired full-time staff to focus on industries that have such needs.

One of the main concerns voiced by companies considering school-to-work initiatives is what it will cost them, not in wages for the students, but in time their employees will spend. The good news is that once companies are convinced to participate, they seem to find that the costs can be partially, if not fully, offset by the contributions students make to the ongoing work of the site and by the growth that their older employees experience as a result of their participation as mentors and supervisors to youth. "Frontline workers who serve as mentors and supervisors often become more excited about their work, more diligent in their responsibilities, and more productive," according to the results of an employer survey conducted by Jobs for the Future.[5]

This has certainly been the case for the employers who offer the Rindge internships. At a recent graduation ceremony of Harvard interns, their mentors were very clear that the "kids help to get the work done." They also talked about how rejuvenating it is for them to work with adolescents. Rather than expressing concern about how much employee time is going to teaching interns, our partners have been pleased by the extent to which employees "feel better about themselves and their work."

Another promising pattern is the tendency of participating employers to expand the number and type of work-based learning opportunities that they offer over time. When the Manpower Development Research Center did a follow-up study in 1995–96 with the same employers involved in sixteen pioneering programs first studied three years earlier, the researchers found a wide range of offerings, including: job shadowing, internships, academic study in the workplace, and occupationally related projects with employer participation in the classroom. While in 1992–93 the companies might have offered one of these, the follow-up study revealed that in the intervening years most had broadened the opportunities available. Participation in one aspect of collaboration with schools seemed to result in a willingness to do more.[6]

Finding Underutilized Resources

Employers are not the only ones to worry about the bottom line. If schools are to embrace project-based and work-based learning, they too will have to find a way to do so without greatly increasing the costs. Projects of the sort described in this book are people-intensive; and, of course, staffing is the major expense in education. The challenge for schools is to make use of the human resources available to them in a very different way. A key strategy at Rindge has been to recognize and enhance the capacity of the vocational faculty.

As Executive Director of Rindge, Larry Rosenstock made a key decision early on that resulted in a redirection of resources. Rather than run the old model (shop exploratories) alongside a new one (vocational-academic integration), he replaced the freshman exploratory with CityWorks. This meant that the vocational teachers who used to staff that program now had two periods free to devote to designing and teaching the new program.

In addition, the CityWorks room (a large space, divided into smaller studios) was constructed in a way that lends itself to the full participation of paraprofessional staff (the vocational department has several bilingual technical assistants to ensure access to the large number of new immigrant students in the school). As long as there is at least one certified professional teacher in the room, it is legally possible for para-professionals to work with small groups of students. With a combination of vocational and para-professional staff, we were able to achieve an ideal student teacher ratio in the studio groupings which guaranteed that for at least one period a day, freshmen would get to work closely with an adult who could help them to tackle project work.

Although most high school communities do not realize it, their vocational, technical, and business teachers are a valuable underutilized resource. Trying to simulate on-the-job conditions, vocational teachers tend to make use of teaching strategies that more closely resemble apprenticeship relations (e.g., coaching, performance assessment) than traditional classroom interactions. And, because they are viewed as integrally involved in job placement, high school vocational teachers tend to be in regular contact with a variety of people beyond the school walls—including, employers, internship sites, community colleges, and jobs programs.

But the value of the vocational faculty goes beyond the teaching methodologies they use and their contacts with the outside world. They can also become a valuable resource in reaching academic goals. Why, then, have vocational teachers remained so invisible in the school reform efforts of the past decade? In her studies of comprehensive high schools, Judith Warren Little has noted that academic and vocational departments are so separate that they constitute "two worlds."[7] At best these two worlds operate in isolation from one another; at worst, they find themselves competing for students and resources. While vocational teachers see themselves as preparing students for careers, academic staff believe that the mission of the high school is to prepare students for college. Viewing vocational students as those who cannot make it academically and hence have become "non-college bound" they see vocational programs (and the teachers who staff them) as much lower on the status hierarchy of the school.

As anyone who has spent time teaching in a high school knows, it is very difficult to overcome the barriers to communication created by the subdivision into subject departments and curricular tracks. Furthermore, there is what Little calls an "architecture of time, space, and task" that literally divides the staff.[8] Students do academic work in classrooms and vocational work in shops which, in many schools are in a separate wing of the building or below ground level; since shop work is seen as requiring longer periods of time, even the schedule may be different.

One approach at Rindge was literally to change the architecture. Carpentry, drafting, and electrical teachers worked with students on the design and construction of new spaces that were neither strictly vocational nor academic. We have already seen the importance of the architectural design in CityWorks. The same has been true of the new technology lab, built in half of what used to be a very large carpentry shop. The lab is a space in which students can do hands-on projects, using equipment ranging from computers to power tools, but it also works well for discussion and even the traditional "chalk and talk." As a result, it is comfortable for both vocational and academic teachers. To ensure such a mix, we also made fundamental changes in some job descriptions.

Consider, for example, the case of Roy Carter, a landscape architect, sculptor, and science teacher, who leads the Rindge technology team. When we first began the reforms and wanted to offer more academic courses, we assigned him to teach science five periods a day. In this way, roughly one hundred students would receive science credits. Now, this teacher leads a technology team composed of four vocational teachers (the electrical teacher, the electronics teacher, a woodworking teacher, and a drafting teacher), who collectively offer various project-based science/technology courses five periods a day.

To plan for this change, the team met together (and with a curriculum designer and local scientists) for almost a year, on a paid, weekly after-school basis, as well as in a summer workshop. Their goal was to move from an analysis of the operating procedures and rules of thumb of their trades to constructing knowledge of how their particular technical areas could be used to teach important underlying principles of science and technology. The result was a new science and technology course, as well as some new curricular units within their technical areas of expertise. Because Carter is a co-teacher in each of the periods, not the sole adult in a room with twenty or more students, he is able both to teach particular science concepts when they are relevant to the project at hand and to carry out the other parts of his role. The lesson here is that by changing one person's job description, it is sometimes possible to maximize the effectiveness of other people.

II. THE BIG PICTURE OF HIGH SCHOOL REFORM

The Restructuring Agenda

The strategies shared here are not sure-fire; nor are they equally available to all schools or communities. Some high schools may not have any vocational faculty (the education reforms of the 1980s resulted in the elimination of many vocational programs). Others may have budgetary crises or teacher contracts that obviate the possibility of considering reduced teaching loads or new roles for teachers. Certainly some communities are more resource rich than others in terms of the number of potential partners. The challenge is to figure out how to tap the potential that exists for providing vital educational experiences for young people, experiences that extend beyond the walls of the school.

It is somewhat encouraging to see the degree to which restructuring is now on the agenda of an increasing number of high schools. For close to a century, the high school has been a very tradition-bound institution. Many of the institutional "givens"—from requirements about "average teaching load" (the number of students a teacher instructs each term) to the scheduling of the high school day and year, stand in the way of work-based and project-based learning. It is difficult to envision students doing coursework that is fully integrated with real work if no period is longer than forty-five or fifty minutes, or if students are always taking disconnected courses, or if no credit is available for this work.

Ideally, restructuring efforts in a school go hand-in-hand with the introduction of more project-based methodologies and more integration of academic and vocational learning. Among the restructuring proposals surfacing in many schools are ones focusing on site-based management, increased "consumer" choice, smaller learning communities, more active learning, increased professionalism of teachers, and alternative means of assessment. In a study of eight schools that were "early innovators" in the movement to integrate vocational and academic education, a group of researchers found that the schools were able to use their integration efforts to give focus and more specific content to all of the proposed restructuring reforms.[9]

Thus, for example, clustering students by career or other themes and/or creating school-within-a-school academy structures is one way to achieve smaller learning communities and increased choice for students. When groups of academic and vocational teachers work together to combine their content into new curricular projects, their professionalism is enhanced. Most substantial approaches to integration depend on teachers collaborating on the development of curriculum materials and the design of local programs related to career interests, points out Norton Grubb, a University of California economist who has written extensively on curriculum integration. In Grubb's view, focusing schools on broadly defined occupational purposes and integrating academic and vocational education provides a way to undo many of the weaknesses of the "shopping mall" model of high school.[10]

Of course, the reality in the schools makes this a complex undertaking. Academic and vocational integration, and project-based methodologies are sometimes seen as competing with, rather than helping to focus other broad-based structural reforms. Restructuring is unlikely to result in the removal of obstacles to "venturing out" unless the school people and parents involved in these efforts share a broad vision of the desirability (and perhaps the urgency) of moving towards more community-oriented, project-based, and work-centered forms of learning. If the teachers advocating such a vision are seen as a special interest group, representing "just a few kids" in a marginal program, restructuring will not result in more authentic teaching or learning.

Changing the Schedule: Teachers who do integrative projects are among the most vocal advocates in a school for changing the schedule. In my visits to schools over the last year, I have been struck by how many schools are in the process of changing or at least debating changes in the schedule. After years of offering seven or eight periods per day, each approximately forty-two to fifty minutes, many high schools have recently made, or are considering a change, particularly toward some form of block scheduling—increasing the length of the periods by having courses meet every other day or only for a semester rather than a year.

Because the school schedule also structures the work day of teachers, they tend to have very strong feelings about which schedule is best. Teachers often ask for advice as to the best schedule for doing projects or for providing integrated work-based learning experiences outside of school. While some schedules certainly seem more "friendly" to project methodologies than others, in my experience it is less important to become identified with advocacy for a particular schedule than it is to focus everyone on agreeing to certain priorities. The schedule should promote more coherence and focus in the student's day; provide day-of-the-week predictability for ensuring that the school can interact with the outside world; permit the clustering of small groups of students and teachers; include regular common planning time for teacher teams and at least some long blocks of instructional time. If teachers agree to such design priorities, the exact length of periods and configuration of blocks will not matter.

Career clusters or academies: The formation of career academies or cluster teams built around broad career themes is a restructuring reform that is directly beneficial to integrative projects. In both the ComAcad and Oakland Health Academy, teachers are able to envision more permeable walls between the school and community because they work together in career academy or cluster teams with the same group of students for a significant portion of the day. The team agrees on the types of local experts who would enrich an integrated unit of study by providing a real world context for cross-disciplinary project work. In a sense, an academy or cluster structure provides a natural design team of teachers working with the same group of students over several years. Still, the structure itself does not guarantee permeability with the outside world, nor does it necessarily follow that teachers function as a design team.

It is important to try to ensure that there is both provision for clustered teaching blocks and common meeting time. Lacking regular opportunities to dream and design together, teachers are likely to remain within the boundaries of the traditional curriculum, even within a small learning community. Again, the issue is not just achieving a particular structural design, but articulating the purpose of the design and the belief system behind it. Common planning time is not just there for sharing information on students the teachers have in common. Teachers need to see their team as having both the responsibility and the authority to bring more coherence to the educational experiences of their students by connecting learning in school to learning outside of school.

Beyond Carnegie Units: One of the most serious barriers to curricular and pedagogical change is the system of Carnegie units and the ways credit is given in our schools. Projects such as those described here are, of necessity, multidisciplinary. Yet in most schools, the system for giving credits is discipline-based. If the chemistry class conducts a study of water quality, the science that students learn will be recognized in the course credit they get. But what if their study also involves them in the many potential social studies lessons about town government or the ownership of land and water rights? What if they end up writing and giving speeches at the town hall or organizing a petition campaign? There will probably not be a way for the chemistry teacher to recognize the learning in these other areas.

Some of the class and individual projects described in this book carry no academic credit at all, offering only "elective" or "technical" credits. In the case of internship projects and senior projects where a lot of writing and oral presentation is involved, students might be offered language arts credit, while the actual domain-based work they do as part of the project goes unrecognized. Usually, credit is based on the certification of the teacher in charge. If an English teacher leads the senior project seminar, the credit will probably be in English. If a vocational teacher is in charge (as in Cityworks), students can only get technical credit for the course.

One interim step in addressing that problem is to have students invite one of their academic teachers to serve as an advisor to their project. In exchange for playing a role in defining the project, the teacher agrees to count the student's work on the project as a part of their grade in the course. This is a strategy currently being tried by the Cornell Youth and Work Program and the career internship program at Noble High School in Maine. (See chapter 3 for more information on these programs.)

High schools have not been quick to embrace more ambitious reforms in alternative assessment and graduation requirements, such as graduation portfolios and performance-based assessments that tie credit more to what students can demonstrate they have learned than to the particular certification of the teachers in whose classes they sat. Thus far, it has been mostly in small schools, such as the Central Park East Secondary School in New York City (CPESS), that such methods have replaced more traditional graduation requirements.

One of the most common reasons high school counselors and teachers give for not changing credit systems is that the colleges will not accept alternative methods as legitimate. The assumption is that they (the colleges) will accept only a traditional transcript, listing grades for the traditional programs of study. Concerns about college admission and college preparation are also leading some high schools to increase the number of Advanced Placement (A.P.) courses they offer. In some schools, this is making it even more difficult to garner support for alternative forms of instruction or assessment. For example, a student with a strong interest in health sciences cannot participate in a health academy because the time blocks conflict with A.P. biology. A teacher who has planned to take all of her students to a nearby pond to do water quality tests learns that several of the students cannot go because they will fail their A.P. American History class if they miss a session.

One strategy that the Oakland Health Academy has used to maintain a hetereogeneous group of students is to offer its own alternatives to A.P. courses. For example, students can earn college credit in psychology by signing up for extensive fieldwork with developmentally disabled teens, combined with a course in human development, offered after school at Oakland Tech by a community college professor. Such a course does not carry the same opportunity to "place out" of a particular freshman course in any college, but it does give students a chance to try their hand at a college level course, and show the colleges to which they are applying that they are serious about doing the work.

In all of the debates within a school community about "what colleges want" or what they will accept, it is important to point out that there are thousands of different colleges, public and private, large and small, with vastly different traditions and expectations. There have always been a few colleges which are themselves quite innovative—for example, using a cooperative education model of joining school and work, using performance-based systems of credits, or offering experiential and community-based programming. Although I've seen no research on the subject, my own review of college catalogues suggests that an increasing number of colleges are themselves no longer "purely academic," and are offering new integrative majors (e.g., in career-oriented areas such as environmental studies), internships, and other routes to develop real world or "marketable skills."

If nothing else, colleges are being forced to make such changes, as parents become angered by the high costs associated with a college education, and the increasing number of college graduates floundering in our economy. This is a somewhat ironic situation, given how many of these same parents are afraid to allow anything that seems practical or vocational in the high school curriculum. Perhaps as more colleges move in that direction, it will also become more acceptable for high schools to offer such programs of study.

It is also important to point out that even the most traditional colleges are sometimes willing to negotiate ways around the standard transcript and testing requirements in order to accommodate innovative high schools. For example, schools based entirely on performance-based graduation standards, such as CPESS, are working successfully with college admissions officers to find ways of representing what their students have accomplished. The college-going rate from CPESS rivals that of well-regarded suburban schools.

Finally, although such programs may not give students an exactly standard transcript, they do give young people a priceless resource—adults in the community who are ready to advocate for them, write references, put in an important phone call, and generally help with the whole process of applying for college admission or for jobs. The benefits of adult advocacy on behalf of a particular student is likely to far outweigh any problems that might be created by a deviation from the standard transcript.

The Standards Movement

The national push to raise the standards in our schools, as exemplified in the Goals 2000 legislation, and the many pronouncements of policy leaders about the importance of high expectations and academic rigor, creates another set of opportunities and some major pitfalls for school-based advocates of work-based and project-based learning. One of the major results of standards-based systemic reforms has been to strengthen the role of the national subject matter councils and associations. Within the high schools, this can translate into reinforcing the divisions between the subject matter departments, which may then result in additional barriers to multidisciplinary, integrative approaches.

Some subject matter associations, such as the National Council of Teachers of Mathematics (NCTM), are emphasizing aspects of their discipline that go far beyond content coverage. Thus, for example, both NCTM and the National Science Education Standards refer in their documents to the importance of focusing on in-depth learning of a limited number of powerful concepts, emphasizing understanding, reasoning, and problem solving, rather than memorization of facts, terminology, and algorithms. They emphasize the value of engaging students in meaningful activities that help them to construct and apply their knowledge of key science and mathematics concepts to real-world phenomena.

At the local level, however, where teachers and administrators worry about scores on various state tests and national standardized tests, the pressure to raise standards is most likely to result in an increased emphasis on the coverage of traditional academic subject matter. Teachers pushing for school-to-work programming or integrative projects are seen as a special interest group for vocational education or the lowest track; to the extent they talk about "all students" learning in this way, their ideas may even be seen by parents or other teachers as a threatening distraction from the academic agenda.

Just how real this dilemma is for teachers can be seen in the questions asked in workshops, even by those who see value in school-to-work approaches: "What about my honors classes?" "How can I do this and not shortchange the academic content of the course?" "How do we create real-work projects that meet high academic expectations?" "Will colleges approve of this type of program?" "If I use portfolios, how will my students do in college?"

In response to concerns about the quantity and quality of academic learning in programs incorporating work-based or field study approaches, I am tempted to ask: "Compared to what?" At this point, schools are relegating far too many students to courses that prepare them neither for college nor productive employment. In some subject areas, such as science, few students end up feeling they are "good enough" at mastering the content matter to pursue coursework beyond the minimum requirements for high school graduation or college entrance. Similarly, it is often only in "honors" English classes that students are invited to grapple with the great concerns of the humanities. (See chapters 4 and 5 for a full discussion of these issues.)

In contrast, programs that help students connect what they are learning to the world, and particularly the world of work, appear to have the potential to increase significantly the number of students taking demanding courses while in high school. The Oakland Health Academy is a good example of that. Instead of simply meeting minimum requirements in science, students complete advanced courses in human physiology and bioscience. Other promising programs report similar results, particularly when the courses themselves, as in Oakland, make use of innovative methods such as case studies and projects.

Still, if we cannot successfully address the concerns raised by teachers and parents, work-based and project-based programs will intensify, rather than mitigate the pernicious effects of the tracking system that is so prevalent in high schools. Many people still seem to share the belief that school-to-work programs are the latest attempt to provide an appropriate (if lesser) education for the non-college bound. This is neither the intent of the School To Work Opportunities Act, nor the reality in many communities starting school-to-work programs.

The only way through this dilemma is for school-to-work and standards-based reformers to come together around a vision of a more engaged, deeper, and richer education. As Margaret Vickers points out in chapter 4 of this volume, if "better" science means more abstract science, the result will be that very few students will continue their studies in the sciences and that most will only take a few years of high school science and will remain in lower level courses that are watered down versions of academic subject matter. The opportunity will be lost to redefine academic rigor to mean not just that students know a lot of concepts and facts, but that they know how to use their knowledge in real-world settings.

In a few communities, school-to-work reformers have become involved at the district level in defining new learning standards, assessments, and graduation requirements. The result has been policy documents that incorporate an emphasis on more applied and integrated learning. In Boston, for example, the new learning standards include both the mastery of disciplinary content, and the development of approaches and methods of disciplinary inquiry, which can be acquired in project-based learning. The graduation requirements stipulate a series of products students must complete and document by the end of their senior year. Because such requirements are being phased in over a four-year period, it is too early to tell how such standards and requirements will be implemented in the schools. But at least there is a platform on which advocates for integrative projects can build.

A Changing Economy

For the past several years, businesses have been saying with increasing vehemence that they need a more prepared and educated workforce to emerge from America's schools. Thus far, this is not a message that has had much effect in the schools, other than to reinforce the already strong push to get students to apply to college. There is a tendency among school personnel to be suspicious of what businesses say, especially if they feel that schools are being blamed for what seem to be economic issues and problems.

In fact, criticisms of business pressure on or involvement in schools is also in evidence in the press. The basic argument is that this trend is subverting the purposes of education away from broad preparation for democratic citizenship and towards more narrow, vocational skills, enabling businesses to hire a more docile workforce so that they do not have to spend much money on training. These same views make some educational commentators suspicious of school-to-work arrangements as still another way that businesses get their foot in the school door.[11]

Unfortunately, these accusations and arguments on both sides obfuscate the reality that there are indeed changing skill requirements in the workforce that are starting to have profound effects on American young people. A number of case studies have been conducted which describe the work content and processes of various jobs. Such studies indicate that decisions and quality control are moving away from middle managers and more to the "front-line workers," who consequently are engaging in less well-defined activities and are expected to be actively problem solving and contributing ideas and initiatives to furthering organizational goals.

These findings were confirmed most recently by two economists, Richard Murnane and Frank Levy. In their recent book, *Teaching the New Basic Skills,*[12] they explain how it can be true at the very same time that: 1) schools are doing a better job than they used to (e.g., standardized test scores are modestly higher today than they were fifteen years ago and the gap between African-American and white students has shrunk somewhat); and 2) that there are serious problems in our schools that demand immediate fixing.

The problem as they describe it is that the economy is changing much faster than the rate of improvement in the schools. Murnane and Levy estimate that half of recent high school graduates have an education that is no longer in demand: "During the past twenty years the skills required to succeed in the economy have changed radically, but the skills taught in most schools have changed very little." The end result, conclude the two economists is that a high school diploma is no longer a "ticket to the middle class."

In their study, Murnane and Levy singled out five companies that offer relatively high wage jobs in industries (e.g., automobile manufacturing and insurance) that have long offered a living wage to young people with a high school diploma. In the hiring, training, promotion practices, and policies of these companies, the researchers found a remarkable consistency in the skills that they sought out and rewarded in their workers.

The "new basic skills" as Murnane and Levy have called them include:[13]

- The ability to read at the ninth-grade level or higher.
- The ability to do math at the ninth-grade level or higher.
- The ability to solve semistructured problems where hypotheses must be formed and tested.
- The ability to work in groups with persons of various backgrounds.
- The ability to communicate effectively, both orally and in writing.
- The ability to use personal computers to carry out simple tasks like word processing.

Significantly, this list does not just emphasize the "hard" skills that are usually at the core of the "back to basics" agenda. Despite the fact that reading and math skills are easier (and considerably cheaper) to measure, all five firms search for evidence of a broader set of abilities. Based on their own research, as well as surveys of managers in large metropolitan areas, Murnane and Levy conclude that skills such as problem solving and working in groups (labeled "soft" because they cannot be measured by multiple choice tests) are becoming increasingly important.

Their point is not that all workers are expected to show initiative and apply knowledge on the shop floor or in the office, but that these new basics are absolutely essential to earning a decent, "middle-class" wage. Workers who lack these skills are likely to earn much less over their working lives than those who do have these skills, according to Murnane and Levy. To find workers with the right set of skills, some companies have switched to hiring only college graduates, not because the jobs require knowledge learned in college, note the researchers, but because the companies feel they cannot be confident that a high school diploma indicates students have the requisite abilities.

Nearly half of American high school students graduate without the level of reading and math skills required by the five companies studied. Murnane and Levy arrive at this conclusion by comparing the tests several of these companies give as part of their hiring process to the National Assessment of Educational Progress tests in reading and mathematics. An applicant for a good entry level job in those firms (e.g., a production associate) would have to score roughly three-hundred points or more on both of the NAEP tests to meet the company cutoff. (Once applicants meet the cutoff, their exact score is not considered.) They found that only three of five students could do this on the 1992 NAEP math test, and only two of five could do it on the reading test.[14]

Murnane and Levy provide evidence that a young person's mastery of these skills matters in the labor market, although not necessarily in the first job new graduates get. Looking at individuals whose highest qualification was a high school diploma, the researchers found a relationship between wages six years after high school and the scores high school seniors got on a basic mathematics test at school. In one analysis, the researchers compared those finishing high school in 1972 to those finishing in 1980. Six years after high school, for both groups, the higher the old test score, the higher the earnings reported. Most significantly, the test scores made *more* of a difference in the 1980s than they did in the 1970s. Graduates in the class of 1972 with strong math scores earned 53 cents per hour more than those with low scores, while for the class of 1980, the difference was $1.33 per hour. The researchers find similar patterns when students' scores on a test of reading comprehension are used.

Furthermore, the boost to wages associated with strong basic skills explains a significant percentage of what most people assume to be a wage premium only available to those who graduate from college. One of the reasons for the strong "Go to college" message of the 1990s is an increasing gap between the earnings of high school and college graduates. Between 1978 and 1986, the difference in wages of a twenty-four-year-old female with a B.A. and one with only a high school diploma increased by 20 percent and for males by 50 percent. But, the researchers find that this wage premium decreases significantly when they control statistically for each student's score on the math test taken as high school senior.

Does this mean that it may not be as essential as most parents and teachers think it is for all young people to go to college? Only if public schools can figure out how to ensure that all students learn the new basic skills in twelve years, rather than the fourteen or more it now takes. This is not an argument against students going to college, but rather an argument against the waste of valuable years (and dollars) on skills that could and should be developed sooner.

Historically, schools have offered watered down academics to the "non-college-bound," delivered via pedagogical approaches that emphasize worksheets and drills. If this approach were effective, one would expect more than half of the seniors to be prepared for the kinds of basic skills tests given by companies recruiting entry-level workers for career track jobs. Yet many students continue to graduate from high school without the "hard" skills. At the same time, the individualized nature of traditional instruction and its priority on getting the right answer does nothing to develop the "soft skills" that Murnane and Levy find are being rewarded in today's workplace.

Although well over two-thirds of high school students now go on to college, only one-third are adequately prepared for college level work, according to another researcher, Kenneth Gray, who bases his conclusion on a review of both NAEP test results and high school transcripts. Gray also notes that 90 percent of private and 95 percent of public colleges offer remedial courses, and over half of all college entrants enroll in them. Although such courses help students make up for skill deficits, enrollment in them is still a powerful predictor of dropping out and defaulting on their loans.

Based on such data, it is possible to make a very strong case for building curriculum around integrative projects that are work-based and/or community-focused. The types of projects described in this book clearly require students to practice the "hard skills." Students write journals, logs, newsletters, and brochures, as well as more traditional papers. They use computers to do research and to present their work; they analyze data, make graphs, and use spreadsheets. In addition, the hard skills are reinforced in a way that also builds the soft skills. Collaboration, teamwork, and communication are all vital components to completing a complex group project.

To support such arguments, those of us advocating this position need to become better at capturing and documenting what students are learning through projects. Even granting that standardized tests provide some measure of mathematics and reading skills (and there are certainly many who argue that the tests are not accurate indicators even of these skills), these tests offer little or no information on all of the other skills included in the new basics: communication skills, teamwork, the ability to handle semi-structured problems, the ability to use computer technology appropriately, or even writing (unless there is an open-ended writing sample, which many tests do not include). In fact, Diamond Star Motors' job entrance exam showed no correlation whatsoever between workers' scores on soft-skill assessments they gave and the workers' scores on the multiple choice cognitive skills test.[15]

Increasingly, school districts have begun to recognize the need for the types of skills listed among the "new basics." In a recent survey of four large urban communities, Jobs for the Future found that all four required some version of the "soft skills" as well as the hard ones on the list. Still, there is a great deal of work to do in translating this into school-based practice. One of the most important tasks is to become more explicit about the mix of skills we are trying to teach by using projects and to develop a variety of ways to measure whether students have achieved those skills.

There are some examples of assessment instruments that measure such skills as "being a collaborative worker." Some are in the form of rubrics, with characteristics listed on a scale of novice to expert (usually one to four). There are others in the form of teacher observation logs, where the teacher checks on what groups are doing, making notations regarding a student's communication skills or problem-solving skills, (as they see them demonstrated). Still other instruments are in the form of self-assessement instruments for students or more open-ended writing prompts. At this point, the best approach is probably to use a variety of such methods.

Some schools have begun to experiment with including career portfolios as a graduation requirement. These usually include such items as a resume, cover letter, sample of a filled out job application and college application. An important next step would be also to include the results of the assessments and self-assessments described above, as well as an account written by the student of a work-based or field-based project that s/he carried out and an evaluation from at least one outside supervisor who has seen the student on the job or in a community placement.

The Small Schools Movement

The struggle to change an existing institution—especially one as large and bureaucratic as the public high school—can seem overwhelming. Creating a new school presents a different set of challenges and opportunities. In the last few years, several small high schools in New York City have caught the public eye and encouraged similar experiments elsewhere. For example, the education reform act in Massachusetts makes it possible for parents or teachers with an idea for a new school to apply for charter school status. Each year a small number of such schools gain approval to begin. Once approved for a charter, the school receives funds for each student equal to the average cost per child in the sending district—monies that are then lost to that district. Perhaps, in part, to stave off the departure of dollars from the city schools, Boston now has a provision to allow "pilot schools" to form within the public system.

Although the terms used to describe these new schools, and the exact provisions for funding them and regulating their quality may differ, a number of districts and states have similar policies to encourage the formation of small schools. The small size (most have four-hundred students or under) means the school is less likely to be a world unto itself, and hence, the surrounding community becomes a more attractive and necessary source of stimulation, interaction, and experience. Furthermore, many of the barriers to connecting with the outside world are removed: it becomes a much simpler matter to make arrangements to go out, from the scheduling of teacher and student time to finding work-based placements.

Of course, this is not the first time in recent history that there has been a movement to start small schools. In the late 1960s and early 1970s hundreds of alternative schools were started, mainly in reaction to large impersonal institutions and bureaucratic modes of acting and thinking. Early on in my own career in education, I spent ten years creating and teaching in such a school. In fact, many of my ideas about the potential of connecting school to work, and of doing projects that link school learning to community needs derive from my experiences at The Group School. Not surprisingly, it proved very hard to sustain these schools, most of which were not funded through the local tax base.

Today new small schools are being built on a somewhat sturdier financial foundation, since most are directly funded via state coffers and local school funds. In addition, anyone with a laptop computer can go onto the internet and hence have access, literally, to a world of information. Although it is not yet clear exactly what this will mean in educating youth, it does seem evident that it changes the economies of scale argument for large, comprehensive high schools.

One of the most intriguing of these new schools opened in the fall of 1996, in Providence, Rhode Island. The Metropolitan Regional Career and Technical Center (MET) is interesting because the curriculum is totally project-based and because of how it was formed and how it connects to a larger plan for state-wide school reform. In the summer of 1996, the legislature of the state of Rhode Island, approved start-up funds to accept the first group of students into the MET, a public high school with the legal status of a local education agency. Several years earlier, the voters had passed a $29 million bond issue for a statewide technical/vocational high school. Many people expected the process to follow the route a number of other states had taken in the 1970s, developing state-of-the-art facilities for technical education that would attract students from a fairly wide geographic area. Instead, the legislature accepted the results of an unusual planning process, involving Peter McWalters, the Commissioner of Education, and literally several hundred citizens of the state, and spearheaded by Dennis Littky and Elliot Washor.

Although both Littky and Washor had a long history of working in and reforming secondary schools, neither came from within the community of vocational education advocates or professionals. In his previous job as principal of Thayer High School in Winchester, New Hampshire, Littky had shepherded a rural school in a conservative community through some major changes of philosophy and structure. His work attracted national attention both because Thayer was held up as a best practice example by the

Coalition of Essential Schools and because the school board tried to fire Littky, whose successful struggle was described in a book (*Doc*) and a television movie of the week ("A Town Torn Apart").

Littky and Washor had come to Rhode Island as Annenberg Fellows of Brown University in order to work on designing a new urban high school. Their basic premise was that no high schools—vocational or academic— were doing enough to prepare young people to work and live in the world of the twenty-first century. "As a principal for nineteen years I'd been doing all the innovative things," says Littky. "We had a great advisor system, and we were working on integrated, interdisciplinary learning. I wasn't a critic from the outside saying 'this isn't working.' But I realized that the best examples of learning happened when the kids did real work or solved real problems, like when they registered people to vote, or developed new school rules, or apprenticed with someone in the community, or traveled and met people, or set up their own businesses."

Individual or Group Projects: Guiding Questions[16]

Problems: What are the problems or issues (on the job, in the school, or in the community) that you care about addressing? Why are they important to you? Who else are they important to and how do they view or experience them?

Personal Questions: What are your compelling questions about these problems/issues?

Goals: What product, service, or other action do you want to produce in relation to the problems? Who is the audience for the products or services? What does successful completion of the project look like to you?

Approaches: How does past experience or history help you solve this problem? How do observation and data collection; modeling and logic; different perspectives; trial and insight; or creativity help you solve this problem?

Tools: What skills and technologies are needed to complete the project? How will you go about getting the skills you need?

Steps and Tasks: What do you need to do in order to reach your goal and complete the project? What are the biggest priorities or hurdles to overcome? What needs to happen first? Next? Who else is needed to work with you? How will you hold one another accountable?

Logistics: What amount of time do you estimate it will take? What special facilities, equipment, or supplies do you need?

Ongoing Assessment: What kind of record would help you organize and keep track of your work? What would help you demonstrate what you are learning?

Final Evaluation: How will you show the results of your project? What criteria will you use? Who else should be involved in reviewing your work? How do you expect to use your new skills and knowledge after this project is completed?

The MET opened in the fall of 1996 with 52 ninth-graders. The plan is to continue growing in increments of 50, until it reaches 900 students. But even at full size, the design calls for each group of 50 to constitute its own home base or learning center. Littky feels very strongly that this is the way to maintain the personalization and organizational agility that are vital to the school's success. These features are very much in evidence today. Each student at the MET has an individual learning plan, built around his or her passions, interests, and needs. Students, parents, and teachers meet regularly to review what the student has done and to revise the plan. The MET is a school without any regularly scheduled classes. The main structure for learning is provided by individual and group projects, growing out of the student's internship experiences, and their evolving assessment of the needs and resources of their own community (the school) and of the larger community.

A group of 50 is small enough that teachers and students can start the day together. Each morning, everyone gathers for a "pick me up," which often consists of a student reading a poem or leading the group in a quick exercise, followed by announcements about the day's activities. What students do next depends on the day of the week and on their individual learning plans. They may meet in an advisory (twelve or fifteen students with one teacher), proceed directly to a community placement, or stay back at their "home base" to work on an individual or group project.

To receive approval for a project, students must submit a written proposal to their advisor, who then helps them clarify both the "what" and "how" of the work. If the project involves a worksite or field placement, an adult mentor from that site also contributes to the definition of the work. The availability of computers at the "home base" makes it possible for students to do research on the internet, as well as to create proposals and final written products with a polished look. The use of computers and video cameras is especially intense just before a presentation day. Periodically, students share the results of their efforts with peers, parents, teachers, mentors, and other invited guests.

The work is not graded, but staff at the school are trying to help students see their efforts in terms of three yardsticks—their own personal standards, school standards, and real-world standards. For example, a student might be preparing a questionnaire, preliminary to doing market research for a bakery where he is doing a work placement. If he is going to present the questionnaire at school, he knows that the standard is that it be word-processed, and accurately spelled and punctuated. But, he also becomes familiar with the real world standard for such instruments by talking to people who do market research for a living and looking at some of the surveys that they use. "This tells you what the work looks like when an expert does it; it gives you some perspective on where you are, where your skills are at this moment," explains Washor.

Although this is a very unusual design for a high school, Washor and Littky are quick to point out that many of these same elements can be found in home schooling, which is highly personalized, and in graduate schools like Oxford, where a student is expected to write a project proposal and then meet with the professor regularly to talk about the progress of the work. "We know that most kids do not learn sitting in a class with twenty-five or thirty people," notes Littky. "Kids learn around their passions."

One of the most unusual aspects of the MET is that it is part of a larger state-wide strategy to change high school education. Along with the school, Littky and Washor direct a nonprofit organization, called The Big Picture Company, which works closely with the Rhode Island State Department of Education (RIDE) to help all of the high schools in the state rethink their practices and policies. Thus far, a leadership center begun by The Big Picture and RIDE has sponsored a series of conversations, forums, and workshops—attended by teachers, principals, superintendents, and parents throughout the state.

Sessions range from workshops on portfolio assessment or project-based learning to targeted conversation among superintendents as to how they can help their districts set and carry out reform priorities. The idea is to use the MET as a "laboratory school" for the state, rather than a model of what everyone should be doing. Despite the fact that these sessions are usually held at four in the afternoon, hundreds of people have come, with representation from the majority of high schools in the state—evidence, as Littky puts it, that "there's clearly a need" for this kind of talk. Although it is much too soon to tell what effect the MET will have on the other schools, the idea of making the work public, from the beginning, and forming a broad network of people who take a direct interest in the work, sets this effort apart from the more typical (and understandable) tendency to build a wall of protection around a new, fledgling school.

Lessons from the 1970s

By opening themselves up to intense public scrutiny from the beginning, the MET staff are staking the future of their school on their ability to make a convincing case for their unusual mixture of work-based learning, mentoring, technology, community experiences, and personalization. Ultimately, the case rests on whether they can provide evidence that the school is indeed preparing graduates with the habits, skills, and knowledge necessary to succeed in college or at work. There is good reason to believe that they will be able to do so. Although what the MET is proposing takes advantage of new technology and new interest stirred up in the business community in support of school-to-work programs, there have been similar experiments in the not-so-distant past, producing evidence of good outcomes.

Here, for example, are excerpts from an article written over fifteen years ago about "experience-based career education" (EBCE). The first few paragraphs bear a striking resemblance to materials being produced by the MET: "While students in traditional programs attend classes all day, experience based career education students spend a major portion of their time on learning projects in the community. Activities are tailored to individual student needs, abilities, learning styles and goals. Students are guided in their learning by ongoing relationships with working adults. . . . Subjects needed for graduation are learned as much as possible through individualized projects, planned for each student in the context of working life in the community. . . . Staff are managers and facilitators of student learning, not teachers in the traditional sense."[17]

Sample Student's Day[18]

8:30 Jack arrives at the learning center, signs in and checks his mail box. There's a note in it to see Sue, a staff person, to review a project and negotiate target dates. Sue is with another student so Jack goes to the study area to work on a fire escape plan for his Emergencies competency.

9:00 Sue says she is ready to talk. They spend twenty minutes looking over activities and setting dates for their completion. Jack thinks one activity will take a lot longer than Sue expects it to take; they talk about it and set some interim target dates for portions of the activity. After the first interim date they will meet again to renegotiate some of the activity's requirement if it does prove to take too long.

9:30 Jack walks with several other students two blocks to the fire station where they have an appointment with the fire marshall to demonstrate skills they have acquired for the Emergencies competency. Jack shows the marshall his fire escape plan and demonstrates fundamental first-aid techniques. The marshall signs competency certification forms for Jack and one of his companions. The third student was asked to return again after more practice in bandaging techniques.

10:30 Jack takes a city bus to a daycare center where he's made an appointment to spend an hour on a special placement observing story time. He has a project pending on children's literature and needs to research different techniques for telling stories to small children. On the way he starts his journal entry for that week.

12:00 Lunchtime at the learning center.

1:00 Jack gets a ride in the program van to his learning level site—a local landscape nursery. There he spends the rest of the afternoon on several project activities for that site: an experiment in plant growth and practice at the counter dealing with customer questions and ringing up sales.

3:00 Jack has his employer instructor sign his time slip and takes a bus home.

First developed in 1971, the idea of experienced-based career education was sponsored by the National Institute of Education (now defunct, but in the 1960s and 1970s the research arm of the United States Department of Education), and then developed and implemented through the four regional laboratories (still funded to carry out research and development for the U.S. Department of Education). In other words, there was some governmental and institutional support behind the premise that a comprehensive curriculum exists outside the walls of the school.

Each lab established at least one demonstration site between 1971 and 1975; these received substantial federal funding, operated under common guidelines, and were carefully monitored to assure compliance with the

EBCE model. Furthermore, program and student outcomes at each site were carefully evaluated by the labs themselves as well as by the Educational Testing Service (ETS). The ETS evaluation was comprehensive, employing multiple measures including the Comprehensive Test of Basic Skills, in-depth interviews with students in the EBCE programs and students who applied but did not end up going (the control group), survey questionnaires of teachers, parents, business people, and students, and ethnographic studies by anthropologists.[19]

The good news is that this research turned up very positive outcomes for students. Among their conclusions: compared to the control group, for example, students in the EBCE programs felt significantly more confident that they had some control over their choice of careers, were knowledgeable about a wider variety of careers, and knew more of the required characteristics and abilities necessary for entry into a career path. While there was no significant difference between the two groups in their scores on tests of reading or math achievement, the EBCE students were better able to respond orally to complex questions raised by the interviewers. Other more local studies revealed similar results. For example, a study of Philadelphia students conducted by Research for Better Schools (1975–77) found that students in EBCE for two years were not only superior to control group students in career maturity, learning-related attitudes, and self concept, but also surpassed them in reading comprehension.[20]

Building a Constituency for Change

These results lead to an obvious question: Why weren't these ideas embraced by more people twenty years ago? Why do they still seem "radical" today? In most places, educators saw EBCE as an alternative for a few students (often those who were lower-achieving) rather than a way to reorganize the way education was delivered to many students. Where the ideas were brought into the main institution of the high school, they were watered down into little more than a system for enhancing career awareness. The time was not ripe for the basic assumption of EBCE—that the educational environment itself should and could be restructured to take advantage both of the value of direct experience and the special potential of community institutions to help young people prepare for adult work and life.

There is some reason for cautious optimism today. The fact that the economy itself is going through major restructuring and the enormity of the shifts that are occurring in the nature of work are contributing to a climate that can support similarly fundamental changes in the schools. In addition to growing numbers of educators who see the importance of going "beyond tinkering," business groups have become powerful advocates for restructuring schools. Although there is not yet a broad constituency for making such changes, several factors may contribute to its growth.

Parents tend to be conservative about changing the schools their children attend, especially when they see their kids learning as much (and many of the same things) as they did. But parents are also workers in our changing economy. If you ask a group of adults how many of them are in organizations that have restructured in the past five years, many hands go up. While this might not immediately transfer into an impulse to change the schools their children attend, over time, they will become aware of the mismatch in skills and hence more open to considering other models of schooling.

In the throes of economic upheaval and change, we may not yet have discovered a metaphor for high school as powerful as the one provided by the assembly line of the industrial era. But current attempts to personalize learning, to eliminate layers of bureaucracy and flatten out the hierarchies, to tranform large high schools into smaller, more autonomous units where student groupings, schedules, activities, and assessment tools are created and recreated to take advantage of learning opportunities—all have their analogues in major sectors of the United States economy.

Today, the assembly line no longer represents all that is modern, powerful, and efficient. Perhaps the time has come when we can remove its legacy from our high schools. Economists tell us that our long-term health and prosperity—personal and collective—depend upon a different organization of work, one in which employees frame problems, design their own tasks, plan, construct, evaluate outcomes, and cooperate in finding new solutions to problems. Yet, the schools that seem so familiar and inevitable to us today continue to reward individuals for performing well on tests that measure the passive accumulation of bits and pieces of knowledge.

Cognitive scientists, such as Howard Gardner, tell us that a person's intelligence is not something that can be measured by a single score on a test, but rather that each person has the potential to *become* smart in multiple domains. The determining factor in whether an individual reaches his or her potential is the extent to which the community values and nurtures the abilities of that person. In other words, we will not have a more capable, intelligent workforce until schools, working with communities, find a way to help all young people discover their interests and develop their intelligences.

Of course, the purposes of schooling go far beyond preparing students for economic success. As one of the only surviving public institutions, schools also have a critical role to play in preparing young people for the demands of citizenship. Although always great, these demands continue to increase. To ensure a vital democracy in the coming century, the next generations will need to understand and evaluate complex issues and alternatives, and find ways to live in harmony with others of different backgrounds and value systems.

These words seem almost impossibly idealistic in our world of increasing social complexity and decreasing social support, where children are left to fend for themselves at younger and younger ages. But we will never mend the rips in our social fabric if we do not enlist community-wide support for developing the skills and talents of all students. There is no way to know whether the programs described in this book—either those attempting to transform existing institutional arrangements, or those starting anew—will succeed in creating a new model of high school. We only know how urgent it is to do so.

NOTES

1. Judith Warren Little, "What Teachers Learn in High School: Professional Development and the Redesign of Vocational Education, *Education and Urban Society* 27: 3 (May, 1995), 288.

2. Little, 288.

3. Samuel Everett, ed. *The Community School,* Paul Pierce, "The School and the Community It Serves," 110.

4. Lynn Olson, "School to Work," pre-publication manuscript, chapter 5, p. 2.

5. Hilary Kopp and Richard Kazis, *Promising Practices,* A Study of Ten School-to-Career Programs (Jobs for the Future, 1995), 8.

6. Edward Pauly, Rachel Pedraza, and Hilary Kopp, *Home Grown Progress: The Evolution of Innovative School-to-Work Programs* (unpublished manuscript, Sept. 1996).

7. Judith Warren Little, "Traditions of Teaching and the Transformation of Work Education," in W. Norton Grubb, ed. *Education Through Occupations in American High Schools: The Challenges of Implementing Curriculum Integration,* Volume 2 (New York: Teachers College Press, 1995), 59.

8. Judith Warren Little, "What Teachers Learn in High School: Professional Development and the Redesign of Vocational Education," *Education and Urban Society* 27: 3 (May, 1995), 283.

9. Kimberly Ramsey, Rick Eden, Cathleen Stasz, and Susan Bodilly, "Integrating Vocational and Academic Education: Lessons from Early Innovators," in Grubb, ed. *Education Through Occupations,* Volume 2, 7–34.

10. Erika Nielsen Andrew and W. Norton Grubb, "The Power of Curriculum Integration: Its Relationship to Other Reforms," in Grubb, ed. *Education Through Occupations,* Volume 1, 39–56.

11. Gerald W. Bracey, "Schools Should Not Prepare Students for Work," *Rethinking Schools,* Summer, 1996, 11.

12. Richard J. Murnane and Frank Levy, *Teaching the New Basic Skills: Principles for Educating Children to Thrive in a Changing Economy* (New York: Martin Kessler Books, The Free Press, 1996).

13. Murnane and Levy, *Teaching the New Basic Skills,* 32.

14. Murnane and Levy, *Teaching the New Basic Skills,* 36.

15. Murnane and Levy, *Teaching the New Basic Skills,* 37.

16. Abridged from The Big Picture Company: Implementation Plan for the Metropolitan Center: Discussion Draft (Dec. 1995).

17. Education and Work Program, "Experience-Based Career Education," (Portland, Oregon: Northwest Regional Educational Laboratory), 2.

18. "Experience-Based Career Education," 3.

19. Thomas R. Owens, "Experience-Based Career Education: Summary and Implications of Research and Evaluation Findings," *Child and Youth Services* 4: 3/4 (1982).

20. Owens, "Experience-Based Career Education."

Contributors

Robert C. Riordan is a long-time teacher, administrator, and teacher trainer. He was named National School to Work Practitioner of the Year in 1994. He is now Project Director for *Changing the Subject: the New Urban High School,* a joint initiative of the Big Picture Company and the U.S. Department of Education.

Adria Steinberg has worked for 30 years to understand why adolescents disengage from school and what educators can do about it. She has pursued this work as a teacher, curriculum designer, founder of an alternative high school, writer/editor of *The Harvard Education Letter*, and academic coordinator of a high school nationally recognized for integrating academic and vocational approaches to learning. She currently directs a project on quality work-based learning for Jobs for the Future, a national policy, research, and school-to-work development group in Boston, Massachusetts.

Margaret Vickers is a Senior Scientist at TERC in Cambridge, Massachusetts, and Director of Working to Learn, a program through which students learn challenging science and technology concepts by integrating classroom learning with relevant workplace and community contexts. She is also a co-author, with Senta Raizen and others, of *Technology Education in the Classroom: Understanding the Designed World.*

Index

L

language arts, 71-72, 134-39, 170
Layton, David, 115-16
learning performance standards, 79
"Learning Site Analysis Form" (NWREL),
87-88
learning space as studio, 18, 165, 166
LeGault, Joel, 52
Lesley College, 82, 134-36
Levy, Frank, 175-77
life vs. school, 2-6, 54-56
literature, work-based learning in, 134-39
Littky, Dennis, 180-81
Little, Judith Warren, 156, 166
Lividoti, Tom, 52-53
lowered expectations, avoiding, 16, 17,
105-106, 123-25, 166, 177-78

M

MacDonald, Joe, 96
McLaughlin, Milbury, 63
Manpower Development Resource
Center, 165
manual training, 16-17
mapping backward into disciplines, 27
market analysis project, 97
Masters, Edgar Lee, 135
mathematics, 110, 113-14, 118-25
mediation training, 65
Meier, Deborah, 61
Mejia-Blau, Javi, 41, 61
Metropolitan Education and Career
Training Center (MET), xvii, 180-84
middle-school, community projects in, 58
mini-projects, 83-84
Montero, Javier, 133
Morales, Dio, 88
Morrison, Toni, 8
motivation vs. challenge, 2
multicultural education, 139-40, 153
multimedia projects, 8-9
Murnane, Richard, 175

N

National Assessment of Educational
Progress (NAEP) tests, 176, 178
National Association for the
Advancement of Colored People,
50-51
National Association of Manufacturers,
14
National Center for Improving High
School Education, 118

National Center for Research in
Vocational Education (NCRVE), 75,
160
National Center for Restructuring
Education, Schools, and Teaching
(NCREST), 95
National Council of Teachers of
Mathematics (NCTM), 172-73
National Education Association, 14
National Institute of Education, 185-86
National Science Education Standards,
111, 172-73
Nation at Risk, A, 77
Newmann, Fred, 103-106
Noble High School, 109-25, 170
Northwestern Regional Education
Laboratory, 87-88

O

Olson, Lynn, 164
opposition to school-to-work, xiii
oral history, 153
"output," student response as, 15-16
Outward Bound, 161

P

panelists for senior project committees,
92-93, 95-96
para-professional staff, 165
partnerships
with community or industry, 11-14,
33-35, 38-39, 44-66, 76-86, 160
creating, 163-65
with supervisors, 113-14
with universities, 56-57, 59, 66
Pathways program, 98-101
pedagogy of place, 47-48
Penrose, Billy, 80-81
performance-based graduation, 172
Perkins, Carl D., Vocational Education
and Applied Technology Act of
1990, x-xii
Pew Charitable Trusts, 109
Physical Sciences Study Committee
(PSSC), 116, 117-18
Plato, 4
Polaroid Corporation, 80, 130-33, 163
poor study habits, 1
portfolio-based assessment, 38-39,
94-96, 179
presentations, oral, 84
Private Industry Council, 77-79, 102
problem-solving strategies, 22

INDEX

defining, 23
design principles for, 20-39
individual vs. group, 181-82
increasing complexity of, 10
as instructional strategy, 29
in internships, 80-86
mini-projects, 83-84
proposals for, 11
"real enough," 27
selection of, 88-92
senior projects, 12-13, 30-31, 66, 92-101
strategies for, 70-71
teams in, 11-14, 33
project-based learning
and academics, 25-28
and disengagement, 1-6
programs in, 5-20
vs. projects as demonstration, 29
as risky, 37
Project Zero, Harvard, 26
Protech collaboration, 77-79
purposeful contexts for learning, xi

Q

quality work, conditions for, 36-37, 102-103
Quality Work-Based Learning Network, 102-103

R

Rachel's Children (Kozol), 55
racism, 133, 139
Raizen, Senta, 119
Ranya, Rohit, 71-72
"real enough" projects, 27, 160
real time vs. school time, 54-56, 71-72
Red Cross, 12
Reid-Cunningham, Allison, 81-82
Research for Better Schools, 186
Resnick, Lauren, 106, 125
resources, 165-67
Responsive Schools Project, Institute of Responsive Education, 44
restructuring of high schools, 155, 167-72
Rhode Island Department of Education, 183-84
Rindge School of Technical Arts, x-xii, xiii-xv, xviii, 5-6, 14-20, 41, 47-56, 60, 80, 91, 157-58, 162-63, 165-67
Riordan, Robert C., xvi-xvii, 28, 129-54
Rodene, Fritz, 143-44
Rosenstock, Larry, x-xi, 131, 165

rural communities, projects in, 42-47, 67
Rural Entrepreneurship Through Action Learning (REAL), 47
Rusk County Committee on Aging, 42

S

scaffolding, 10, 30
schedules
issues in, 159-61
restructuring, 169, 182
Scheffler, Israel, 62
Schneider, Barbara, 2
School Mathematics Study Group, 116
School of Environmental Studies, xviii
School to Work Opportunities Act, xi, xii, 69, 74, 76
Science Education for Public Understanding Program, 114
Science for All Americans (AAAS), 118
sciences
inclusive vs. exclusive approach, 122-25
projects in, xvi-xvii, 109-14
pure vs. applied, 115-18
in schools, 114-25
SciTeks modules (ACS), 114
Seidel, Steve, 26
seminars
in school, 86-88
at worksite, 82-83
semistructured problems, 28-31
senior projects, 12-13, 30-31, 66, 92-101
Shea, John, 162
Sher, Jonathan, 47
simulated activities, use of, 58-59
Sizer, Theodore, 31
skills
acquired through applying, 85-86
vs. competencies, 79
derived from subject matter, 34-35
new basic, 175-77
"soft" vs. "hard," 176-79
Sloan Study of Youth and Social Development, 2
small schools movement, 155, 179-84
Smith, Hedrick, 131
Smith Hughes act, 14, 67, 68
"social reconstruction," 63
sports, 4
standardized tests, 38, 175-79, 186
standards
community and personal, 183-84
in humanities, 151-53
movement to raise, 155, 172-73

197